ASIA'S
ENVIRONMENTAL
MOVEMENTS

—— **ASIA AND THE PACIFIC** ——

series editor: Mark Selden

This new series explores the most dynamic and contested region of the world, including contributions on political, economic, cultural, and social change in modern and contemporary Asia and the Pacific.

ASIA'S ENVIRONMENTAL MOVEMENTS
Comparative Perspectives
edited by Yok-shiu F. Lee and Alvin Y. so

CENSORING HISTORY
Perspectives on Nationalism and War in the Twentieth Century
edited by Laura Hein and Mark Selden

CHINA'S WORKERS UNDER ASSAULT
Anita Chan

THE CONTENTIOUS CHINESE
Elizabeth J. Perry

THE POLITICAL ECONOMY OF UNEVEN DEVELOPMENT
The Case of China
Wang Shaoguang and Hu Angang

THEATER AND SOCIETY
An Anthology of Contemporary Chinese Drama
edited by Haiping Yan

WOMEN IN REPUBLICAN CHINA
A Sourcebook
edited by Lan Hua and Vanessa Fong

ASIA'S
ENVIRONMENTAL
MOVEMENTS

Comparative Perspectives

Yok-shiu F. Lee and Alvin Y. So
Editors

An East Gate Book

M.E. Sharpe
Armonk, New York
London, England

An East Gate Book

Library of Congress Cataloging-in-Publication Data

Asia's environmental movements : comparative perspectives / edited by Yok-shiu Lee
and Alvin Y. So.
p. cm.—(Asia and the Pacific)
"An East Gate book."
Includes bibliographical references and index.
ISBN 0–56324–908–1 (cloth : alk. paper)—ISBN 1–56324–909–X (pbk. : alk. paper)
1. Environmentalism—Asia. 2. Environmentalism—Asia—Case studies.
3. Environmental policy—Asia. I. Lee, Yok-shiu. II. So, Alvin Y., 1953– . III. Series:
Asia and the Pacific (Armonk, N.Y.)
GE199.A78A784   1998
363.7′0095—dc21
99–12310
CIP

Printed in the United States of America

The paper used in this publication meets the minimum requirements of
American National Standard for Information Sciences—
Permanence of Paper for Printed Library Materials,
ANSI Z 39.48–1984.

BM (c)   10   9   8   7   6   5   4   3   2   1
BM (p)   10   9   8   7   6   5   4   3   2   1

Contents

Preface

This project was truly collaborative in nature right from the beginning and throughout its life. The project was conceived in early 1995 when we, in response to a research grant program that encouraged collaborative research projects between the East-West Center and the University of Hawaii, were trying to identify a significant issue in the Asia-Pacific region that could bring together our respective research interests: environment and sociology. We then identified environmental movements in Asia as an emerging social phenomenon that had enormous social and political implications but whose patterns of social and cultural origins had yet to be fully understood. Moreover, given Asia's extremely diverse social, cultural, and political backgrounds, we believed that the contours and consequences of environmentalism in the region could only be fruitfully explored from a comparative perspective. We therefore invited researchers from several Asian societies—South Korea, Taiwan, Hong Kong, Thailand, and the Philippines—where some forms of environmental movements could be discerned. We also invited an American sociologist to examine the Asian experiences collectively from the U.S. perspective.

We are thus very grateful to the case study coordinators. The project would not have been possible without their enthusiasm and full cooperation. From preparing the preliminary case study papers to contributing to the comparative analyses, they were actively involved in every phase of the project. While we have prepared the overall project research framework, the research framework for the comparative analyses was the product of intensive and extensive discussion among all the participants in our first workshop. All the case study coordinators were in fact brought together at two international workshops where the preliminary case study papers, the revised case study papers, and the comparative analyses were critiqued and suggestions made for their revision. Through these workshops all the project participants have therefore contributed to the entire manuscript in one form or another, making this edited volume a truly collaborative product.

We are grateful to the following organizations for awarding us research and conference grants: University of Hawaii–East-West Center Collaborative Research Grant Committee, Department of Sociology at the University of Hawaii, and the Hui Oi-Chow Trust Fund at the University of Hong Kong. Their financial support has made it possible for all the project participants to meet at two international workshops, the first one held at the East-West Center in November 1995 and the second one at the University of Hong Kong in February 1997.

We would like to thank our colleagues at several institutions for their support for and interest in the project and its two workshops. At the East-West Center, Bruce Koppel and Terry Rambo took an early interest in the project and gave us encouraging words and unfailing support throughout its life. As discussants, James Nickum and Michael Dove (of the East-West Center) and Herb Barringer (of the University of Hawaii) made invaluable contributions in the first workshop. At the University of Hong Kong, Victor Sit and C.Y. Jim gave their full support to see the project through to its fruitful completion. At the second workshop, useful comments for the project were offered by Simon S.C. Chau, Ho Kin-Chung, Man Si-Wai, Ng Cho-Nam, Clement Lam, and Yan Wing-Lok. Moreover, the two workshops would not have been successfully organized without the efficient administrative and logistical support provided by June Kuramoto and Karen Yamamoto at the East-West Center and Tommy Liu at the University of Hong Kong. Furthermore, we would like to thank the following graduate students for their assistance in organizing the two workshops: Miroo Brewer, Shelly Habel, Alyssa Miller, Cecilia Yuen, and Lee Ka-Man.

Last but not least, we would like to thank Mark Selden, who has read through several earlier drafts with great care and has given us invaluable suggestions on how to improve and strengthen the manuscript. We alone, of course, will be responsible for any shortcomings that may still remain.

Yok-shiu F. Lee
Alvin Y. So
July 1998

ASIA'S
ENVIRONMENTAL
MOVEMENTS

1

Introduction

Yok-shiu F. Lee and Alvin Y. So

Acronyms

ANGOC Asian NGO Coalition
APPEN Asia Pacific People's Environ-
        mental Network

NIEs   Newly Industrialized
        Economies
SCMP South China Morning Post

As East Asia's high-speed export-oriented economic development strategy enters its third decade, many Asian citizens have begun to ask themselves whether the price they have paid for rapid economic growth was worth it. For despite the constant self-congratulation of government and business for creating economic "miracles" in East Asia, accumulating evidence suggests that the other face of high-speed growth is an environmental tragedy of massive proportions (Bello and Rosenfeld 1992). In South Korea, for instance, where the highest priority of the dictatorship from the 1960s forward was economic expansion, and all perceived barriers to that growth were brutally suppressed, rapid industrialization left indelible marks on the landscape; the consequences of environmental neglect are found in the country's poisoned air and water (Eder 1996). In Taiwan, rapid economic development has also put tremendous pressure on the island's resource base. Whereas the most visible symptoms include water and energy shortages and various types of pollution, the most critical issue centers around abuses of land-use zoning that adversely impacted fragile areas like slope lands and coastal fishing grounds (Edmonds 1996). In Hong Kong, where the industrial restructuring process led to a relocation of industry from Hong Kong to Southern China in the last two decades, the job of identifying the causes of environmental problems in the territory itself—such as ambient air and surface water pollution—has been made more complicated (Ng and Ng 1997).

Throughout Southeast Asia, a region that experienced high rates of economic growth and rapid urbanization in the 1970s and 1980s, the mass media report daily on concerns about choking air and water pollution, the impact of large-scale infrastructure projects on the indigenous people, deforestation of the uplands and soil erosion, dumping of industrial wastes, traffic congestion, and a host of other environmental issues (Brookfield and Byron 1993; Parnwell and Bryant 1996). To a great extent, most of these trade- and investment-induced environmental degradation and pollution problems in Southeast Asia can be traced to multinational corporations that are either exploiting raw materials in or have shifted their industrial production operations to the region. The very process of extracting natural resources has led to environmental disasters such as deforestation, massive soil erosion and desertification, and pollution of water supplies, and the penetration of industrial technologies and projects has frequently exacted a heavy human toll in industrial accidents and poisoning from toxic materials (Ezenkele 1998; Khor 1992).

In Thailand, for example, double-digit growth rates over a decade prior to the country's 1997 economic collapse were achieved at the cost of severe damage to the environment, including industrial pollution, deforestation, and the encroachment on national parks and wildlife (Komin 1993). Moreover, along with other developing countries, Thailand has been the recipient of substandard industrial plants and hazardous production processes that have been shifted there by transnational corporations to escape health and pollution standards in their home countries (Athanasiou 1996; Khor 1992).

In the Philippines, the imperatives of economic growth have allowed the island nation's natural resources to be ravaged and extracted by mining and logging companies and agribusiness groups, leaving behind rainforests and coral reefs depleted of fuel and food for struggling farmers and fisherfolks (Broad and Cavanagh 1993). To be sure, many of the environmental problems were the product of the Philippines' colonial history. Transnational interests from Spain,

Japan, and most importantly the United States have been accused of causing considerable damage to the country's resource base during their reigns. At the present, nevertheless, access to natural resources is still primarily determined by a semi-colonial structure that permits the national elite and multinational corporations such as Atlas, Benguet, Philiex, and Marcopper a substantial control over the country's mineral resources (Rosario-Santos 1992).

In any event, by the early 1970s, one could detect a growing, albeit highly limited, public concern in Asia over the inability of the state to address the environmental consequences of postwar population and economic growth. By the late 1970s, numerous non-governmental organizations emerged throughout East and Southeast Asia, often serving as a vehicle for grassroots communities to express their political dissent and socioeconomic grievances (Howard 1993). Since the 1980s, the increasing deterioration of the living and natural environment all over Asia has led to a gradual emergence of environmental consciousness among the citizenry and the evolution of various types of environmental movements throughout the region (Karan 1994; Williams 1992; Weller and Hsiao 1994; Hung 1994).

Very often, grassroots environmental resistance organizations in the region have emerged from a variety of oppositional political movements motivated by anticolonial, national independence, Marxist, and feminist aspirations (Taylor 1995a). Many started as groups to address common socioeconomic and religious concerns. Some, discovering the inextricable linkages between and among poverty, domination by outsiders, and environmental degradation, have become ecologically and politically radicalized. One prominent example is that of the popular movements in the Philippines, which, despite the diversity of their original grievances, have all established strong environmental agendas and rationales (Porio and Taylor 1995). In some other countries, traditional moral and religious motivations, in the face of increasing deterioration, have helped contribute to the increasing "environment" character of many popular movements. Religions "have been mutating into forms capable of inspiring (or reinforcing) ecological activism, both by articulating ideals that participants find compelling (and thus legitimations for resistance) and by providing concrete institutional resources for ecological struggles" (Taylor 1995b: 337). In short, it is the realization of the connections between rapid industrial development, environmental degradation, and deteriorating life prospects that has led to the "environmentalization" of many popular social movements.

Similar to their counterparts in Europe and the Americas (Collinson 1996), environmental movements in Asia represent a variety of issues, point to a wide range of solutions and a multitude of problems, and include a daunting diversity of interest groups, activists, and constituents operating on many levels of action and policymaking (Cribb 1988; Hirsch 1994). Asia's environmental movements have not developed uniformly throughout the region. In Japan, for instance, citizens' groups have successfully rallied around some location-specific environmental issues, although a national-level movement similar to that in the United States has yet to materialize (Hoffman 1996). On the other hand, in post-Marcos Philippines, non-governmental organizations have become an especially significant feature of political and social life, and many such organizations have been active agents in addressing local, regional, and national environmental issues (Howard 1993).

In a nutshell, the advent of Asia's environmental movements has stirred regional controversies. Given that these movements are manifest or latent alternative modes of expression and political mobilization for the working class, political parties, as well as others traditionally found in the opposition, and that the environmental conditions in much of Asia have now reached crisis proportions (Eder 1996; Howard 1993), it is imperative that we gain an improved understanding of these movements' real and potential impacts as well as their limitations.

Hong Kong's Controversial Environmental Movement

"Warning by Academic: Majority See Green Groups as Enemy" (emphasis in original). This was the headline in the *South China Morning Post* (*SCMP* 1997a)—the leading English-language newspaper in Hong Kong—on February 18, 1997. The *SCMP* story began with this statement: "Green groups have failed to convince and are seen by the silent majority as 'the enemy,' an academic says."

Stephen Chiu, who had presented a paper at a workshop on Asia's environmental movements, was quoted as saying that "green groups [in Hong Kong] had adopted a consensual approach, lobbying and working with the Government at the expense of mobilizing grassroots support. Hong Kong has so far failed to develop a dynamic environmental movement capable of mobilizing broad-based public support, to exert significant influence on public policy, or to transform popular environmental consciousness." Chiu was further quoted as saying that "[t]he most glaring failure of Hong Kong's environmental movement was the failure to communicate effectively with the silent majority— they see [the greens] as their enemy." The *SCMP* cited a case in which "fishermen protesting against the new airport appealed to social activists, not green groups who focused on the plight of Chinese White Dolphins instead." Finally, the *SCMP* quoted Chiu as saying that "green groups should fuse livelihood issues with environmental problems, such as the conservation of Hong Kong's marine resources."

This newspaper account was accompanied by an *SCMP* (1997b) editorial stating that "Hong Kong sociologists, who have just presented a paper to Asian environmental groups, surprisingly blame conservationists for this. They say green groups are not reaching the hearts of the public because they are thought to be hostile to livelihood issues which are everyone's main priority." The editorial went on to argue that the root of public disregard for the environment is actually "not livelihoods, but part of the price for the drive for affluence which has made the territory so prosperous. For instance, take the insatiable local appetite for exotic fish which is emptying the seas and destroying coral reefs as far afield as Indonesia." The *SCMP* editorial in the end called on the government "to involve people on issues about which they do feel strongly. Land reclamation is one such example. Air pollution is another."

On 19 February 1997, Chiu and his coauthors, in a letter to the *SCMP,* insisted that their view had been distorted: they never "blamed conservationists for the appalling record of environmental concern." They certainly "are not prepared to make the claim that a majority of [Hong Kong] people see the green groups as their enemy at all times." What they did say is that the work of local greens "has been hampered by the political structure in Hong Kong and their own organizational weakness and that it could be improved by trying to reach out to the grassroots. The trouble for our [Hong Kong] environmental movement is that we have environmentalists, who espouse the so-called 'post-materialist' values (i.e., putting the environment and quality of life ahead of economic growth and material prosperity), striving to influence a materialist society and a colonial polity which put growth and prosperity on top."

The above debate is interesting not because the *SCMP* misinterpreted Chiu's presentation at the environmental movement workshop; newspapers make such mistakes all the time. What is significant is that the debate raised several critical issues pertinent to the study of Asia's environmental movements.

Critical Issues for Asia's Environmental Movements

Movement Origin: Affluence or Degradation?

Environmentalism is widely associated with affluence in industrialized societies. (The *SCMP,* for example, argues that affluence in Hong Kong—which led to insatiable local appetites for exotic fish, emptying the seas and destroying coral reefs—is a major cause of environmental problems in that city.) In industrializing economies such as those in East Asia and part of Southeast Asia, some analysts suggest that afflu-ence has laid the foundation for the emergence of a large middle class which, in turn, provided the major impetus behind the rise of en-vironmentalism in the region. In a study of Southeast Asian countries, Webster (n.d.: 5) states that "[i]t is the middle income group that seems most concerned about environmental problems," because they are "at a point in their lives where they can focus on concerns other than sur-vival." Similarly, Hirsch (1994: 6) points out that "environmentalism is often seen to be the product of Thailand's rapidly growing middle class. It is commonly assumed, not only in the Thai case, that a combi-nation of education, increased concern over quality of life issues and the leisure to reflect beyond immediate survival questions all give the middle class a key role in environmentalism." The implication of this argument is that environmental concerns are a luxury of an affluent society, pertaining to the middle class, that will appear at an advanced stage of industrial development.

However, looming over Asia's more politicized environmental cam-paigns are environmental degradation issues. In terms of human conse-quences, in the 1990s, environmental degradation poses a far more serious threat in Asia than in the West. In the West, adverse effects of environmental destruction concentrate primarily on human health and on natural habitats protected for their scientific, aesthetic, or leisure value. In Asia's developing countries pursuing high-speed, profit-oriented growth, the multiple impacts of environmental degradation are far greater: the destruction of life chances of millions of people, especially underprivileged groups in urban slums and the countryside (Hirsch 1994). Consequently, the urban poor, local communities, aborigines, and villagers throughout Asia have in significant instances all shown strong concern for issues related to environmental degradation. Brechin and Kempton (1996) and Kaimowitz (1996) recently presented new evidence of the proliferation of Third World grassroots environmental organizations and cross-national opinion surveys suggesting that concerns for the environment are not simply the product of a postmaterialist cultural shift, but also a matter of serious environmental degradation. The distinction between an environmentalism rooted in affluence versus one rooted in misery or dislocation has important implications for the overall discourse and strategies of Asia's environmental movements.

Movement Discourse: "Postmaterialist" or Livelihood Issues?

Chiu and his coauthors argue that some of Hong Kong's environmentalists espouse "postmaterialist" values that put quality of life concerns ahead of livelihood issues. Inglehart, too, maintains that materialist values in Western industrialized countries have been replaced by postmaterialist values, resulting in a shift in basic values from physical sustenance and safety toward belonging, self-expression, leisure, and quality of life (Brechin and Kempton 1994: 247).

Whereas environmental discourses in Korea, Taiwan, and Hong Kong resemble Western environmental discourses, which characteristically center upon negative impacts on human health, leisure, and natural habitats, environmental discourses in the Philippines and Thailand are primarily fueled by conflicts over livelihood issues vital to the survival of the poor. Whereas quality of life issues (such as the protection of natural ecosystems) assume greater prominence than economic disputes as the motivating factor behind collective environmental actions in East Asia, as in the West, environmental conflicts in Southeast Asia often remain another form of economic battle over livelihood issues. Whereas environmental movements in East Asia, like their counterparts in the West, typically reify a consumer society or at least rarely question its socio-ecological basis, some Southeast Asian environmental movements—given the centrality of livelihood discourse and survival issues—provide a more thoroughgoing critique both of consumerism and of uncontrolled economic development.

Although not included in this volume, a brief review of India's environmental discourse is highly instructive for our discussion. Gadgil and Guha (1994: 120) point out that environmental groups in India launched "an incisive critique of the development process itself" through "the process of struggle, the spreading of consciousness, . . . constructive work" as well as their efforts outlining an alternative development framework for a more sustainable and equitable society. Gadgil and Guha identified three strands within the dominant ideologies of India's environmentalism. The first trend is heavily influenced by a moral and religious perspective that rejects modernity. It urges an end to the wasteful life-styles inspired by capitalist and industrial development, arguing that social and ecological harmony can only be found through a return to India's precolonial village life. The moralists reframe traditional social justice discourse, such as inequitable development policies, in environmental terms. The second tendency, informed by Marxist ideology, argues that ruthless capitalist exploitation of resources and the poor are at the root of degradation. Marxist environmentalists, convinced that the creation of an economically just society is a logical precondition for social and ecological harmony, thus concentrate on organizing the poor to redistribute political and economic power. The third trend is "appropriate technology," which strives for "a working synthesis of agriculture and industry, big and small units, and Western and Eastern technological traditions." This trend designs and promotes technologies that are "resource conserving, labor intensive and socially liberating" (Gadgil and Guha 1994: 128).

Whatever the utilities of theories of an emergence of postmaterialist values in accounting for rising environmentalism in more developed countries, they are unable to explain the appearance of widespread grassroots concern for environmental affairs in poorer societies, including the nations of Southeast Asia. This may stem in part from the fact that environmental degradation is seen, especially in poorer nations, not as a postmaterialist quality of life issue but as a basic threat to human survival (Dunlap and Mertig 1995: 135). As Brechin and Kempton (1994: 265) remark, "Today, an expanded notion of environmentalism is often considered as integral to the economic development process. . . . [R]ather than being a postindustrial luxury, a healthy environment is now widely viewed as essential for a sound economic base. . . . Instead of being a postmaterialist value, environmental values have become integrated with materialist values." Seen in sociological terms, the environmental groups helped (re)define the scope of an environmentalism which Asia's societies now recognize as part of their understanding of the complex society–environment relationship. It would be interesting to examine how such materialistic values were incorporated into the environmental discourse and the extent to which such values have been successfully utilized in making claims in Asia's environmental movements.

Movement Strategy: Toward the Top or the Bottom?

An environmental organization's choice of strategy is largely influenced by its degree of commitment to the environmental cause as well as the direction and intensity of its political orientation. Generally speaking, many environmental organizations in Asia are part of a larger social movement opposing authoritarianism and advancing more direct forms of democratic participation. This is, of course, not meant to deny the existence of a diversity of political inclinations within the movement. Some organizations are relatively neutral politically and willing to work within the existing system to bring about marginal improvements to the environment, while there are those who are politically more assertive in demanding greater environmental and democratic changes at a faster pace but basically share the same prodevelopment stance adopted by the state and the private sector. Then, there is a third major group of organizations committed to a more radical environmentalism and advocating an alternative, idealized life-style that is centered around simple technology and social equity (Buttel 1992).

It is also important to recognize that, unlike most old or new social movements, the environmental movement does not have a natural constituency. For many environmental issues, those acting on behalf of an environmental cause do not expect personal material benefits. A healthier environment tends to be a public good which cannot be denied to anybody, including those who resisted environmental improvement. Yet, because the movement does not enjoy support from a readily recognizable natural constituency, environmental organizations face at least one major dilemma: whether to mobilize support on an elite or mass level (Breyman 1993). While "[i]nstrumentally focused elite groups might question the investment of resources required to 'explain the science' to the general public," some analysts argue that sharing basic ideas about the nature and dimensions of a problem and its remedy with the general public are "essential for effective and sustained citizen movement" (Breyman 1993: 141).

For illustrative purposes, let us look at the case of Hong Kong again. Although the *SCMP* editorial called upon the Hong Kong government to involve more people in the deliberations of environmental issues, its rush to endorse the view that most Hong Kong people perceived environmental groups as "enemies" in fact revealed the editors' preference for a strategy of the local environmental movement to ally with the government at the top in order to influence policy outcomes. Assuming that one of the major weaknesses of Hong Kong's environmental movement was that local environmentalists did not enjoy strong support from the mass media and general public, the editors at the *SCMP* thus concluded that an alliance with the government offered the most viable tactic for Hong Kong's environmentalists.

Chiu and his coauthors, however, urged environmental groups to tap into the potential of mass support by following a vastly different strategy of grassroots mobilization from below. They argued that an effective linkage with the government without a similarly strong connection at the grassroots community level was one critical weakness of Hong Kong's environmental movement. Not only have the environmental groups failed to communicate effectively with the silent majority due to the groups' postmaterialistic discourse, but their lobbying effort, directed wholly at the Hong Kong government, was conducted at the expense of mobilizing effective grassroots support.

Again, India's experience is instructive. The Indian case is frequently seen as a model for the strategy of grassroots mobilization at the bottom. Through organizing the victims of environmental degradation, environmental groups introduced three distinct sets of initiatives: the prevention of ecologically destructive economic practices; the promotion of environmental messages through skillful use of the media; and the design and implementation of environmental rehabilitation programs to restore degraded ecosystems. This three-pronged social action program (i.e., struggle, publicity, and restoration) served as the strategic backbone of India's environmental movement (Gadgil and Guha 1994).

In short, the strategies that environmental groups consider and adopt depend on these groups' specific origins and political orientations, plus the broader social, political, and cultural contexts in which they operate. Additionally, movement organizations have a choice with regard to the modes through which they engage the state. "Possible modes include bypassing, challenging, pressuring, and supporting the State" (Breyman 1993: 147). While the decision to select from these modes of operation is partly a function of the knowledge available to an organization and also other factors internal to the organization, the state can have a major influence over the course of actions taken by movement organizations by (re)structuring the overall incentive system.

Movement Impacts: Significant or Minimal?

Given the significance of environmental movements, one major issue has been the extent to which these movements turn into important, transformative, social forces. There are both strengths and weaknesses in the emerging modes of political mobilization by movement organizations. In the West, for instance, the support base for environmental movements is usually articulate, politically skilled, and able to exercise influence disproportionate to its numbers. Moreover, environmental mobilization in the West focuses around Green Political Parties (in Europe), or takes the form of multiple, overlapping grassroots organizations as well as lobbying and high-powered think tanks. As such, these groups are a predominant and broad-based political force with major impact on environmental policies.

There are, however, major limitations to the political strength of environmental movements. Environmental concerns, when expressed in the political arena, "essentially involve either pursuing public goods (e.g., environmental integrity) or consumptionist goals (reducing health risks by limiting nuclear power)" (Buttel 1992: 13). In other words, these concerns are not easily translated into and combined with the other material interests that are more readily transposed into entitlements of citizenship. Moreover, most environmental issues can be coopted by the state or the corporate sector, as either could easily take a particular environmental issue as its own, trivializing or commercializing the issue for its own benefit.

What is clear is that local environmental groups are able to strengthen their movements by joining with international groups. Since the 1980s, for instance, international development agencies, influenced by a new awareness of global ecology, have tried to integrate local organizations into a global environment-and-development framework. In Asia, local NGOs in the developing countries have organized regionally and formed regional coalitions such as Asia Pacific People's Environmental Network (APPEN) and the Asian NGO Coalition (ANGOC) (Finger 1992).

The struggle against the Narmada dam project in India vividly illustrates the power of building alliances with international actors by the local groups. "According to World Bank officials in charge of Narmada, the international links were crucial in forcing the Bank to drop funding for the project" (Akula 1995: 144). By sending faxes to international organizations such as the Environmental Defense Fund in Washington, D.C., Survival International in London, and Friends of the Earth in Tokyo, local protest groups in India were able to solicit support from these organizations which, in turn, put pressure on politicians in the respective countries to stop the Bank from providing further funding for the Narmada project.

Although support from international networks such as Greenpeace and Friends of the Earth is important to many local environmental groups in Asia, this overseas linkage has also made them vulnerable to criticism, especially from local governments sensitive to any questioning of their adopted developmental models. Some of the region's governments have complained that many global environmental initiatives directed at their countries resemble a new form of neocolonialism imposed on them by the world's richer countries to maintain the latter's dominance over the former. For instance, the Malaysian government, one of the more vocal critics of the environmental movements in the region, has accused "its critics of paternalism, neocolonialism, and of being political rather than scientific" (Howard 1993: 16).

Looking at the case of Hong Kong once more, neither the *SCMP* nor Chiu saw Hong Kong's environmental movement as an important agency for solving Hong Kong's environmental problems. In the early 1990s, fishermen protesting the construction of Hong Kong's new airport apparently appealed to social activists, not green groups, for help. Nevertheless, the societal impact of environmental movements is not simply limited to specific policy changes. By fostering a debate—like that in Hong Kong's mass media—on the difficulties, shortcomings, and limited scopes of the dominant and alternative models of development on the level of action—environmental movements make available the relevant interactions, interpretations, and discourses for public scrutiny. In this respect, the larger significance of these movements stems from their real and potential influence in shaping state–society relations through efforts to structure forms and contexts of public discourses on development-related issues.

Comparing Movements: Convergence or Divergence?

The *SCMP* implicitly argues that as Hong Kong's society grows more affluent, the development of its environmental problems and movement will follow paths of Western industrialized countries. In fact, many of Asia's environmental movement leaders and activists have received their education in the West, and are obviously strongly influenced by Western environmental discourses and strategies.

Nevertheless, Asia's environmental movements have emerged from totally different political, economic, and cultural contexts from those of their Western counterparts. Economically, whereas Western environmental movements evolved in advanced industrial economies, many Asian movements appeared either in the so-called "newly industrializing economies" (NIEs) or economically backward countries. Culturally, whereas environmental groups in the West flourished in civic cultures dominated by Christianity, Asia's environmental organizations developed either in predominantly Chinese Confucian culture or in cultures permeated with Hindu, Buddhist, or Islamic beliefs. Politically, whereas Western environmental movements emanated from advanced democratic institutional settings, most Asian variants arose either in countries undergoing the initial phase of democratic transition or in authoritarian states where civil rights are highly restricted.

In this respect, Asia's environmental movements have apparently emerged from very different structural contexts, have proposed different discourses and strategies, and have exercised different impacts on their countries in contrast to their Western counterparts. For example, within the domain of Southeast Asian authoritarian states and East Asian countries undergoing the initial phases of democratic transition, the debate over environmental issues is not limited to the question of how to resolve a society's growing environmental problems but has far wider political implications. The debate on the environment may open up a whole new political discussion on the need to restructure the existing political regime to allow increasing levels of public participation and democratic control over the government's policies on environmental issues (MacAndrews 1994).

Moreover, given the diverse social and cultural roots of environmentalism within the region, it would be interesting to examine the extent to which interests and concerns of Asia's multitude of environmental groups converge. What are the prospects of transnational complementarity within and between environmental movements across the region, in advancing the theory and practice of environmentalism? Conversely, how have movement antagonists in different countries attempted to stymie coalition-building by environmental groups within and across national boundaries in the region? To what extent and why have different states facilitated or hindered movement activities? To what degree and why has greater mobilization occurred around certain issues in one particular country than in some other countries?

Objectives and Significance of the Book

The objectives of this book are (1) to identify the political, economic, and socio-cultural conditions under which Asia's environmental movements have emerged; (2) to outline the characteristics of Asia's environmental movements; (3) to trace the history and transformation of these environmental movements over the past three decades; (4) to examine the impacts of these movements on the state, economy, and society; and (5) to examine the similarities and differences between and among Asia's environmental movements.

In meeting these objectives, the book examines assumptions regarding the meaning and origins of the rise of environmentalism in Asia. While a limited number of publications trace the advent of environmental movements in Asian countries, little analysis substantiates these presuppositions and critically examines the social roots of environmental movements.

Second, this book assesses the transformative impact of different types of environmental movements. Much research and literature exists on how environmental movements in the West have impacted on environmental attitudes, environmental legislation, and the resulting quality of life. While similar movements in Asia possess great transformative potential, thus far much less is known about the implications and actual impacts of the activities of different environmental groups on the quality of the environment and the well-being of different segments of the population. The issue of whether these movements can maintain their platforms or be suppressed or coopted by the state will have profound consequences on the prospect of Asia's environment and development.

Lastly, a comparative analysis of Asia's environmental movements in different social, political, economic, and cultural contexts will enable social scientists to clarify issues related to social movements, such as the question of mass mobilization in authoritarian and newly democratizing states, the built-in weaknesses of environmental movements that contain diverse and sometimes confrontational elements, the response of the state to grassroots initiatives, and the difficult policy task of striking a balance between economic growth and environmental protection.

Research Strategy and Research Questions

Despite the growing importance of Asia's environmental movements, the literature on both Asian area studies and environmental studies in general have yet to provide in-depth information and comparative analysis on the above critical issues. As a recent book reviewer (Roberts 1995) of *Asia's Environmental Crisis,* edited by Michael C. Howard noted, "compared with the avalanche of literature on the Americas, Europe, and even Africa, Asia has remained a virtual blind spot in attempts to understand environmental change and environmental social movements from a global or comparative perspective."

This volume will not just examine these critical issues, but will also undertake a systematic investigation into the origins, transformation, and the real and potential impacts of environmental movements in East Asia and Southeast Asia. To achieve this larger objective, two sets of countries/territories were selected to illustrate the diversity of the development of environmental organizations in the vast and heterogeneous Asian region. The first set of research sites includes Hong Kong, Taiwan, and South Korea, all of which are "newly industrializing economies" (NIEs) that have just gone through democratic breakthroughs and are heavily influenced by Confucian cultural values. The second set of research sites includes Thailand and the Philippines which, compared to the NIEs, are less advanced economically and are dominated by Buddhist and Catholic cultural values, respectively. Given their diverse economic, political, and cultural configurations, these five countries/territories provide fertile ground for an examination of how societal, structural contexts shaped the origins and transformation of environmental movements in Asia.

The research was accomplished in two stages. First, a workshop in Honolulu in November 1995 brought together social scientists from these research sites to a common research agenda on each country's environmental movement. After the Honolulu workshop, these researchers were given a broad set of guidelines, flexible enough to permit each to do justice to his/her own country's unique circumstances, but structured to ensure that each author would organize his/her materials to address a common set of research questions within a shared analytical framework. The country case study reports were specifically asked to address the following research questions:

Structural and Historical Context. What are the political, economic, and cultural contexts that gave rise to the movements? To what extent are these structural contexts similar to (or different from) the contexts that gave rise to environmental movements in the West? What accounts for the different streams, the rise, and the decline of the movements?

The Characteristics. What are the goals and concerns of the movements? How do movement organizations define the "environment" (broadly or narrowly)? In what ways are environmental issues linked to livelihood and human rights issues? What are their working relationships with the grassroots communities, the state, and other political institutions?

Strategies and Politics. What types (e.g., seminars, protests, lobbies) and what level (e.g., local, provincial, and national) of activities are conducted by the movements? Do they advocate a confrontational strategy? To what extent, and how, do movement organizations achieve coalition-building with political parties, labor unions, and professional groups?

Impacts. What are the impacts of the movements' activities on environmental policies, environmental behavior, and the distribution of costs and benefits of environmental improvements? What are the impacts of the movements on political institutions, electoral politics, state–society relationships, the economy, and indigenous culture?

Comparative Studies

After the country reports that paid attention to the above research questions were completed in 1996, we identified the distinguishing features of Asia's environmental movements that set them apart from their Western counterparts and examined the similarities and differences between environmental movements in East Asia and Southeast Asia. In other words, to what extent do we see characteristics that are unique to Asia among the region's environmental movements? How can we account for similarities and differences between East Asian and Southeast Asian environmental movements? To what extent could Southeast Asian environmental movements learn from the experiences of East Asian environmental movements? What kinds of coalitions are possible between environmental organizations in the region?

We invited Andrew Szasz, an expert on the American toxic waste movement (Szasz 1994), to read the various country case study reports on Asia's environmental movements. We asked Szasz to contribute a paper examining and evaluating the Asian cases from the perspective of grassroots environmentalism in the United States, with special attention to how the Asian experiences resemble or differ from the American case.

Based on the findings of the country case study reports presented at the original workshop, we identified four crucial factors that helped shape Asia's environmental movements, namely, the process of democratization, culture, the business sector's reactions to rising environmentalism, and the pioneering efforts of the anti-nuclear movement.

Depending on their research interests, two to four country report authors teamed up to collaborate on a comparative analysis on each of the above topics. A team leader, identified for each comparative chapter, drafted an introductory section and formulated key research issues for the topic under investigation. Then, collaborating team members, following the team leader's guideline, wrote a short report on the issue at hand about his/her own country. The editors of this volume were responsible for collecting all of these sections, editing them, writing up the first drafts of the comparative chapters, and finalizing these drafts into their existing form.

A second workshop was held in Hong Kong in February 1997 to discuss the findings of the draft comparative chapters. This workshop enabled the chapter authors and the volume editors to review and critique one another's sections and formulate a coherent explanation to account for the divergent patterns and converging trends of environmental movements in East Asia and Southeast Asia. As such, the comparative chapters are truly a collaboration between chapter authors and volume editors.

Organization and Major Arguments of the Book

This book is organized into two parts: part one includes five country case study chapters and part two contains five comparative analysis chapters. The first part, which consists of five country case studies on South Korea, Taiwan, Hong Kong, Thailand, and the Philippines, attempts to examine the origins, the transformation, and the impacts of environmental movements in these countries/territories.

Su-Hoon Lee claims that South Korea, after three decades of nonstop, high-speed industrial growth, suffers from an extreme environmental crisis. He notes that while the environmental movement in South Korea was concerned primarily with the two principal issues of pollution and nuclear power, the anti-nuclear campaign will increasingly become a dominant national issue, because the country's economy has become structurally dependent upon nuclear power and, despite increased environmental consciousness, South Korea's highrate, export-oriented development model remains deeply entrenched in the minds of the state elite and business sector leaders.

In Taiwan, Hsin-Huang Michael Hsiao observes that while the environmental movement, compared with other social movements, enjoys a high level of public support, it is unclear whether and to what extent the short-sighted "victim consciousness" can be transformed into a broader "environmental consciousness" by which the people in Taiwan continue to mobilize to safeguard the environment for the long term. Hsiao also notes that although the government in Taiwan has become more responsive and accountable in dealing with local environmental problems, its pro-growth ideology has hardly been challenged.

Stephen Wing-kai Chiu and his coauthors discover that all environmental groups in Hong Kong contributed to the cause of environmental improvement of the city, but duplication and competition between and among these groups led to disarticulation for the movement as a whole. They also raise concerns over three outstanding issues that will impinge upon the prospects of Hong Kong's environmental movement—namely, the impact of industrial restructuring on environmental quality, cross-border pollution, and the scope of social advocacy for environmentalism under Chinese rule.

Alvin So and Yok-shiu Lee point to increasing levels of collaboration and cooperation between and among the government, nongovernmental organizations (NGOs), and the private sector in addressing environmental issues in Thailand. Indeed, they claim, perhaps to the surprise of many, that both government and the business sector in Thailand have started playing an important and supportive role in that country's environmental movement, even though the NGOs are recognized as the key players in initiating the movement in the first place.

Given that environmental issues in the Philippines tend to be framed in terms of livelihood and equity concerns, Francisco Magno sees environmental movement leaders maintaining community control over resources as a vital component of any strategy to promote equitable and sustainable development. With the recent transformation of local governments into a major locus of decision-making processes affecting the environment, Magno observes that local coalition-building efforts assume a crucial spot in the movement's repertoire of strategic actions.

The book's second part, devoted to comparative analyses, starts with a chapter relating the principal findings of a study of the U.S. toxic waste movement to the Asian case studies, to highlight major similarities and differences between America's and Asia's environmental movements. Andrew Szasz argues that, with Americans and Asians subscribing to the logic of unfettered economic growth, it is not surprising to see a similar sense of victimization and militant responses. However, Szasz contends that these similar motivations and actions generated different movement trajectories and impacts. For instance, with the possible exception of the Philippines, local protests have not led to an overall shift in the state's economic and environmental policies in the other case study societies.

Szasz's chapter is followed by four additional comparative chapters that examine, respectively, the transformation of the nature of Asia's environmental movements in various phases of the democratization process, the role of culture in the formation and mobilization of Asia's environmental movements, the pioneering role of the anti-nuclear campaigns in environmental movements, and the different patterns of the business sector's responses to environmental movements. It should be noted that the topics selected for these comparative chapters, in fact, correspond to the four principal factors identified in this analysis as being the most important determinants influencing the contours of Asia's environmental movements. As such, let us first summarize our findings derived from the case study chapters, which are detailed in the concluding chapter, and then specify the nature and extent of how the principal factors (such as democratization, culture, the anti-nuclear campaign, and the business sector) have helped shape the contours of environmental movements in Asia.

On the basis of the in-depth case study chapters, we have been able to delineate the distinctive features of Asia's environmental movements, and identify similarities and differences between environmental movements in East Asia and Southeast Asia. In brief, our analysis shows that Asia's environmental movements are complicated phenomena. They are comprised of several different strands of environmental activities conducted by a diversity of social groups to achieve a variety of political goals. While they may share some similar outlooks, the fundamental interests, motivations, and agendas of these social groups may not converge. Moreover, while Asia's environmental movements can be traced to some Western roots, they have been culturally indigenized. In East and Southeast Asian countries, local environmental activists have all engaged in a process of indigenization through which salient religious symbols, cultural values, and rituals are effectively incorporated into the movements' repertoire of protest activities. And this indigenization of Western environmentalism provides a major source of empowerment and legitimization for local activists to challenge dominant ideologies and culprits of environmental degradation in the region.

Our study further identifies three major distinctive paths of environmental movements in the countries concerned—namely, the populist movements in Taiwan, South Korea, and the Philippines; the corporatist path in Thailand; and the postmaterialist mode in Hong Kong. In summary, the populist course taken by environmental groups in Taiwan, South Korea, and the Philippines is marked by its emphasis on promoting grassroots activism, community empowerment, livelihood concerns, confrontational tactics, and social discourses on sustainability. In contrast, the environmental movement in Thailand has embarked on a totally opposite track—that of corporatist environmentalism. Designed to contain radical environmental protests and to promote a socially responsible corporate image, the dominant actors of the corporatist environmental movement in Thailand—the business sector and the state—have strived to promote cooperation, as opposed to confrontation, among the major stakeholders in defining the country's environmental agenda. Advocating a non-confrontational, consensus-building approach to resolving environmental disputes, Hong Kong's dominant environmental groups have chosen the postmaterialist path. Such a strand of environmentalism—with the promotion of a "green life-style" at its core and the sponsorship of a variety of environmental education programs at its periphery—has helped raise the public's environmental awareness. However, most of the prominent environmental groups have shied away from initiating and maintaining any sustained linkages with grassroots communities in challenging the environmental actions ensuing from the dominant power structure.

As already alluded to earlier, our analysis has identified four major factors—democratization, culture, the anti-nuclear campaign, and the business sector—that, singularly and interactively, have helped shape the contours of Asia's environmental movements. The principal arguments of these comparative analyses are briefly summarized below.

On the issue of the impact of democratization on environmental movements, we observe in Chapter 9 that, being the two strongest social movements in society, democracy and environmental movements share similar societal goals of overthrowing authoritarian regimes and creating a better living environment. Although there was at times a fusion of leadership and members between the two movements, there are a variety of patterns of the relationship between democracy movements and environmental movements during the phases of democratic transition and consolidation. In countries where democracy has been consolidated and achieved, such as Taiwan, South Korea, and the Philippines, environmental movements have acted either as partners or as guardians of the democratic camps. On the other hand, in societies where the democratization process has been barred from being fully developed and consolidated, such as the case of Hong Kong, the role of the environmental movements was reduced to that of a bystander and detached from the democracy movement.

Chapter 8, on the role of culture in the social mobilization of environmental movements, asserts that Western environmentalism was indigenized in Asia through the incorporation of radical Asian religious and cultural values and rituals. Religious discourses (folk religion, Catholicism, and Buddhism), cultural values (familism, Feng Shui cosmology, and indigenous traditions), and rituals (religious parades, funerals, and the Catholic mass) have all played an important role in "framing" the environmental debates as well as in legitimizing protest activities in the region. The fusion of these native religious and cultural symbols with the environmental movements has led to the creation of distinctive styles of Asian environmentalism and the empowerment of local environmental protests, enabling the latter to effectively challenge dominant authoritarian states. As such, the analysis disputes Pye's conception of the paternalistic nature of Asia's political culture, which supposedly cherishes the status quo. Instead, it shows that Asia's religions, cultural values, and rituals have proven to be fertile ground for environmental discourses and movements to take root.

The opening up of the political process in Taiwan, South Korea, and Hong Kong in the 1980s, as exemplified by a decentralizing state and a changing pattern of political opportunities in each society, has had significant implications for the environmental movements in general and for the anti-nuclear movements specifically in all three countries/territories. Chapter 10, on anti-nuclear campaigns, advances the view that the anti-nuclear movements have been one of the most potent forces in galvanizing the general population in all three societies toward supporting the environmental agenda. However, unable to sway the pro-growth ideology solidly upheld by the state in all three communities, the anti-nuclear protests have at best been able to delay the implementation of the respective nuclear energy programs. Nevertheless, as the links in the nuclear chain in countries like South Korea and Taiwan—such as identifying acceptable sites for new power plants—will remain incomplete or weak in the foreseeable future, they will have to continue to seek solutions outside their territorial boundaries. As such, the anti-nuclear protests will in all likelihood continue to gain momentum and possibly develop into a regionwide project.

On the business sector's response to rising environmentalism, Chapter 11 argues that the differential trajectories of environmental movements are influenced by pro- or counter-movement strategies adopted by international and local corporations. In Thailand and Hong Kong, for instance, the environmental movements were heavily influenced by the corporate strategy of appropriating the social space for environmental discourse through the sponsorship of environmental education activities. In both Thailand and Hong Kong, corporate sponsorship of non-confrontational environmental programs is now commonly used by companies in the private sector as a public relations strategy to enhance their corporate image. Many environmental NGOs in these two places, saddled with the problem of financial constraints, are highly receptive to and influenced by corporate sponsorship. In Taiwan, private and public firms are sheltered from the impact of global environmentalism because the Taiwan government is not a signatory of various international environmental agreements. Taiwan's business sector is therefore not under any political pressure to liaison with the environmental groups to address the latter's concerns. As such, the experience of Taiwan's movement suggests that environmental groups would need to liaison and organize with grassroots social groups to maintain their own identities and independence in order to resist the corporate sector's counter-movement tactics.

By the late 1990s, Asia's environmental movements have created an environmental discourse that extends to both societies and states. The general public is increasingly receptive to and supportive of the agendas of environmental groups. States and elites in the region have also been forced to adopt a pro-environmental stance, at least rhetorically, which has led to some, if limited, actual policy impacts. While environmental awareness in these societies has been heightened, the governments in the region have, however, all remained deeply committed to the pro-development ideology with the result that environmental conditions in Asia are continuing to deteriorate. We believe that movement activists have to articulate an effective and thorough critique of the rampant developmentalism that has been subscribed to indiscriminately by both the elite and the general population in the region. The first aspect of such a critique relates to the unmasking of the concept of "progress" that lies at the heart of the ideology of industrial society. A second, related, aspect pertains to the refutation of Japan as the exemplary "industrial development model." The fact that Japan's affluence has brought little sense of fulfillment but profoundly empty and alienated lives to many Japanese would need to be brought to the attention of the rest of Asia (McCormack 1996). Only through a broadening of objectives and strategies can Asia's environmental movements move closer to achieving the larger societal goal of building socially just and ecologically sustainable communities.

References

Akula, Vikram. 1995. "Grassroots Environmental Resistance in India." In *Ecological Resistance Movements: The Global Emergence of Radical and Popular Environmentalism,* edited by Bron Taylor, pp. 128–145. Albany: State University of New York Press.

Athanasiou, Tom. 1996. *Divided Planet: The Ecology of Rich and Poor.* Boston: Little, Brown.

Bello, Walden, and Stephanie Rosenfeld. 1992. *Dragons in Distress: Asia's Miracle Economies in Crisis.* San Francisco: The Institute for Food and Development Policy.

Brechin, Steven R., and Willett Kempton. 1994. "Global Environmentalism: A Challenge to the Postmaterialism Thesis?" *Social Science Quarterly* 75(2): 245–269.

Breyman, Steve. 1993. "Knowledge as Power: Ecology Movements and Global Environmental Problems." In *The State and Social Power in Global Environmental Politics,* edited by Ronnie Lipschutz and Ken Conca, pp. 124–157. New York: Columbia University Press.

Broad, Robin, and John Cavanagh. 1993. *Plundering Paradise: The Struggle for the Environment in the Philippines.* Berkeley: University of California Press.

Brookfield, Harold, and Yvonne Byron (Editors). 1993. *South-East Asia's Environmental Future.* Tokyo: United Nations University Press.

Buttel, Frederick. 1992. "Environmentalization: Origins, Processes, and Implications for Rural Social Change." *Rural Sociology* 57(1): 1–27.

Collinson, Helen (Editor). 1996. *Green Guerrillas: Environmental Conflicts and Initiatives in Latin America and the Caribbean.* New York: Monthly Review Press.

Cribb, R. 1988. "The Politics of Environmental Protection in Indonesia." Victoria: The Centre of Southeast Asian Studies at Monash University.

Dunlap, Reiley, and Angela Mertig. 1995. "Global Concern for the Environment: Is Affluence a Prerequisite?" *Journal of Social Issues* 51(4): 121–137.

Eder, Norman. 1996. *Poisoned Prosperity: Development, Modernization, and the Environment in South Korea.* Armonk: M.E. Sharpe.

Edmonds, Richard Louis. 1996. "Taiwan's Environment Today." *The China Quarterly,* 148: 1224–1259.

Ezenkele, Agochukwu. 1998. Untitled. *The Earth Times,* May 23.

Finger, Matthias. 1992. "The Changing Green Movement—A Clarification." In *Research In Social Movements, Conflicts, and Change: The Green Movement Worldwide,* edited by Matthias Finger, pp. 229–246. Greenwich: JAI Press.

———. 1994. "NGOs and Transformation: Beyond Social Movement Theory." In *Environmental NGOs in World Politics: Linking the Local and the Global,* edited by Thomas Princen and Matthias Finger, pp. 48–66. London: Routledge.

Gadgil, Madhav, and Ramachandra Guha. 1994. "Ecological Conflicts and the Environmental Movement in India." *Development and Change* 25: 101–136.

Hirsch, Philip. 1994. "Where are the Roots of Thai Environmentalism?" *TEI Quarterly Environment Journal* 2(2): 5–15.

Hoffman, Steven. 1996. "The Influence of Citizen/Environment Groups upon Local Environmental Policy Process in Japan." Unpublished Ph.D. dissertation. Madison: University of Wisconsin.

Howard, Michael C. (Editor). 1993. *Asia's Environmental Crisis.* Boulder: Westview Press.

Hung Wing-tat. 1994. "The Environment." In *The Other Hong Kong Report,* edited by Donald McMillen and Si-wai Man, pp. 254–264. Hong Kong: The Chinese University of Hong Kong Press.

International Society for Ecology and Culture. 1992. "The Future of Progress." In *The Future of Progress: Reflections on Environment and Development,* edited by Edward Goldsmith, Martin Khor, Helena Norberg-Hodge, and Vandana Shiva, pp. 1–22. Bristol: International Society for Ecology and Culture.

Kaimowitz, David. 1996. "Social Pressure for Environmental Reform." In *Green Guerrillas,* edited by Helen Collinson, pp. 20–32. New York: Monthly Review Press.

Karan, P.P. 1994. "Environmental Movement in India." *The Geographical Review* 84(1): 33–41.

Khor, Martin. 1992. "Development, Trade, and the Environment: A Third World Perspective." In *The Future of Progress: Reflections on Environment & Development,* edited by Edward Goldsmith, et al., pp. 27–45. Bristol: International Society for Ecology and Culture.

Komin, Suntaree. 1993. "A Social Analysis of the Environmental Problems in Thailand." In *Asia's Environmental Crisis,* edited by Michael C. Howard, pp. 257–274. Boulder: Westview Press.

MacAndrews, Colin. 1994. "Politics of the Environment in Indonesia." *Asian Survey* 34(4): 369–380.

McCormack, Gavan. 1996. *The Emptiness of Japanese Affluence.* Armonk: M.E. Sharpe.

Ng, Cho-nam, and Ting-leung Ng. 1997. "The Environment." In *The Other Hong Kong Report,* edited by Joseph Y.S. Cheng, pp. 463–504. Hong Kong: The Chinese University of Hong Kong Press.

Parnwell, Michael J.G., and Raymond L. Bryant. 1996. *Environmental Change in Southeast Asia: People, Politics and Sustainable Development.* London: Routledge.

Porio, Emma, and Bron Taylor. 1995. "Popular Environmentalists in the Philippines: People's Claims to Natural Resources." In *Ecological Resistance Movements: The Global Emergence of Radical and Popular Environmentalism,* edited by Bron Taylor, pp. 146–158. Albany: State University of New York Press.

Roberts, J. Timmons. 1995. Review of "Asia's Environmental Crisis." *Contemporary Sociology* 24: 211–212.

Rosario-Santos, Filipina del. 1992. "The Philippine Environmental Crisis." In *The Future of Progress: Reflections on Environment and Development,* edited by Edward Goldsmith, Martin Khor, Helena Norberg-Hodge, and Vandana Shiva. Bristol: International Society for Ecology and Culture (no page numbers printed in publication).

South China Morning Post (SCMP). 1997a. "Warning by Academic: Majority 'See Green Groups as Enemy'." *South China Morning Post,* February 18.

————. 1997b. "Time for Action." *South China Morning Post,* February 18.

Szasz, Andrew. 1994. *Ecopopulism.* Minneapolis: University of Minnesota Press.

Taylor, Bron. 1995a. "Introduction: The Global Emergence of Popular Ecological Resistance." In *Ecological Resistance Movements: The Global Emergence of Radical and Popular Environmentalism,* edited by Bron Taylor, pp. 1–7. Albany: State University of New York Press.

————. 1995b. "Popular Ecological Resistance and Radical Environmentalism." In *Ecological Resistance Movements: The Global Emergence of Radical and Popular Environmentalism,* edited by Bron Taylor, pp. 334–353. Albany: State University of New York Press.

Webster, Douglas. n.d. "The Rise of the Urban Middle Income Group: Implications for Reversal of Urban Environmental Degradation in ASEAN Cities." Bangkok: Natural Resources Program, Asian Institute of Technology, 12 pp.

Weller, Robert P., and Hsin-Huang Michael Hsiao. 1994. "Culture, Gender, and Community in Taiwan's Environmental Movement." Paper presented at the Workshop on Environmental Movements in Asia, International Institute for Asian Studies and Nordic Institute of Asian Studies, Leiden, 27–29 October 1994.

Williams, Jack. 1992. "Environmentalism in Taiwan." In *Taiwan, Beyond the Economic Miracle,* edited by Denis Simon and Michael Kau, pp. 187–210. Armonk: M.E. Sharpe.

Country Case Studies

2

Environmental Movements in Taiwan

Hsin-Huang Michael Hsiao

Acronyms

CEPD	Council for Economic Planning and Development	EPA	Environmental Protection Agency
DPP	Democratic Progressive Party	GP	Green Party
		KMT	Kuomintang (Nationalist Party)
EIA	Environmental Impact Assessment	NCP	New China Party
		NGOs	Non-Governmental Organizations
EOI	Export-Oriented Industrialization	TEPU	Taiwan Environmental Protection Union

---

Introduction

Outside Taiwan, books and journal articles assessing the "Taiwan miracle" now begin to address its environmental costs, but most attention is still paid to the magnitude of environmental pollution and nature depletion problems faced by the island; very few concern public attempts to cope with the pressing social problems affecting their lives. Any serious study on a society's environmental movement requires long-term observation, and an in-depth understanding of the complexity of the data on different events organized by various environmental groups. Therefore, the best studies to date have been produced by researchers who are local scholars with direct contacts with environmental groups and are sympathetic to the grassroots movements.

Among the increasing literature on the Taiwanese environmental

Table 2.1

Taiwan's Three Streams of Environmental Movements

Conceptions	Awareness/Consciousness	Collective Action
Immediate home	Awareness of pollution leads to: "Victim consciousness"	Anti-pollution protest movement
Larger living environment or ecosystem	Awareness of nature degradation leads to: "Conservation consciousness" and "Public safety consciousness"	Nature conservation movement Anti-nuclear movement

movement, there are available empirical reports of public environmental awareness and consciousness. Hsiao (1982; 1986; 1989; 1991) conducted four waves of national surveys of public awareness of Taiwan's environmental problems and attitudes toward the growth versus environment controversy. Hsiao also formulated a research framework in linking different conceptions of the environment (immediate home domain versus large living environment and ecosystem) with the different awareness levels of two types of environmental problems (pollution versus nature degradation), and in turn associating them with distinguishable magnitudes of three types of collective action for the environment (anti-pollution versus nature conservation versus anti-nuclear). A causal diagram of the conception–awareness–action relationship is therefore adopted in this chapter to guide the following analysis of Taiwan's environmental movements (Table 2.1).

The Making of Taiwan's Environmental Movements

The Overall Background

Since the 1980s, Taiwan has seen the emergence of three distinctive yet interrelated streams of environmental movements; the anti-pollution protests (since 1980), the nature conservation movement (since 1982), and the anti-nuclear movement (since 1988). The aim of this chapter is to offer a systematic portrayal of the history, social base, and the actors of Taiwan's three streams of environmental movement. These movements were staged, first, to raise the Taiwanese people's awareness of worsening ecological problems caused by rapid industrialization and economic growth, and to mobilize the public into organized social movements to protect the quality of life and the environment, and, second, to engage in the discursive conflicts against the pro-growth state and the profit-seeking industrialists over values related to the environment.

A search of Taiwan's economic planning documents from the early 1950s to the present discloses no mention of the need for environmental protection or nature conservation until the late 1970s, when planning bureaucrats began to consciously articulate nature as a resource to be exploited or used for recreation. Some local scientists and intellectuals did their best in the 1970s to warn the public and the government about environmental dangers. But their voices were largely unheeded (Hsiao 1987). As serious problems developed at an alarming speed, accumulations of solid and hazardous wastes, air and water pollution, and destabilized natural resource systems have brought discomfort, pain, and loss to ordinary people on a large scale beginning in the 1980s. People experienced the costs of the postwar era's hyper-growth under the authoritarian developmental state of the ruling Nationalist Party (KMT).

Thirty years of commitment to capitalist growth at any cost left the environment, almost unprotected, to absorb the by-products of production and consumption. According to one estimation in the late 1980s, if production and consumption are not reorganized to reduce environmental stress, the GNP's 6.5 percent and the population's 1.1 percent annual growth rates—targets set by the Council for Economic Planning and Development (CEPD)—will more than double current pressures on Taiwan's environment by the year 2000 (Taiwan 2000 Study Steering Committee 1989). The public has become increasingly aware of, and impatient with, how worsening environmental problems affect the quality of life, and public discontent over Taiwan's environmental degradation has become a major source of discord and even disorder since the 1980s. Many recent surveys have found that environmental problems rank high among the social concerns of the Taiwanese; that environmental consciousness has increased rapidly in the mid-1980s; and that the public is extremely pessimistic about Taiwan's environmental future. For example, in 1983, 70 percent of the respondents rated environmental problems as serious or very serious; by 1986, the figure jumped to 88 percent. In the 1990s, more than 50 percent expect environmental problems will continue to worsen in the near future (Hsiao 1991; Chiu 1994).

The Local Anti-Pollution Protests

In the early 1980s, anti-pollution collective actions first coalesced into movements in many contaminated local communities. These started as localized pollution victim protests organized solely by victim residents of the communities. With the help of media exposure to a wider public, in the mid-1980s these anti-pollution actions turned into a noticeable nationwide grassroots social movement. The success of the victims' self-mobilization in one locality had the immediate effect of inspiring other communities to get organized to stage similar protests. The primary actors involved in this type of environmental movement were the local victim residents in villages, townships, or cities. Concerned new middle-class intellectuals and university professors, college students, and the younger generation newspaper reporters rendered their sympathy and support to the victims' collective actions against the polluting industries. The primary social base of the local anti-pollution movement consisted of community residents and their existing social networks of kin, neighborhoods, temples, and local voluntary organizations. Though the leadership was in the hands of existing local elites or new grassroots elites, the supporters consisted of people of different classes. The new middle-class segment's support from the outside served to legitimate the protests from within. Some nationwide environmental organizations, including the prominent Taiwan Environmental Protection Union (TEPU) and its local chapters, also provided necessary professional know-how and mobilized popular support.

Based on the 1,211 local anti-pollution protests that took place between 1980 and 1996, Taiwan's environmentalism can be characterized as victim activism (Hsiao 1997). The frequency of the victims' protests reflected one critical factor: the retreat of authoritarian control over civil society. That 90 percent of the 1,211 protests took place between 1988 and 1996—that is, after martial law was lifted in July 1987—demonstrates how victims took advantage of newly opened civil space to voice their grievances. Most actions mobilized against, or sought compensation for, existing injuries or losses to residents. Existing injuries arouse people much more than potential ones: 84 percent of the total proclaimed protest objectives were reactive rather than preventive or preemptive; the latter accounted for only 16 percent. However, the significant increase in preventive protests in the post–

martial law era indicates residents' lack of confidence in the state's policies and the corporate sector's pollution control practices. Out of 243 preventive protests, only four cases occurred under martial law. All the local protests were mobilized by the collective "victim consciousness," derived from immediate or perceived victimization by pollution. Local temples are important sites of anti-pollution protests. Local deities, religious parades, and ghost festivals are all crucial components in this stream of the environmental movement.

The frequency of anti-pollution populist protests also reflects the density of industries in different parts of the island. Three-quarters of all protests took place in northern and southern Taiwan, where polluting industries were concentrated. The great majority of local populist movements were organized against existing industrial facilities and corporations. The second largest target was local government. Though not directly or explicitly, the central state's industrial and pro-growth policies were implicated as the prime cause of many local communities' environmental problems. Sometimes protests generated the formation of permanent local anti-pollution or environmental protection organizations. This was not, however, the norm, as only 157 cases (13 percent) have established more or less formalized civil society organizations as the centers for long-term struggles against polluters. In most cases, energetic and persistent organizations that sustained the protests quickly atrophied when the immediate threat was withdrawn.

As pointed out, the primary actors involved in this type of environmental movement have been the local victim residents and their organizations. "Outside" environmental organizations and concerned environmental activists thus served as supporting actors in some of the local movements. However, only 229 cases (19 percent) were assisted by these outside forces. Through local protests, a new breed of grassroots elites and leadership was created in the early 1990s. Compared to Hong Kong's environmental movement (Chan and Hills 1993), in which existing local administrative organizations and their leadership played a crucial role in presenting local grievances to the colonial British government, Taiwan's anti-pollution protests are similar to what Andrew Szasz (1994) characterized as an "environmental populist movement."

Such anti-pollution populist movements generated both direct interest conflict and normative conflict between local residents and ordinary citizens on the one hand, and business and the state on the other

(Hsiao 1998). The victim consciousness was such that residents suddenly realized that the air they breathed, the water they drank, and the natural commons on which they depended for their livelihood (as farmers, fishermen, and other growers) were commodified to serve the political and economic needs of the state and industry (Hsu 1995; Hsu and Hsiao 1996). The rapid industrialization of Taiwan's many localities also undermined long-existing local institutions, relations, norms, and values, and a new sense of community was constructed in opposition to the state's ideology of economic and industrial growth at the sacrifice of the environment and people's life quality.

The Nature Conservation Movement

The second stream of Taiwan's environmental movement is concerned with the destruction of Taiwan's natural resources. This also became a movement in the early 1980s shortly after the above-discussed anti-pollution protests. Many rescue campaigns were organized by nature conservationists who were mainly writers, scholars, and scientists. These were later joined by many other local, concerned, middle-class groups in the late 1980s. These campaigns were conducted to rescue endangered migratory birds, mangroves, rivers, forests, coastal wetlands, and the ecologically significant gorges from excessive industrial development projects and careless human actions. The key actors in this nature conservation movement, in contrast with the anti-pollution protests, have been non-governmental organizations, including the Bird Society, Homemakers' Union and Foundation, Green Consumers' Foundation, the Society of Wildlife and Nature, and the Nature Conservation Union.

The Bird Society was originally organized by people who enjoy birdwatching. By the 1990s, the Society developed into one of Taiwan's biggest environmental organizations, with more than a dozen local chapters islandwide. This formerly apolitical organization was gradually drawn into political activism because of the increased destruction of Taiwan's natural environment, which sharply contradicted the Society's fundamental beliefs.

Here, it is important to note that women make up the membership of several national conservationist groups, separate from the women writers who started raising conservation concerns in Taiwanese civil society. Women are not usually the public leaders of local anti-pollution protests, yet they are often active in stressing the value of nurturing nature during protests. But in the conservation movement, they have played more important roles. Among the women's conservation-environmental groups, the Homemaker's Union and Foundation is the most noticeable example of this. With a popular base among middle-class housewives, this group is not inclined to take on the controversial political issues, nor interested in the more strictly academic lectures and roundtables of the other groups. Rather, it attempts to root environmentalism in issues of household and motherhood, valuing environmental protection and nature conservation as means to protect the health and future of all children.

A few Buddhist organizations also appeal to nurturance (Weller and Hsiao 1998). Usually, Buddhist organizations for the environment take on no radical issues such as corporate power and abuse of state policies and address fewer controversial issues concerning control of individuals and households. But they often speak of a need to preserve nature and not destroy it. A Buddhist monk and his civil society organization have been very active, successfully forming the above-mentioned Nature Conservation Union. To the Union, one of the most pressing issues is saving Taiwan's west coast and coastal wetlands from environmentally damaging large-scale industrial projects planned by the state in recent years. The natural ecology along Taiwan's west coast was severely polluted and eroded by ill-planned industrial development and fisheries. The state's new plan is to build a chain of coastal industrial zones on those ecologically sensitive areas, its hidden agenda to launch redevelopment after the destruction on the coast. Therefore, the nature conservation movement is increasingly taking on the state's pro-growth policies and developing conflicting discourses against the state and big industry.

The Anti-Nuclear Movement

The third stream of Taiwan's civil society environmental movement concentrates on one specific goal: fighting the construction of a fourth nuclear power plant planned by the powerful state-owned Taiwan Power Company. The proposed plan had been approved by the state before it was made public. The debate peaked during a public forum in the summer of 1985 organized by the Consumers' Foundation, the first social movement organization, established as early as 1980. In that heated debate, Taiwan Power Company officials present were critically questioned by concerned scholars and environmentalists about the feasibility of such a new plant, in terms of safety and economic considerations. Following that, an accidental fire in the third nuclear power plant at the southern tip of Taiwan in late 1985 once again drew public attention to the nuclear power issue. Local residents even organized meetings and rallies to demand that authorities promise a safer energy plan and provide compensation to communities surrounding nuclear plants.

As a result of these developments in 1985 and intensive media coverage of nuclear-related issues, people were provided with ample opportunities to learn more about the pros and cons of nuclear power generation. Ironically, this needed public education did not come from the voluntary provision of accurate information from the nuclear power regulatory authority. The Taiwanese people were forced to be educated about the nuclear power issue by potential nuclear disasters in Taiwan and abroad. The tragic Chernobyl nuclear power accident in Russia was another lesson by default. Under the state's pro-growth strategy, nuclear power generation was considered a necessary national industrial project. Before the controversy over the fourth nuclear power plant became public in 1985, the Taiwan Power Company even planned a total of twenty reactors on the small island by the year 2000. In 1985, Taiwan had already constructed three nuclear power plants, with a total of six reactors in operation; together they generated 52 percent of Taiwan's electricity. This made Taiwan, after France, the world's second leading nuclear-power-dependent country.

Conflicts over the nuclear power issue between the new middle-class liberal intellectuals and concerned environmental groups on the one hand, and the Taiwan Power Company on the other, were intensified after 1986. However, the anti-nuclear voices mainly came from academic and social movement circles. From 1988 onward, anti-nuclear voices were joined by active participation of residents of the proposed site of the fourth nuclear power plant on the northern coast of Taiwan. Since then, the third stream of Taiwan's environmental movement against nuclear power has become a social movement backed by new middle-class intellectuals and civil society organizations and local residents. The main force behind the anti-nuclear movement has been the TEPU, which has devoted organizational resources to combat the proposed nuclear power plant since the mid-1980s. The TEPU was established by volunteers, mostly university professors and students. It also established a local chapter at the proposed site in order to sustain the mobilization of local residents for this specific cause. Over the years, the anti-nuclear movement has turned into a nationwide no-nukes movement to take on the state's energy development policy and the pro-growth myths behind it.

The Taipei County Government controlled by the oppositional Democratic Progressive Party (DPP) even organized a countryside referendum on the fourth nuclear power plant in 1995. But the result of the referendum was not validated due to an insufficient turnout. The capital Taipei City Government, which was also under the DPP's rule, once again held a referendum on the nuclear power issue along with the presidential election in March 23, 1996. The result revealed that 52 percent of the Taipei voters cast a "no" vote on the issue. Obviously, the anti-nuclear movement had developed a clear coalition with this major opposition political party. The opposition DPP even wrote in its charter the anti-nuclear position opposing construction of nuclear power facilities on the island. The New China Party (NCP) is also inclined against nuclear power generation for Taiwan's future energy needs. The most recently formed Green Party (GP) even took a "total rejection" position toward Taiwan's nuclear power policy. In other words, conflicts over nuclear power generation have merged into a political conflict between the pro-nuclear KMT and the anti-nuclear DPP, NCP, and GP. Recently, the movement also adopted a more confrontational approach, commonly used by the anti-pollution protests, in staging protests against the Taiwan Power Company and the state. A coalition between the anti-nuclear movement and the nature conservation movement has also been developed, as both are concerned with the protection of Taiwan's nature and ecology, and both have targeted the state and its pro-growth and anti-environmental ideologies.

Characterizing the Political Economy of Taiwan's Environmental Movements

Comparing the Three Streams

Among the three streams of Taiwan's environmental movements, the anti-nuclear movement has produced the largest volume of written

campaign materials, books, and journal articles. It reflects the complexity of the nuclear power controversy around the world. The rich
materials were written entirely by movement activists. The nature conservation movement also produced an abundant amount of information
and records put out by the conservation groups themselves. These two
streams of environmental movements have used these materials to persuade the public to support their causes, a common strategy for both
conservation and anti-nuclear movements.

By comparison, the anti-pollution movement has generated much
more conflict in its protests. Both non-confrontational and confrontational strategies and tactics have been employed by such local protest
movements. Yet, this stream of the environmental movement produces
very few materials written by movement activists themselves. Instead,
the supporting intellectuals and reporters document many important
stories on their behalf.

Since anti-pollution protests and the nature conservation movement
began in the early 1980s ahead of many other social movements, they
actually took the lead in encouraging other social groups and sectors to
organize for other causes. In a way, the two streams of environmental
movements played an important role in accelerating the rise of
Taiwan's emerging social movements in the 1980s. The consumer
movement led by the Consumers' Foundation since 1980 set the stage
for concerned middle-class intellectuals to speak out for social reforms; thus, the conservation movement had sprung out of the
consumers' movement. But the local anti-pollution movement
emerged independently in different localities. In retrospect, these two
environmental movements accelerated Taiwan's initial political liberalization process that has taken place since the early 1980s. The anti-
nuclear movement, on the other hand, was the product of political
liberalization as it became a movement in 1988, right after the lifting
of martial law on July 15, 1987.

The coalition of these three lines of Taiwan's environmental movement can be found in the occasional overlapping leadership between
the conservation movement and the anti-nuclear movement. It also can
be found in that the same environmental activist groups are often behind anti-pollution protests and the anti-nuclear movement. In recent
years, as conservation efforts have moved into protecting various
coastal wetlands, more and more local residents were organized. As a
result, the conservation movement has become much more locally

based and decentralized in character. To protest against an environmentally damaging project on coastal wetlands, the conservation movement began to be a preventive anti-pollution action group.

Anti-pollution protests generated support from local politicians, especially elected opposition leaders. The conservation movement, in general, has been less politicized, while the anti-nuclear movement had overt political implications from the start. Therefore, the anti-nuclear movement in Taiwan developed a clear coalition with the opposition parties.

There are few strong and obvious alliances between the environmental movement as a whole and other social movements. The role of labor unions in the environmental movement has been ambivalent; in some cases, the unions' antagonistic sentiments toward anti-pollution protesters were even expressed.

Democratization and Environmental Movements

In the late 1980s, one of the most discussed topics in Taiwan's social science circles was the causal relationship between pervasive civil protests since the early 1980s and the subsequent democratization process. Many scholars share the view that the emergence of various social movements that the state hesitated to repress by coercive means challenged the long-standing authoritarian rule, and, in turn, created a set of collective action repertoires and a "public sphere," which political dissidents and social activists could utilize to facilitate the reorganization of political structures (Hsiao 1994; Wu 1990). Following this main theme, it is important to address in what way Taiwan's environmental movement greatly contributed to the democratization process and how reciprocal relationships between the two emerged, especially after Taiwan's significant political transformation settles.

Between 1980 and 1987 (the so-called "liberalization" period of Taiwan's democratization), various social movements, including those of consumers, environmentalists, women, aborigines, and students, emerged and grew. Compared to other social movements emerging during the same period of time, the importance of the environmental movement rested on its ubiquitous nature and direct impact on local politics. The anti-pollution protests of the environmental movement were never limited to certain locations (such as the urban/rural dichotomy) but occurred nationwide, in almost every city and county. According to a calculation of the number of protests launched by seven listed social movements from 1983 to 1988, environmental movement protests occurred 582 times and made up about one-fifth of all protests (Wu 1990: 57–59). Among social movements, the environmental movement has been the most widely extended and most localized.

Since the environmental protests reflected the suffering of local residents, whether or not they successfully eliminate or control the source of pollution and bargain with the polluting industries depends on how well they mobilize and utilize all necessary socio-cultural resources and networks long dominated by KMT-affiliated organizations. They have successfully transformed and reinterpreted the academic debate into simple statements and slogans compatible with existing cultural schemes (folk religions, familism, and traditional aborigine beliefs) and therefore reached a wider audience. These local, self-organized protests can be viewed as an act not only challenging the KMT's "top-down" rule since the 1950s, but also demanding resource redistribution of local politics—on political (votes), social (civil mobilization), and economic (polluting industries versus suffering residents) levels. A new kind of "participatory political culture" was generated and formed in the course of these protests.

Thus, the pervasive grievances of anti-pollution residents were soon transformed into hostility toward the KMT state, which had been unable to either effectively control the polluting industries or quickly alleviate the victims' pain. These grievances also metamorphosed into support toward opposition political leaders who strongly challenged the KMT. Though political scientists seldom study party affiliation and preference among movement constituents in general, it is safe to say that those angry anti-pollution residents have contributed to increasing gains of votes for anti-KMT candidates, and that the protests have served as a tool to shake and break down the cohesiveness of the KMT's local control. On the one hand, these protests, as a test of the tolerance level of the ruling party, lowered the risks of other social movements that adopt similar action repertoires. On the other hand, the challenge toward long-existing, rigid social control created a broader public space that further facilitated politically oppositional forces and the establishment of opposition parties. This meant that the one-party domination was gradually replaced by a fledgling, truly functioning, multiple-party system. In short, the environment-related anti-pollution, nature conservation, and anti-nuclear movements have contributed directly or indirectly to Taiwan's democratization, and this in turn has opened new space for these and other movements.

During the last decade, hundreds of regional and national protests regarding environmental issues challenged the myth of "Taiwan's miracle" by revealing social costs behind the unconstrained pursuit of economic prosperity. Numerous residents suffered greatly due to industrial pollution and hazardous wastes, and their lived-in environment and natural landscapes were rapidly destroyed by highly polluting industries. All the grievance and anger are directed to the causes of recent environmental catastrophes: modern profit-seeking enterprises and corporations.

Business and Environmental Movements

Starting from the early 1980s, Taiwan's enterprises, private or state-owned, faced new challenges: victims of pollution demanded compensation; protesters blocked entries to factories so that no workers or goods flowed in or out; more and more local residents and activist scholars opposed the establishment of new petrochemical/plastic factories and nuclear power plants; politicians, NGOs (non-governmental organizations), opposition parties, labor unions, and consultant groups got involved in various pollution disputes, facing conflicting interests and demands.

Response patterns of the business sector shared little common ground; they differed by size, market (domestic or overseas), products (pollution-affiliated or not), and available resources. Though Taiwan's business sector is heterogeneous and the strategy that each corporation may adopt varies greatly, it is reasonable to say that the "green industry" option is not yet a popular choice. Though accepting the notion of "not to pollute the planet where we reside" in a very broad sense, most of Taiwan's entrepreneurs still view "greening strategies" as counterproductive, costly, and undesirable. To comply with the new environmental regulations and respond to the environmental movement meant to increase production costs (e.g., upgrading technology, replacing equipment, reorganizing production processes, etc.), and few enterprises are willing to do so in the absence of external pressure.

Most strikingly, Taiwan's business sector has unanimously adopted an "opportunist strategy" to deal with challenges from environmental populism. In essence, this opportunist reaction has largely discredited

Taiwan's business sector in its stand on environmental protection. However, the opportunist stand again varies by the size of the enterprises in question and is also related to governmental policies.

Since the late 1980s, challenged by cheaper labor in Southeast Asia and mainland China as well as greater competition in the world manufacturing market, Taiwan's state has begun to implement the second EOI (export-oriented industrialization) policy to reorganize the domestic economy, including providing incentives for conglomerates to expand domestic investments, financing selected medium-sized enterprises to produce higher value-added products, and indirectly encouraging medium/small-sized enterprises of "sunset" industries to move out of Taiwan. The purpose of the policy is to strengthen Taiwan's competitive capacity by producing "high value-added items that are skill-intensive and require a more fully developed local industrial base" (Gereffi 1990: 17).

The impact of such policies on the relationships between enterprises and the environmental movement has been great. Medium- and small-sized enterprises not having sufficient capital to invest in pollution abatement equipment are motivated to move overseas, contingent on the government's encouragement. As a result, these runaway enterprises have escaped from domestic environmental regulations and transferred the social costs of industrial pollution to less developed countries with more relaxed regulations. This is the first type of "opportunist strategy of exit," very similar to what some transnational corporations did to Taiwan prior to the 1980s.

On the other hand, most big conglomerates and some medium-sized enterprises able to afford pollution-preventing investments are unwilling to do so. They still gamble against the government's seriousness about the environment. Facing rising labor costs, increasing environmental-awareness, and pressure of environmental regulations, many conglomerates have threatened to retreat from Taiwan; they staged an "investment strike" in order to bargain for "a better investment environment." Such an "opportunist strategy of bargaining" has an immediate impact; the Taiwanese state and its political elites believe in keeping big industries (i.e., petrochemical, nuclear power, and other highly polluting industries) as necessary signs of national economic strength. Despite the great opposition of local residents and environment-minded academics and professionals, the government still opts for providing cheaper land and water supply, and for simplifying (and/or loosening up) the EIA (environmental impact assessment) procedures in order to accommodate business demands. For years, the government also took suppressive attitudes and actions toward local protests in order to facilitate the construction of naphtha crackers (a polluting industry that refines oil products into a precursor of plastics), nuclear power plants, and industrial parks that might destroy wetlands and forests around this small island.

Realizing the government's ambiguous stand in the contest between economic growth and environmental protection, the big conglomerates and large enterprises then adopted the second type of opportunist strategy by pressing the state to lean to the side of business to favor further growth at the expense of the environment. Moreover, Taiwan's big business also took a variety of less costly and short-term tactics to deal with protests. Instead of paying serious attention to long-term environmental management, they chose to trade "the right to pollute" with (1) immediate fines or compensation when pollution was disclosed by victims or environmental agencies; or (2) promises of rewards or funds for local public facilities in order to gain public support for the new construction of industries. In these businesses' mentality, money may buy the right to pollute. Enterprises of all sizes that choose to stay in Taiwan invest less than 5 percent of total investment on pollution abatement equipment, and the running costs of this equipment have been less than 0.3 percent of the total business expenditures for years (EPA 1996).

Conclusions: Assessing the Impacts and Limits

The impact of Taiwan's three environmental movement streams can be evaluated in several ways. The first is to see how the environmental movement has been understood and supported by the general public. The second is to assess what normative and organizational impacts it made on individuals, communities, and the wider society. Finally, the third focuses on the policy effects the environmental movement has had on the state.

Public Support

Compared to other social movements, the environmental movement as a whole has been perceived by Taiwanese people with the highest level of understanding; it has also enjoyed the greatest public support. The Social Attitudes Surveys conducted in 1991 and 1992 clearly reveal the public's positive attitudes toward the environmental movement. In both years, the environmental movement topped nine other ranked social movements among publicly understood movements. In 1991, 68.3 percent of the respondents reported that they were aware of and understood the environmental movement; the figure rose to 79.5 percent a year later. Again, in both 1991 and 1992, the environmental movement was the most supported social movement among the ten listed movements; 82.4 percent and 87.7 percent of the respondents expressed their support respectively (Hsiao 1996). This has shown that the environmental movement generated the most public understanding and support since its emergence in the 1980s.

Though the survey data cannot directly distinguish the differential awareness and support that each of the three streams actually gained, it can be hypothesized that, among the three, nature conservation is best understood and supported, while the anti-nuclear movement is the least understood and supported. The social consensus over nature conservation is the least questionable. Misunderstanding and mistrust of some individuals and groups to the two "anti" causes in the environmental movement are often detected. Generally speaking, the middle classes, especially the new middle-class segment, have greater empathetic understanding and positive support of the environmental movement as a whole.

Normative Impact

The victims have learned that protest brings results; the majority of local anti-pollution protests achieved at least some of their immediate objectives. The polluting factories were forced either to improve conditions or to compensate the victims or their communities. Some factories were even forced to shut down or move to another location. A few preemptive protests succeeded in stopping planned construction projects or delaying them for further evaluation. But what is unclear is the long-term impact of transforming short-sighted "victim consciousness" into broader and long-term "environmental consciousness" by which the people of Taiwan can continue their self-mobilization to safeguard the future environmental and living quality. More often than not, with the removal of immediate pollution, local anti-pollution efforts ceased to exist and no further pro-environment collective action was sustained. Nevertheless, the emerging sense of community induced by collective protest experiences in many localities should, in the future, serve as the normative foundation for constructing a sustainable, pro-environment consciousness.

On the other hand, the nature conservation and anti-nuclear movements successfully raised overall social consciousness of a new dilemma facing today's Taiwan. The public became more aware of the high environmental costs incurred by rapid industrialization and modernization. Public debates have been staged on the environmental impact of several large-scale industrial projects, including that of a state-backed nuclear power plant. More people in Taiwan are forced to realize that beneath the modern and efficient life-style they enjoy lie increasingly intolerable environmental and living conditions. People are now caught between two equally desirable values for individuals and society: a good material life and a clean, safe environment for them, their children, and their grandchildren. In other words, the nature conservation and anti-nuclear movements successfully forced the people to face a normative dilemma by making necessary a prioritization of two societal values. Taiwanese people no longer single-mindedly support pro-growth beliefs and values that were so deeply embedded in society's accepted notions. A slow, yet firm, public recognition of the dialectics of economic growth and environmental quality can be discerned (Hsiao 1998).

Policy Impact

The policy impacts of the three streams of Taiwan's environmental movement again differ. The widespread, local anti-pollution protests forced the central government to speed up changes to various environmental policies. Tougher pollution controls were adopted, a specific Pollution Disputes Resolution Law passed, the Environmental Impacts Assessment Act enacted, and the Environmental Protection Basic Law is now under review in the Legislative Yuan. Though local and central governments are also more responsive and accountable to local environmental problems, their pro-growth ideologies have not been effectively challenged. That the state is willing to take care of the immediate environmental problems does not mean its long-pursued pro-industrial, pro-growth strategies will be modified in the short run. It is quite evident, judging from the continued, increasingly ambitious industrial polices, that the democratizing KMT state has no clear intention to redirect its priorities of national development.

In addition, though the government reformulated "stricter regulations" to prevent pollution, whether these regulations and punishments were really stringent enough is questionable. Scholars and activists have long challenged the adequacy of the given regulations, especially crucial pollutant control standards found to be much lower than those of other developed countries (Chang 1994: 296–297). Also, the extent to which these regulations are fully implemented appears even more questionable. For example, in the last four years (1992–95), the number of petition cases on pollution nuisance increased from 77,547 to 117,788, but the total amount of fines actually collected from pollution-causing enterprises dropped approximately 11 percent (EPA 1996).

Also, the EPA and local environmental agencies intervened in an intimidated way, seeming afraid to offend either enterprises or victims, such that these agencies did not take sides or make any concrete conclusions. As a result, the EPA has angered people on all sides, establishing a reputation as weak and ineffective among environmentalists, and troublesome within the government and among enterprises (Weller and Hsiao 1998). Thus, outraged victims and environmental activists were forced to take more disruptive actions. While the confrontation heated up, many pollution-causing enterprises finally stated, "we are willing to pay." Given the generally negative reputation of Taiwan's enterprises on environmental issues, it is not difficult to understand why grievances were so pervasive among pollution victims and why most environmental activists were distrustful when dealing with enterprises.

Until recently, Taiwan's business sector did not establish any direct dialogue or relationship with environmental groups through cooperation or sponsorship. Though many conglomerates, in their attempts to change their corporate images, established themselves as philanthropists by setting up non-profit welfare or charity organizations or by sponsoring cultural and charitable activities, they are still not viewed as taking progressive attitudes toward the environment.

The nature conservation movement faces the same difficulty of effectively changing the state's pro-growth policy. This movement, with the timely help and pressuring from global conservation groups, pushed the state into passing the Wildlife Protection Law. But due to the lack of necessary supporting manpower and political determination on the part of local governments to implement the protection of wildlife and natural resources, the new law has become an empty promise. As pointed out earlier, the state and its capitalist allies have even planned to construct more industrial zones along the already endangered northern and southern coastal areas. Though nature conservation groups voiced their disagreements, and conflicts over the proposed large-scale coastal industrial facilities intensified, the state's determination has not been affected at the present. If the ambitious, ruthless plan of building up a chain of coastal industrial zones is eventually implemented, Taiwan's natural coastal ecology is doomed to complete destruction, including its remaining few wetlands. The Nature Conservation Union and many other environmental-conservation organizations, with the backing of concerned intellectuals and scientists, now fight to rescue Taiwan's coastal areas from being turned into a "Cement Great Wall" to be built along the west coast. The movement is confronting not only the KMT state, but local government and industrial interests, all of whom see such projects as necessary for upgrading Taiwan's industrial capability and increasing Taiwan's competitiveness in the world manufacturing market.

Finally, the anti-nuclear movement, in alliance with the opposition parties, still struggles to postpone, if not stop altogether, the construction of the fourth nuclear power plant. However, Taiwan's anti-nuclear movement has not fully engaged in the major discourse of the nuclear power controversy for the following reasons. First of all, the state has neither openly engaged in public debates with anti-nuclear groups nor approved a nationwide referendum to decide the fate of the construction of the new power plant. Second, by manipulating public ignorance, the pro-nuclear KMT state has instilled in the general public the belief in "the inevitability of building the fourth nuclear power plant" by creating the mass illusion of an energy shortage. For example, whenever the anti-nuclear movement has appeared influential, Taiwan Power Company has "coincidentally" limited and rationed the electricity supply to ordinary residences so as to aggravate public fear of an electricity shortage. Third, under the pro-growth ideology upheld by the state and big business, the aggressive publicity campaign to promote "nuclear energy safety" and "nuclear industry as leading industry and a must infrastructure" has been quite effective in neutralizing anti-nuclear claims and consequently decreasing public suspicion of nuclear power.

As a result, Taiwan's anti-nuclear movement has not been able to shake the determination of the state's pro-nuclear executive branch. In

1990, the construction of the new power plant was first officially promoted as one major project in the "Six-Year National Development
Plan," which meant the state would do whatever it could to materialize
the plan for the new power plant. In the following two years, in spite of
the rising anti-nuclear voice in civil society, the Ministry of Economic
Affairs and its highest executive body, the Executive Yuan, further
approved the concrete plan and had its environmental impact assessment review passed.

The ruling KMT still controlled more than half of the seats in the
Legislative Yuan and successfully won enough votes in the legislative
body to approve the consecutive yearly budgets for the proposed plant
in 1995, 1996, and 1997. The opposition DPP and NCP legislators
have, however, declared that they would continue the battle against the
yearly budgets for subsequent years. As of now, the opposition's move
can be read more as a political symbol of protest than one of substance.
Nevertheless, the battlefield of the conflict over the future of nuclear
power has now moved from civil society to political society.

In the summer of 1998, during the National Energy Conference, the
vice-premier openly yet implicitly hinted that future energy policy
would be re-directed and that nuclear power would not be the only
priority. What this announcement means is that the government wishes
to persuade opposition legislators and anti-nuclear movement groups
not to halt the fourth nuclear power plant with a promise that there will
be no further nuclear power projects. In other words, the fourth nuclear
power plant currently under construction is the government's last nuclear project. Responses so far from DPP, NCP, and anti-nuclear
movement activists to this new policy promise are rather quiet, and no
radical opposition has been voiced. One can only wait and see if the
state will take such a new energy policy initiative seriously and officially refrain from proposing any further nuclear power development
projects. To the anti-nuclear movement, the fight against the fourth
nuclear power plant may not succeed in the end, but it has however
forced the state to downgrade nuclear power in future energy policy
agendas. Of course, this is not the end of the story; the controversy
over nuclear power will still continue for years to come.

Nevertheless, Taiwan's anti-nuclear movement has sparked a sharp
cleavage among elites (KMT versus opposition elites; technological
bureaucrats versus environmentally inclined academics) in the matter
of nuclear policy, and has succeeded in erecting barriers to developing

nuclear energy by the state. Due to widespread opposition, the proposal of the new power plant has been deferred three times in the past, and the Legislative Yuan even froze the government budget for the new plan twice (Central News Agency 1995: 212). More important, considering the steady growth of domestic electricity consumption (an average 8 percent in increases per year) and total electricity generated (an average 8.4 percent in increases per year) from 1981 to 1994, the increasing rate of electricity generated from nuclear power plants fluctuated significantly from a 30 percent increase (1983–84) to a 7 percent decline (1987–88 and 1988–89). The percentage of nuclear energy in electricity production even dropped over the decade from 52 percent in 1985 to 30 percent in 1994. In short, the rise of the antinuclear movement in the mid-1980s has postponed the expansion of nuclear power and served as an antidote to Taiwan's dependence on nuclear energy.

In the long run, even if the construction of the new power plant is eventually completed and the plant starts working, the expanding amount of nuclear waste will still make the disposal problem a huge headache for the state. The aborigines living side by side with the old dumping site have already refused to take any more storage and have demanded that the government remove the stored waste. The plan to find a new domestic dumping site has not been successful. After the news media broke the story that several heads of poor villages and towns secretly applied as dumping site locations in exchange for huge amounts of compensation, these heads were forced to withdraw their applications under the greater pressure of residents' opposition.

In order to avoid the problem of new dumping sites being associated with domestic "environmental racism" and "environmental classism," the remaining solution is to "export" the nuclear waste to other countries. In the past few years, Taiwan has aggressively negotiated agreements with the People's Republic China, North Korea, Russia, and others. The recent dispute over Taiwan's export of nuclear waste to North Korea raised by South Korea puts Taiwan under great international pressure. Taiwan's exported nuclear waste to North Korea is criticized as "environmental classism" at the international level: a developed country deposits domestically undesirable products in a poorer one.

The export of nuclear waste is only one dispute embedded in the global nuclear politics. The dissemination of the nuclear industry, for military or civilian use, has never been a purely national issue; it is effectively an international one. Taiwan has imported all six nuclear reactors from U.S. vendors General Electric and Westinghouse (Thomas 1998: 71) to balance trade. Now Taiwan plans to trade nuclear waste exports with North Korea for hard currency and food, which causes anger and fear in South Korea. The irony here is that powerful nuclear industries of technologically advanced countries, such as the U.S., make huge profits by selling nuclear reactors and fuels to Taiwan, thus passing on waste disposal problems. The result is that technologically less advanced countries, like Taiwan, North Korea, and even South Korea, are trapped in the waste disposal controversy and force each other to suffer from these undesirable products. The missing link in the whole dispute and the chain of responsibility seems to be the nuclear industries of Western industrial states. The uneasy, awkward relationships between the environmental movement organizations and activists in Taiwan, South Korea, and the U.S. in facing this controversy over Taiwan's nuclear waste export also reveal the fragility of such alliances, and of conflicts between "national sovereignty" and "global environmentalism."

Regarding the effects of global environmentalism on Taiwan's government and enterprises, as Taiwan is not a signatory to various international environmental agreements, most of the consensuses reached in these agreements have not applied to Taiwan's industries; also, Taiwan's unique political situation makes the pressure of global environmentalism less effective. The most salient example of this is that in 1990, Taiwan's government still granted permission for the production of CFCs (chlorofluorocarbons), which had been listed as a soon-to-be-banned product in the Montreal Protocol (Chang 1994: 289–295). Therefore, the linkage between Taiwan's environmental policy and global environmental initiatives will be a new challenge faced by Taiwan's environmental movement in the years to come.

References

Central News Agency (in Taiwan). 1995. *The Chinese World Almanac*. Taipei: Central News Agency.

Chan, Cecilia, and Peter Hills. 1993. *Limited Gains: Grassroots Mobilization and the Environment in Hong Kong*. Hong Kong: Hong Kong University Press.

Chang, Chin-Shi. 1994. "Greenhouse Effects, Ozone Layer, and Taiwan's Petrochemical Industries." (In Chinese.) In *Environmental Protection and Industrial*

Policies, edited by Taiwan Research Fund, pp. 277–308. Taipei: Vanguard Publication Co.

Chiu, Hei-Yuan. 1994. "Changes of Public Perception of Social Problems." (In Chinese.) In *The Social Image of Taiwan: Social Science Approaches*, edited by C.C. Yi, pp. 1–40. Taipei: ISSP, Academia Sinica.

EPA (Environmental Protection Agency). 1996. *1996 Yearbook of Environmental Statistics, Taiwan Area, ROC.* Taipei: EPA.

Gereffi, Gary. 1990. "Paths of Industrialization: An Overview." In *Manufacturing Miracles*, edited by Gary Gereffi and David Wyman, pp. 3–31. Princeton: Princeton University Press.

Hsiao, H.H. Michael. 1982. "Environmental Quality and Environmental Problems: A Report of Public Perception and Attitudes." (In Chinese.) In *Social Change in Economic Development Processes*, edited by Chang-i Wen, Chenghung Liao, H.H. Michael Hsiao, and K.J. Chen, pp. 29–81. Taipei: Community Development Research and Training Center.

———. 1986. "New Environmental Paradigm and Social Change: An Analysis of Environmental Values in Taiwan." (In Chinese.) *Journal of Sociology* (National Taiwan University) 18: 81–134.

———. 1987. *We Have Only One Taiwan.* (In Chinese.) Taipei: Yuan-Shen Books.

———. 1989. "The Rise of Environmental Consciousness in Taiwan." *Impact Assessment Bulletin* 8 (1–2): 217–231.

———. 1991. "Public Perception and Attitudes Toward Environmental Protection." (In Chinese.) In *The Social Attitudes Survey of Taiwan: The Report on the Feb. 1991 Survey*, pp. 90–97. Taipei: ISSP, Academia Sinica.

———. 1994. "The Character and Changes of Taiwan's Local Environmental Protest Movement: 1980–1991." (In Chinese.) In *Environmental Protection and Industrial Policies*, edited by Taiwan Research Fund, pp. 550–573. Taipei: Vanguard Publication Co.

———. 1996. "Social Movements and Civil Society in Taiwan: A Typological Analysis of Social Movements and Public Acceptance." *Copenhagen Journal of Asian Studies* 11: 7–26.

———. 1997. *Taiwan's Local Environmental Protection Movement: 1991–1996.* (In Chinese.) Taipei: Environmental Protection Agency.

———. 1998. "Normative Conflicts in Contemporary Taiwan." In *The Limits of Social Cohesion: Conflict and Mediation in Pluralist Societies*, edited by Peter L. Berger, pp. 320–351. Boulder: Westview Press.

Hsu, Shih-Jung. 1995. "Environmental Protest, the Authoritarian State and Civil Society: The Case of Taiwan." Ph. D. Dissertation in Urban Affairs and Public Policy, University of Delaware.

Hsu, Shih-Jung, and H.H. Michael Hsiao. 1996. "Soil Pollution and Farmers' Protest Movement: A Case Study in Taiwan's Taoyuan County." Paper presented at the "East–West Environmental Linkages" Workshop, University of Oslo, Norway, October 26–29.

Szasz, Andrew. 1994. *EcoPopulism: Toxic Waste and the Movement for Environmental Justice.* Minneapolis: University of Minnesota Press.

Taiwan 2000 Study Steering Committee. 1989. *Taiwan 2000: Balancing Economic Growth and Environmental Protection.* Taipei: Institute of Ethnology, Academia Sinica.

Thomas, S.D. 1998. *The Realities of Nuclear Power: International Economic and Regulatory Experience.* Cambridge: Cambridge University Press.

Weller, Robert, and H.H. Michael Hsiao. 1998. "Culture, Gender and Community in Taiwan's Environmental Movement." In *Environmental Movement in Asia,* edited by Arne Kalland and Gerard Persoon. London: Curzon Press.

Wu, Je-Ming. 1990. *Social Protests During the Period of Transformation of Taiwan's Political Regime.* (In Chinese.) Master's Thesis, Graduate Institute of Political Science, National Taiwan University.

3

Environmental Movements in Hong Kong

Stephen Wing-Kai Chiu, Ho-Fung Hung,
and On-Kwok Lai

Acronyms

ACE	Advisory Council on the Environment	Lands D	Land Department
CA	Conservancy Association	NGOs	Non-Governmental Organizations
CD	Community Development	PADS	Port and Airport Development
COMAC	Commissioner for Administrative Complaints		Strategy
		PMC	Planning and Management Committee
CPA	Country Parks Authority		
EPD	Environmental Protection Department	PRC	People's Republic of China
		SLTDC	Sha Lo Tung Development Company
FoE	Friends of the Earth		
GP	Green Power	TYCG	Tsing Yi Concern Group
KTDB	Kwai Chung and Tsing Yi District Board	WWF	World Wild Fund for Nature, Hong Kong

Note: Authors' names are arranged in alphabetical order. We are grateful for the comments from the editors of this volume, and the participants of the Second Workshop on "Asia's Environmental Movements in Comparative Perspective," February 17–20, 1997, especially the discussants of a draft version of this chapter, Drs. Ho Kin-chung, Man Si-wai, and Ng Cho-nam. We also want to thank all the interviewees from the various environmental organizations. To protect their privacy, their identity will be concealed in this chapter. All errors are ours and opinions expressed herein do not represent those of the editors, discussants, or interviewees.

Introduction

"There is some truth in the saying that we [in Hong Kong] enjoy a First World economy but only a Third World environment" (Lam 1989: 365). Wong (1996: 371–372) further laments that Hong Kong's air quality does not always meet the Air Quality Objectives. Total suspended particulates, respirable suspended particulates, and nitrogen dioxide levels are high. Water quality in the Hong Kong harbor remains poor, with dissolved oxygen about 50 percent saturation, reflecting the large quantity of organic material being poured into the harbor. The number of beaches in the "poor" and "very poor" categories increased in 1995, indicating continuous deterioration of Hong Kong's coastal water. By the 1990s, the massive construction activities of infrastructure and housing developments have left tranquility to few places in the territory. The huge port and airport projects continue to destroy land and water ecologies, producing pollution including contaminated mud (Hung 1995: 341).

Despite the above growing concerns about the environment since the 1980s, Hong Kong has, in fact, experienced less serious environmental degradation than most Third World countries. As a result of the growing economic integration with mainland China, there was an export of over 5 million industrial jobs across the border to Guangdong province in the 1990s. This industrial relocation helps to transfer most of the manufacturing and other polluting industries out of Hong Kong. In addition, Hong Kong has been undergoing industrial upgrading from low value-added, labor-intensive industries to high value-added industries, services, finance, real restate, tourism, and so forth. Most of these high value-added activities are not life threatening like nuclear power plants and petrochemical factories. Of course, the big polluting deforestation and mines are not in Hong Kong in the first place.

As such, this chapter studies how the pattern of Hong Kong's development has affected the contour of environmental movements in the territory. It will be shown that since the 1980s, Hong Kong has witnessed the growth of a number of organizations and spontaneous protest actions directed toward environmental issues, making considerable contributions to conservation, shaping Hong Kong's environmental agenda, and pushing for legislative amelioration of environmental problems. Nevertheless, in contrast to its counterparts elsewhere, Hong Kong has not yet developed a dynamic environmental movement capable of mobilizing broad-based public support, exerting significant influence on public policy, and forging a transformation in popular environmental consciousness.

This chapter will provide a synoptic view of Hong Kong's environmental movement, highlighting the crucial organizations, mobilization campaigns, and the analytical issues involved. We will also offer a few interpretations for the specific trajectories of development of the environmental movement, arguing that the factors molding the environmental movement in Hong Kong include the ideological and political orientations of movement activists, organizational weaknesses, and the changing political opportunity structures since the mid-1980s.

Profile of Major Movement Organizations

The actors in Hong Kong's environmental movement can be roughly classified into two categories: the territorywide environmental NGOs and locally based organizations. The following description of the NGOs is mainly based on Hoi (1994).

Territorywide NGOs

The Conservancy Association (CA) is Hong Kong's oldest environmental NGO. It was founded in 1968 by a group of professionals inspired by the "environmental consciousness" of the West. Throughout the 1970s, the CA defined itself as a pressure group that put outside pressure on the government to improve its environment-related policies. During its early history, the CA also participated in local grassroots environmental struggles such as the Anti–Oil Refinery Plant campaign on Lamma Island, the Anti–Industrial Pollution movement of the Indu River in the New Territories, and the protest against the operation of the airport after midnight. Early intervention into local struggles was so successful that the CA gained a "radical" reputation. In the eyes of the colonial state, the CA was a potentially subversive organization. In fact, the CA came under the tight monitoring of the state in the 1970s.

In 1974, the government established the Advisory Committee on Environmental Pollution and invited representatives of the CA into this businessmen-dominated board. The leaders of the CA thought that the historical role of the CA as a pressure group had already served its time and hence directed the organization into establishing a working relationship with the government. Since then, the CA has combined its role as a critic in various governmental consultative committees with that of being a "good partner" with the colonial state in environmental protection.

Friends of the Earth (Hong Kong) (FoE) was established by a group of expatriates in Hong Kong in 1983. Through the 1980s, it was generally an exclusive group isolated from the Chinese community. Most of its leaders and members were foreign residents in Hong Kong. In its early years, FoE was no stranger to confrontational actions. It participated actively in the Anti–Daya Bay campaign and also organized an ad-hoc campaign against a nuclear-powered freighter moving into Hong Kong. Since the 1990s, however, FoE has begun to focus more on non-confrontational actions. It organized various educational programs like environment exhibitions and recycling campaigns in different residential areas. Despite all these, the most well known activity of FoE was its legal challenge against the government and private developers for damaging protected wetland areas like the Mai Po Marshes. Since the 1990s, the organization has started to broaden its membership and staff base to the Chinese community.

The World Wild Fund for Nature (Hong Kong) (WWF) is a low-profile NGO founded by a group of foreign businessmen and conservationists in Hong Kong in 1981. Most of its works center on managing the internationally renowned Mai Po Marshes and organizing related educational programs. It also conducts research projects related to the protection of wildlife and gives professional advice to the government through advisory channels.

Green Power (GP) is another relatively broad-based environmental group in Hong Kong. It was established in 1988 by a group of young middle-class professionals, including scientists, academics, artists, clergy, doctors, executives, journalists, and former radicals. The popularity of the group was largely built upon its charismatic leader, Simon Chau, who accused the colonial state and corporations of "criminal" acts against the environment, and also criticized other established environmental NGOs for working with the establishment and complicity with the state and big business. Chau captured public attention mainly because of the special, alternative "green life-style" he espoused; he managed to have constant exposure in the media, telling the public how he lived without television, detergents, artificial flavorings, and so on. Under the media's limelight, Chau was constructed as a radical utopian; GP quickly became inseparable from his image.

By the 1990s, both GP and Chau eventually abandoned radical viewpoints. Their sharp anti-establishment criticisms were replaced by a philosophical perspective of "protecting the environment by changing individual life-styles." The "green life-style" soon rose with the popularity of Chau and GP, and became the focus of educational programs, exhibitions, and publications of GP. In 1995, however, Chau resigned as the chair of GP over dissent on the approach to environmentalism and started his own organization, Green Produce Foundation. Since then, GP reverted from an individualized life-style approach to a strategy inclined toward social activism and policy criticism.

Local Actors

Along with territorywide organizations, there are also a few locale-specific actors working toward environmental protection in Hong Kong. They include grassroots communities mobilized to protect their surrounding environment, which is constituted by ad-hoc organizations arising from local communities in response to specific environmental issues. Usually, these rely on a more confrontational strategy in pursuing their ends. Tsing Yi Concern Group is a typical example of a confrontational local grassroots organization. In addition, there is another type of local green group focused on raising the "green consciousness" of the community. This type includes Green Peng Chau Association, Green Lantau Association, green groups in local social service centers, and environmental associations in universities and secondary schools. Most of these groups adopted the promotion of a "green life-style" as their principal aim.

Action Repertoire: Confrontation Versus Consensus

Since an environmental movement manifests itself in different forms, we will, for illustrative purposes, apply the dichotomous classification of the modal approach and strategies employed by movement organizations and campaigns. These are the *confrontational* approach, whereby conflicting actors/organizations and their counterparts are identifiable, and the contrasting *consensual* approach, whereby the involving parties are not positioned as if they are antagonistic or in a zero-sum game. In the former, interests and claims of different parties are construed as contradictory and incompatible, while in the latter, demands are typically conceived as reconcilable and a mutually beneficial solution is always possible. For environmental groups, a confrontational approach would largely rule out possibilities of cooperation with members of the power elite, such as the government and business, while a consensual approach is largely premised on support from the elite. In terms of the means of action, the consensual approach often relies on socially acceptable and legitimate means (such as education and publicity), while the confrontational approach is likely to deploy means regarded as outside the established institutional framework and hence controversial (e.g., protests and demonstrations). With the exception of the Anti–Daya Bay movement, a more confrontational strategy is adopted by community groups in local environmental issues, while the established environmental NGOs normally opt for the consensual approach of education and lobbying in environmental movements.

The confrontational/consensual dimension can be supplemented by a local/territorywide dimension, as developed above in our discussion of environmental movement actors. Local actions/activities are organized by local actors such as locality-based community organizations. Territorywide actions are initiated by organizations not attached to any specific localities. The local/territorywide distinction is important because the two kinds of strategies/mobilizations also differ in their orientation to environmental issues.

In the following sections, we will use different cases to illustrate the different *modi operandi* of societal mobilization on environmental issues. Our discussion will follow the fourfold classification of local/territorywide and confrontational/consensual actions. We will first discuss the two types of confrontational strategies and then move onto consensual campaigns. On the whole, we can see that a few NGOs started out with a more confrontational posture but later shifted to a more consensual mode.

Local Confrontational Mobilization

As illustrations, two locally based protest campaigns with respect to community-specific mobilization will be outlined here, namely, the

	Confrontational	Consensual
Local	• The case of Tsing Yi Island (urban)	• Local campaigns for recyling
Territorywide	• Protection of wetlands: Against Sha Lo Tung Golf Course	• Environmental education Green consumerism and life-style

relocation of hazardous industries on Tsing Yi Island and the protest against pollution in the rural Sham Tseng area. Mobilization against hazardous installations on Tsing Yi Island was an example of community grassroots protest in an *urban* area in support of better environmental and communal resources (such as housing allocation and relocation). Community social workers played a significant role in the mobilization process. In the Tsing Yi case, the principal agency for mobilization was the Tsing Yi Concern Group (TYCG), formed in 1983 by a group of social workers to promote grassroots participation in local affairs. From the beginning, this group combined confrontational strategies with a community mobilization approach in pressing the government to solve community problems.

The proximity of environmental hazards (ranging from petrochemical installations and processing plants to chemical engineering industries) to residential areas, remains the major controversy surrounding Tsing Yi Island's development. The most obvious case was the presence of the Mobil Oil depot storing inflammable petroleum products and liquefied petro-gas, only fifty meters away from private residential blocks of Mayfair Garden. The leakage to the TYCG of a confidential *Hazard Potential Consultancy Report* on the community's hazardous exposure in late 1983 served as a catalyst for mobilizing for the relocation and reduction of hazardous industries in Tsing Yi. The chemical disasters of Mexico City in November 1984 and poison gas leakage in Union Carbide's Bhopal (India) in December 1984 also spurred popular sentiment against the hazardous installations.

An outstanding feature of this case was the TYCG's and its members' involvement in local politics through the Kwai Chung and Tsing Yi District Board (KTDB). The impact of collective protests and demonstrations could then be channeled through elected officials to the District Board for deliberation, even though the KTDB was only a consultative body under the colonial political structure (Kwok 1994). The TYCG hoped to reinforce its chance of success by participating in electoral and institutional politics. Nevertheless, the involvement of TYCG in institutional local politics also backfired by generating internal conflicts, leading to the split of membership between the TYCG and the Tsing Yi Action Group, which was formed by dissident members of the former.

In contrast to the urban conflict in Tsing Yi, Sham Tseng is an old, indigenous village with most of its villages settled before colonization in the late nineteenth century. Since the 1970s, however, traffic networks developed in the area near Sham Tseng so that the village became more accessible to urban areas. The village economy then became more active, with factories and restaurants opening in or nearby the area. Needless to say, pollution arose in the form of noise pollution caused by the highway and the pollution of the Sham Tseng nullah by oily discharge from restaurants (Chang 1993).

A team of community development (CD) social workers began to mobilize the residents and raise their consciousness over environmental problems. A youth community group and a women's group were formed, with the help of the social workers, to discuss channels through which to tackle environmental problems. Like other indigenous villages, Sham Tseng had a close-knit community structure and a powerful and well-respected Village Office. Hence, the mobilization work of the social workers was fettered by the Village Office's conservatism. A social worker once wrote to the government requesting the implementation of measures to reduce traffic speed on a steep slope in Sham Tseng in order to reduce noise pollution. This letter annoyed the Sham Tseng Village Office, which claimed that the social worker had interfered with village administration. Thereafter, the CD team was prevented from taking part in the Sham Tseng nullah and highway noise pollution cases. This Sham Tseng episode shows how rural environmental mobilization can be preempted by local rural elite (Chiu and Hung 1997).

Territorywide Confrontations: The Anti–Daya Bay Nuclear Plant Campaign

The Anti–Daya Bay Nuclear Plant Campaign was the most controversial environmental issue in the last decade. The controversy developed under the shadow of political uncertainty over Hong Kong's future and coincided with the drafting process of the Basic Law of the

Hong Kong Special Administrative Region in 1986. The nuclear accident at Chernobyl in April 1986 also helped the mobilization by changing people's views of nuclear energy.

At the beginning, there was a debate in the local media on the safety of and need for nuclear energy, and a generalized doubt over the PRC's ability to manage a nuclear facility. The debate then quickly turned into a polarized and antagonistic process of politicization between the pro–Daya Bay camp, consisting of a strong coalition among the pro-PRC, conservative, and business interests on the one hand, and environmental NGOs, veteran social activists, and environmentally sensitive middle-class liberals on the other. Both camps were supported by their respective media and press institutions.

Under the leadership of the Joint Conference for Shelving the Daya Bay Nuclear Plant formed by 107 local pressure and community groups, the Anti–Daya Bay movement solicited more than one million signatures in a signature campaign. The Joint Conference was an amalgamation of most pressure and community groups developed in the late 1970s and early 1980s, plus those elected officials eager to try out their mandated role as the people's representative (elections for local-level representative bodies, the District Board, and the Regional Councils were first held in 1985 and 1986). Though the million-strong signatures do not suggest active support for the Anti–Daya Bay campaign, they do indicate the breadth of the resentment over the project and an acceptance of the movement's articulation of the issue.

A peculiar feature of the movement was that the core leaders in the Joint Conference were not strongly associated with established NGOs. Both CA and FoE were members of the Joint Conference, and the latter's spokesman, Reverend Fung Chi-wood, was a member of CA. Nevertheless, the Anti–Daya Bay movement was steered by other veteran pressure groups, such as the Hong Kong Professional Teachers' Union, the Hong Kong Christian Industrial Committee, the Hong Kong Social Workers' General Union, the Hong Kong Federation of Students, and elected officials and community organizations (Sing forthcoming). After the campaign, the leaders of the anti-nuclear campaign retreated from high-profile environmental protests and turned to other rising, contentious social issues on the political agenda. In the late 1980s, the agenda of popular mobilizations was dominated by the issue of political liberalization.

Yet the transient nature of the mobilizations in the Daya Bay case was evident when the protests eventually receded after the movement was counteracted by a corporate (The China Light and Power Co.) public relations campaign and both the British colonial state and socialist Chinese state showed no sign of concession. The Anti–Daya Bay campaign died down rapidly after the Guangdong Nuclear Power Plant Joint Venture Company and the (British and French) suppliers signed contracts for the plant. Still, this was perhaps the only case in Hong Kong where a major campaign of environmental protest was organized by a coalition of social groups with a strong grassroots element. In retrospect, the Anti–Daya Bay campaign successfully developed a sense of solidarity among the core leadership in the Joint Conference. It also contributed to the development of a sense of identity among Hong Kong people vis-à-vis the British colonial state and the PRC.

Confrontation by Legal Means: Sha Lo Tung

The campaign against the development projects in Sha Lo Tung was an outstanding case of green groups blocking an attempt to use country park land for private property development. At the same time, it also highlighted important features of the major environmental NGOs' repertoires of action and mobilization, namely, a limited social mobilization and a narrowly defined scope of environmental actions, mainly through existing legal and administrative channels.

The Sha Lo Tung golf course development began as a small-scale local land-use dispute. Yet with the efforts of environmental groups, it later developed into a widely publicized environmental debate concerning such larger issues as the impact of such developments on the natural habitat and the opacity of governmental land administration (Hong Kong Council of Social Service 1992). The Sha Lo Tung Development Company (SLTDC), after swiftly procuring rights to village land from the local rural elite, submitted to the administration a proposal to construct a nine-hole golf course/country club/residential development project immediately adjacent to the Pat Sin Leng Country Park in 1979. Since its plan involved the use of country park land, the SLTDC's application was forwarded, via the Lands Department (Lands D), to the Planning and Management Committee (PMC) of the Country Parks Board (CPB) for deliberation.

On condition that the developer provide certain public recreational facilities for the community, CPB advised the Country Parks Authority

(CPA) to give formal approval to the Lands D in March 1990 for the proposed use of the country park land. In July 1990, the Lands D approved in principle the land exchange proposal made by the developer. At this stage, six environmental groups including the CA, FoE, Green Lantau Association, GP, the Lamma Island Conservation Society, and WWF protested the proposed development; the groups challenged the administration's decision to give up designated country park land to a private development. More environmental groups were involved in the opposition campaign, which included petitions, a signature campaign (collecting over 22,000 signatures in less than a week's time), submissions to elected and appointed officials (in District Boards, the Legislative Council, and the Executive Council), study tours to Sha Lo Tung, and gathering at the entrance of Pat Sin Leng Country Park. Yet the administration maintained that the proposal was in the public interest.

Dissatisfied with the administration's explanation, FoE and other environmental groups applied for a judicial review of CPA's decision. In April 1992, the High Court ordered that CPA's approval be quashed on the grounds that CPA acted *ultra vires* when it offered to grant approval of the proposed development. The developer subsequently reduced the scope of its project so that no country park land would be involved. The administration ruled that this further application must be processed in the normal manner. Environmental groups also launched a complaint to the Commissioner for Administrative Complaints (COMAC 1994), the Hong Kong equivalent of an Ombudsman calling for an investigation on charges of administrative malpractice. The COMAC eventually found procedural improprieties and poor decision making on the part of the administration.

In this case, the environmental groups' achievements (led by FoE) are at least twofold. First, they halted the development project via application for judicial review and also brought in the COMAC to ensure that all administrative procedures were fulfilled. Second, public articulation of the issue and a media campaign also served as very effective community education in bringing attention to the environmental impact of land development (golf course and residential private property). Nonetheless, this achievement should be qualified against the fact that such legal actions had very limited potential to arouse public participation. Once the case was put into court, most major legal arguments and procedures were hardly comprehensible to the general public. The coalition NGOs in this campaign made few efforts at societal mobilization, instead adopting a legalistic mode of operation in the form of seeking judicial review and complaining to the COMAC. This suggests that the established environmental NGOs in Hong Kong are at their best when they attempt to resolve environmental disputes through existing legal or administrative channels.

Such legalistic actions only brought partial success to the NGOs. The development proposal was delayed but not dropped. More recently, the villagers from Sha Lo Tung argued for the right to re-farm and develop their village. For the environmental groups, re-farming without careful planning was, in fact, destroying the natural habitat, and serving as a legitimate pretext for (inviting) the development of the golf course and residential property. Even though the NGOs, especially FoE, presented conclusive arguments for conserving the area and suggested several concrete actions that the government could have taken, the latter "did not raise even a whimper of protest" against the re-farming. In other words, while legal actions might yield a few concrete results, without sustained and broad-based social mobilization, environmental actions which confine themselves strictly within the legal and administrative framework possess built-in limitations. But at least this mode of environmental movement is less likely to change the rules of the game, which are unfavorable to the articulation of environmental issues and to fostering any structural change within the polity, which puts the environment in a marginal position.

The Consensual Approach

Environmental consciousness-raising is the primary focus of most environmental NGOs, particularly larger and established ones. Fullfledged environmental education programs are now part of the extracurricular activities in schools, civic education topics in the community, and themes for television and radio programs. The FoE invested a lot of time and energy in environmental education. One recent endeavor is the "adopt an estate" program, an eighteen-month program in a public housing estate focusing on "how to minimize waste and how to set up recycling programs for paper, glass and metals." It also organized tree-planting activities and worked with the Body Shop to sponsor secondary student activities to examine their schools' uses of resources and waste management.

The WWF, on the other hand, focused on its conservation program and used its custodian's role over the Mai Po bird sanctuary to inculcate love of nature among the general public. Started in 1985, Mai Po's education program now attracts more than 35,000 visitors annually. Of these, about one-third are primary and secondary students visiting the area as part of their class or extracurricular activities. With three full-time education officers and an army of about fifty part-time guides, WWF offers a large variety of educational activities for visitors. It launched a three-year Primary Environmental Education Development Program "aimed to further develop wetland-based primary level environmental education both at Mai Po and elsewhere in Hong Kong." It also organized a large number of activities for its members, such as overnight stays at Mai Po, bicycle trips, and visits to Malaysian national parks.

These educational activities are strongly supported by the belated arrival of green funds available via both the public and private sectors. For instance, in the Governor's Speech in 1993, concern for the environment was highlighted by the establishment of an Environment and Conservation Fund with HK$50 million and its institutional arm of the Environmental Education Committee (Ng 1997). In the 1990s, corporate sponsorship, such as by Overseas Trust Bank, Caltex, Shell, Esso Green Fund, China Light and Power, Provisional Airport Authority, and so forth, also emerged as the major force behind many environmental education programs. With green sponsorship, environmental NGOs were able to organize educational programs with greater frequency and intensity, which in turn led to a surge in their membership and activities, largely owing to more media exposure and public participation in educational programs. In addition, other community, educational, and social groups also joined the bandwagon and began to provide more environmental education programs (Hong Kong Council of Social Service 1991; Lai 1993). The result was a form of "consensual environmentalism," with an accent on educational activities.

By realigning their operations with state and corporate sponsorship, environmental NGOs obtain much-needed resources for organizational development, in addition to membership subscriptions and donations. On top of this, corporate sponsorships also became another additional source of revenue for covering recurrent expenses. Due to its link to corporate sponsorship, FoE Hong Kong in fact parted company with the international FoE movement on the issue of cooperation with corporate sponsors. In short, green sponsorship follows where environmental education and, to a certain extent, environmentalism, lead.

The Case of Green Power

Apart from the above groups, the case of GP is also interesting because its espousing of an alternative green life-style in many ways exemplified the consensual approach to environmental issues in Hong Kong. Since its formation in 1988, apart from articulating environmental issues in policy arenas and the mass media, GP's activities have been mostly national in nature, with an increasingly alternative life-style approach, namely, appealing to the general public with green and sustainable styles of life for individuals and the community (Fung 1994; Chau 1992). Through these educational programs, GP recruited a large number of members and built up a good public image of environmental expertise. In fact, GP, or more precisely, its most active leader, Simon Chau, is now an environmental celebrity in Hong Kong (Fung 1994).

GP was successful in attracting the mass media's attention to a greener consumption life-style. For example, many green promotional programs are carried out under the themes of:

- paper saving and recycling;
- bring your own bag (BYOB)—use fewer plastic bags;
- organic farming, which allows people to have a taste of "green life";
- organizing eco-tours from 1993 to Malaysian tropical rain forests;
- vegetarianism, avoid consuming sharks' fins, swallows' nests, snakes;
- polluters-pay principle (green tax) on certain consumable items;
- collaboration with religious bodies to promote greener life-styles;
- green concerts;
- promotions and bazaars of green products.

It also devised creative ways of blending green thinking with daily life. For example, under Chau, GP organized talks and seminars on alternative medicine, life stresses, and green and safe offices. By relating the green philosophy with stress and office safety, Chau hoped to raise public consciousness about the importance of green thinking in everyday life.

GP also pushed for the indigenization of environmentalism and ecological ideas, blending them with the traditional Chinese way of consumption and cosmology (Chau and Fung 1990). Its partnership with religious bodies (Buddhist and Taoist) represents a major thrust in the emergence of the consensual environmentalism in Hong Kong. Clearly, GP strove to develop a non-confrontational strategy of mobilization, seeking to work within existing parameters of colonial governance and the capitalist, consumerist society rather than changing them. By promoting an alternative, environment-friendly individual and communal life-style, it aimed to achieve its green objectives without directly challenging the capitalist and colonial structural frameworks (Chau 1990). Cultural transformation was thus given the highest priority in GP's and Chau's environmental agenda.

In 1995, Chau left the organization. The approach of GP shifted away from the focus on cultural transformation to a more pragmatic line after his departure. The activities of the group became more diversified, and it engaged more in policy research and environmental education in Hong Kong as well as China.

Assessing the Impact of the Environmental Movement

We will examine the impact of Hong Kong's environmental movement in terms of two aspects: the government's approach to environmental issues, and environmental consciousness in Hong Kong.

The Impact on Colonial Governance of the Environment

Before the mid-1970s, the government had no known environmental policy. There was also no governmental agency specifically responsible for monitoring the environment and implementing legislation pertaining to the environment. Only in 1977 was the Environmental Protection Unit established. It was later renamed the Environmental Protection Agency in 1981, and then the Environmental Protection Department (EPD) in 1986, reflecting an increase in stature of the administrative arm of environmental protection within the bureaucratic framework. "The restructuring in 1986 enabled EPD to incorporate various pollution control units in other government departments, and to effectively integrate environmental monitoring, policy formulation and enforcement" (Lam 1989: 350) .

One environmentalist also observed that the change in attitude came gradually—after the signing by the Chinese and British governments of the Joint Declaration on the future of Hong Kong, and at the beginning of the decolonization process. By the mid-1980s, the government adopted "a different attitude toward pressure groups" and did not see them as "troublemakers" anymore. The government was simply more ready to "absorb" pressure groups, and a similar consultative machinery was constructed in the area of environmental policies (King 1981). It seems that local and territorywide groups' bringing of environmental problems to public attention was instrumental in prompting the government to overhaul its "non-interventionist" approach to the environment.

Aside from "administrative absorption," the colonial government also showed a renewed commitment to environmental protection. In 1988, Sir David Wilson said:

> I am increasingly convinced that one of our major priorities must be to halt this decline [in environmental quality] and do more to improve our environment. This is because I believe that the conditions in which we live, like the continued growth of our economy, are essential aspects of making Hong Kong what we want it to be—a place where people want to go on working and living (quoted in Siddall 1991: 403).

The governor's words were indeed followed by a flurry of actions. In 1989, a *White Paper on Pollution* was published, spelling out government policies on the environment and setting a timetable for the environmental program of the next decade. By now, the government boasted an elaborate structure of administrative organs dealing with environmental problems. It also established a system of consultation vis-à-vis environmental organizations (see EPD 1996).

On the whole, the environmental movement achieved considerable gains through administrative channels. The establishment of the Environmental Impact Assessment requirement for major development projects was an important victory for environmentalists' lobbying efforts, although the initiative from within the government is equally, if not more, important. The NGOs also worked with the government in supporting the compulsory conversion of diesel to petrol fuel for vehicles, as well as the Wastage Disposal Bill, which was environmentally friendly but socially unpopular. Green groups also played an active role in monitoring the environmental impact of the new airport and restricting the scope of its construction. From time to time, the NGOs also published research reports and the best critiques of the government's environmental policy, which contributed to public discussion of environmental problems.

Nevertheless, the achievements of lobbying and participation in the governance structure were uneven. Attempts by NGOs to block development projects in the countryside by administrative and judicial means met with mixed success. In areas of particular concern to the government, namely, pollution prevention, achievements are few and far between. Water, air, and noise pollution are still not tackled comprehensively (Siddall 1991; Hung 1995). One environmentalist criticized the government's high-sounding emphasis on the need for "fresh thinking" about environmental issues: "Simply thinking is not enough; actions are also required. What the government so far failed most to do is invest adequate resources to comply with the well-pronounced commitments to protect and conserve the environment, especially those related to agreements signed at the Earth Summit" (Hung 1994: 264).

Other critics also pointed out the inadequacy of the government's anti-pollution orientation and command-and-control approach to environmental issues, and the fact that the government lacks a strategy for sustainable development (Ng and Ng 1992: 365). From time to time, the contradictions in the government's approach, its inadequate provisions for enforcing regulations, and the frequent outbreak of administrative blunders and oversights, were pointed out by environmentalists (see, for example, Siddall 1991). The NGOs also recognized the limitations of the present consultative system. The FoE made the following scathing criticism of the Advisory Council on the Environment (ACE):

> Advisory bodies are supposed to be a check on the administration, but time and again they are proving to be rubber stamps. Their "approval" is used to justify unacceptable decisions such as Sha Chau [in which a fuel aviation facility for the new airport will be built which threatens an important dolphin habitat]. After all, if the ACE accepts it, then it must be environmentally sound, right? Advisory bodies are also, arguably, a means of bringing critics such as green groups and academics into the system and taming them (*One Earth* [summer 1995]: 8–10).

More seriously, the government's recent development projects suggest that it still values development and economic growth higher than conservation and environmental protection. As one environmentalist admits, their influence can only be felt in issues directly related and limited to the environment, and their influence is often weaker for issues with broader developmental implications. The massive new airport project was the most notorious example of this. Despite protests from green groups, no proper ecological impact assessment was conducted before the commencement of the project. The result was heavy damage to the ecology and natural habitats in the Chek Lap Kok Island area.

Therefore, although we do not dispute that the lobbying efforts of the NGOs achieved considerable success, the impact of environmental groups within the existing administrative and consultative framework appears limited. In fact, the green groups were among the first to expose the limitations of government consultative and administrative initiatives.

The Paradigmatic Shift of Environmental Consciousness in Hong Kong

People in Hong Kong historically showed a low sensitivity to the environmental impact of human construction, but there are now signs of growing sensitivities to the environment. The new orientation can be seen in the new life-style approach of the Body Shop movement, which has reoriented middle-class consumers' cosmetic and body care preferences (Cheng et al. 1995). As a Body Shop senior executive wrote: "I see the Body Shop's role as setting a good example both environmentally and socially. We are a unique organization which, in a short space of time, has had a profound effect on people's perception of the products they find on their supermarket shelves." Here, the logic is that life-styles and consumption patterns are linked structurally in shaping the reproduction of the environment, as both of them influence the way in which environmental degradation or environmental conservation takes place. In other words, the interplay between production and consumption determines the conditions under which environmental problems occur.

Moreover, educational efforts by groups like the WWF and CA sensitized people to the need for conservation, while the efforts by FoE and GP to promote a green life-style also began to take root in a considerable segment of the local educated middle classes, reflecting their expanding membership. The belated jumping on the environment bandwagon by the corporate sector, apart from the influence of global trends, must also be traced to the painstaking efforts of local green groups in advocacy and education. The formation in 1988 of the Private Sector Committee on the Environment, which aimed at pooling together efforts and resources of a group of leading companies to address environmental problems in Hong Kong, can be seen in this context. As its chair commented: "Environmental groups help to create a climate of opinion which has promoted a clear change in public attitude in recent years" (*Green Productivity* 1990).

Nevertheless, the effect of this consensual environmentalism on actual practices of environmental conservation is largely contingent. On the one hand, recent survey findings indicated that people view positively government and quasi-governmental organizations' assumption of a more proactive role in controlling environmental problems, such as the implementation of the Polluters-Pay Principle (Hung 1995: 346). Yet when the Principle was actually implemented via sewage charges proportionate to the volume of fresh water consumption in April 1995, many people and organizations opposed such preventive measures. Here, there appears to be a dissonance between people's beliefs about environmentalism and their actual behavior in tackling environmental issues (Man 1995a; 1995b).

A 1992 survey comparing environmental attitudes of citizens in fourteen cities reported that Hong Kong people's environmental consciousness ranked among the poorest (Ng and Ng 1992: 375). A recent survey using a standardized index measuring propensity toward environmental protection also showed that Hong Kong is the lowest among forty countries or regions in the world (Lee, Chiu, and Hung 1997). While most people perceived environmental problems as "urgent," the willingness of local Hong Kong people to put up their own money for environmental protection appeared to be much less than in other places. The level of environmental consciousness and the propensity to protect the environment by paying for its cleaning or living a "green" life is still low among the older, less-educated, or lower-income groups. Therefore, as with governmental efforts toward environmental protection, the impact of environmental groups in achieving a cultural transformation in Hong Kong's environmental consciousness is also uneven, despite the increasing emphasis by environmental groups on such endeavors.

The growing dominance of environmental education and media-focused programs was also questioned by some environmentalists in

light of the danger of trivialization and commercialization of environmentalism as well as the possibility of making people environmentally fatigued by over-exposure to educational programs, as there
are now too many environmental education programs sending out
simplistic messages: fairs, festivals, concerts, exhibitions and competitions, and so forth. In short, "environmental" is used as a catch word
for most, if not all, community education programs as well as the
emerging media industries (Ng 1997). There are doubts whether the
educational efforts of NGOs can overcome the inertia of the public
and "deepen" environmental consciousness. By now, as the previously cited studies highlighted, Hong Kong people possess a keen
sense of environmental awareness, but the problem is how to turn this
awareness into action. In fact, one of the strengths of GP's life-style
approach is to link daily life practices with the environment, but its
weakness lies in its advocacy of a limited kind of practice rather than
focusing on the structural constraints on environmental protection or
conservation.

Interpreting the Development of the Environmental Movement

Given the limited gains achieved by the local environmental movement, how should we interpret its development trajectory? Why were
its achievements relatively uneven? Why was the consensual approach
the dominant mode of operation among territorywide NGOs? Why
were they so reluctant to take confrontational actions that directly
challenge the existing institutional framework of governance and the
power structure? Why do they prefer to lobby the government and
argue against officials inside the committee rooms rather than "taking
it to the people" by seeking to mobilize support from a broad spectrum
of the society? Why did NGOs' strategic repertories take a distinc-
tively consensual turn, toward environmental education and lobbying
instead of grassroots mobilization? Here we draw on the recent synthesis emerging from the discussion of social movements, and fashion an
interpretation along the lines of three sets of factors: "(1) the structure
of political opportunities and constraints confronting the movement;
(2) the forms of organization (informal as well as formal) available to
insurgents; and (3) the collective processes of interpretation, attribu-
tion, and social construction that mediate between opportunity and
action" (McAdam, McCarthy, and Zald 1996: 2).

The Changing Structure of Political Opportunities

Since the 1980s, the state progressively incorporated green groups into its consultative machinery. This helped forge among environmentalists a sense of efficacy in the participation in governmental consultation bodies. As one environmentalist told us,

> After the appointment of many of our members into the various consultative committees, welfare again gained a direct channel of communication with the government. Hence in recent years, we have rarely taken issues to the street. In case we have disagreements with the government, we can always argue with them directly in the committees.

Therefore, one reason why environmentalists placed an emphasis on lobbying the government is that they clearly feel it works.

In particular, since the mid-1980s, the government apparently became more open and responsive to demands made by environmentalists. Since 1993, the incorporation of green groups into the consultative machinery was also institutionalized when appointment to consultative committees was made not only on a personal basis but as representatives of the major green groups (Hung 1994: 260). Incremental changes in environmental regulations were implemented from time to time. By now the leading NGOs already have a long experience in dealing with the government through the consultative framework and, in a limited way, through the legislature. Over time, environmentalists developed a *modus vivendi* between themselves and the officials. They appeared to learn when to push, retreat, and compromise. They also learned how to build alliances among themselves to put pressure on the government collectively within the committees. They issued joint statements in commenting on environmental issues, one example being the "Green Groups United Front," formed when major NGOs submitted an Earth Day manifesto to the government in 1993.

Through interactions with the government over the years, they also developed a perception (quite correctly) that the latter is not homogeneous, and that it is possible to build alliances with the relatively pro-environment faction within the government against those officials less sympathetic to their cause. An environmentalist made this point clearly during our interview:

> The government is also not an iron-clad entity. Instead there are many fractions within it. What we are doing is sometimes trying to coordinate our actions with some of the officials. When there is an environmental problem, the Environment Protection Department will often give us the information so that we could criticize the government. With a public outcry, they can then argue for money to address the issue. In one sense, we [the officials and NGOs] are just using each other.

They also think that in the officials' urge to avoid making mistakes, they would seek NGOs' cooperation and opinions. This certainly reinforces the conviction among green groups that it is possible to pursue environmental goals through existing political channels. For them, it is a simple fact that "given the opportunities in the existing institutional arrangement, you will think why not take advantage of them and try to influence the government's policies?" Or as another environmentalist put it: "Communication, consensus and cooperation take the place of distrust, criticism and confrontation" (Hung 1994: 260). However, Hung (1995: 358) points out that "*in order to keep the working relationship with other members in these government organizations, opposition actions have been tuned down*" (emphasis added).

Given the small number of persons involved in the environmental movement and their meager organizational resources, environmentalists find it hard even to keep up with proceedings of meetings or to finish reading all the tabled documents. Little time and few resources are therefore available for alternative forms of action.

Apart from the gradual opening of opportunities for green groups in the consultative machinery, broader changes in the political structure also result from the articulation of environmental issues in the society and polity. From the mid-1980s, Hong Kong's authoritarian colonial political system began to undergo a process of gradual liberalization and democratization. Seats in the legislature and other local-level consultative bodies were gradually opened for popular election. This fundamental change in the rules of the political game had two important effects on the environmental movement. First, from the beginning of the liberalization, issues of the pace and form of reforms in the political structure dominated the societal agenda. The prospective reunification with China also further complicated this process and accentuated the significance of democratic reforms in Hong Kong. As a result, not only did political groups focus their efforts on demanding or opposing a faster pace of democratization before reunification, but the general public did as well, under the influence of such political discourses that highlighted the overriding importance of political issues. Societal attention on other issues not directly related to political reforms is thus likely to be diminished. Not only the environment movement, but other forms of social movements also were affected by this process of politicization (Lui and Chiu 1997).

A second effect of the changes in the political process is competition for resources between environmental groups and other political groupings. One obvious area of competition is personnel. Given the small and restricted number of persons active in societal and political affairs, the demands from different causes and issues for leadership and core membership are likely to weaken the less-appealing cause. Given the overwhelming presence of political issues, it is only natural for the environmental movement to lose personnel to political activities. For example, most leaders (as well as their members) in the anti–Daya Bay campaign switched to another battlefield—the struggle for the 1988 Direct Election for Legislative Council—soon after the movement subsided (Sing forthcoming). Sometimes environmental issues are even exploited by political parties of different shades to further their own electoral interests. The societal exposure and support of environmental groups are hence likely to be restricted. If it is difficult for environmental groups to "claim credit" for raising certain environmental issues, it is similarly difficult for them to enlist popular support by engaging in these issues.

We do not want to write off completely the benefits of democratization on environmental protection; it does make the colonial government relatively more accountable and responsive to popular demands. On the whole, however, the changes in political process "absorbed" environmental groups into institutional politics, made them preoccupied with the details of the consultative process, and prompted them to turn to a more conciliatory approach on environmental issues. As Hung (1994: 261) observes, one reason why the criticisms of the Port and Airport Development Strategy (PADS) and the sewage disposal strategic plan were muted was "too much care [is] given to maintaining a good relationship with the government." We are not saying that the NGOs are not trying to defend the environment as they see fit, but in doing so, the logic of the incorporation process preempts any radical or confrontational actions. The ascendancy of the debate over political reform also led to competition for societal support and resources between green groups and political organizations.

It is, however, insufficient to account for the development of social movements entirely in terms of the political process. For example, why have local green groups been overwhelmingly in favor of a cooperative action repertoire rather than possible alternatives? To answer this question, we need to turn to the other two factors impinging on social movements.

Mobilizing Structures

A general problem for the environmental movement in Hong Kong is its organizational weakness. Most environmental organizations have only a thin layer of staff members; most activities must be entrusted to volunteers whose participation is often intermittent. Turnover in leadership also often produced significant instability in the organization, resulting in abrupt changes in strategies and focus. Both GP and CA, for example, experienced leadership turnover and succession crises during their histories. Some GP members also complained that their leaders were more interested in interpersonal rivalry than the well-being of the organization (Fung 1994: 36, 58).

Some organizations (especially CA), often by their own choice, have a small membership base. The other NGOs actively recruit new members. Even in those cases, however, they have more success in recruiting new members than maintaining them in the organization, or motivating them to take an active part in organizational affairs. In other words, such organizations have not been successful in "deepening" their members' involvement. Some members in fact have developed a consumerist attitude toward participation in GP. They pay their dues and expect to receive a bundle of services. They do not normally perceive themselves as having an obligation or right to take into their own hands the operation of the organization (Fung 1994: 54). Of course, members are also encouraged to be volunteers in other activities, but on the whole, ordinary members do not necessarily feel deeply involved in NGOs, which have a larger membership base. This mode of membership is best suited for consensual environmental education and not prepared for popular mobilization or confrontational actions. A major consequence of a small membership is that the organizations must depend on outside funding to cover operating costs. The educational programs of the major organizations do not always run on a self-financing basis and require subsidies from the organization. Personnel costs are also high in Hong Kong, given the high cost of living. Much energy therefore must be spent on fund-raising.

In recent years, corporate and governmental funding are readily available, but often at a cost. Accepting corporate and governmental funding means that organizations must maintain a friendly relationship with their donors; hence, these types of funding can be used only in less-sensitive programs like educational ones. Corporate and governmental sponsorship are often granted on a project basis, which rarely covers personnel and administrative costs. Thus, while corporate-funded educational programs and fund-raising activities absorb much of the meager human resources (paid and voluntary) in the organization, they still cannot be used to solve the financial bottleneck in most organizations. For example, one reason that CA sought to maintain a small and low-profile organization was to avoid being dragged into this vicious cycle of expansion, fund-raising, and corporate sponsorship.

Sometimes the acceptance of corporate sponsorship can also lead to moral and practical dilemmas between green groups and their leaders. In the campaign against the Nam Sang Wai redevelopment project (Hong Kong's only remaining wetland area, which forms part of the Deep Bay Buffer Zone for Conservation in Mai Po Marshes), the WWF and other NGOs applied for a judicial review of the Town Planning Board decision approving the project. Nevertheless, according to a leading environmentalist, some activists in the campaign accepted offers of consultancy contracts from private property developers in the form of ecological development contracts, or compromised with property developers once their claims for compensation were met: "In pursuing the [Nam Sang Wai development] case, the developer is very active in soliciting the support of the 'green groups'. Some prominent members of the 'green groups' have been involved in preparing the proposal for the developer. Their opinions do carry weight on the decision of the Town Planning Board at its final hearing" (Hung 1994: 261–262; Hung 1995: 357).

In short, it is difficult for green groups to resist the temptation to be involved in profit-driven "ecologically sound projects" sponsored by private developers or the state. While the assumption of advisory roles by environmental groups in development projects might help mitigate their adverse effects on the environment, such involvement might also be construed as an endorsement of the projects by these groups.

Another issue is the relative underdevelopment of confrontational mobilization for the environment at the local level. This can also be traced to a number of organizational problems. First, territorywide environmental NGOs generally are not keen on building networks with community/grassroots protest groups, let alone mobilizing the grassroots community. Though environmental NGOs exhibit different orientations, all seem remote from grassroots mobilization. For instance, FoE works in accordance with formal and legal litigation, CA focuses on scientifically and professionally defined conservation issues, WWF largely focuses on conservation work in the Mai Po area, and GP experiments with a life-style approach. A major case of grassroots mobilization, the Tsing Yi Island campaign, was organized by local community leaders without any external intervention. The campaigns and legal actions against the construction of a golf course, on the other hand, were staged by NGOs without much community involvement.

Second, we mentioned earlier how the growth of electoral politics since 1982 affected environmental organizations. In fact, many community leaders, who previously mobilized residents for community-cum-environmental problems, redirected their efforts to electoral politics, either to support their affiliated candidates or even to participate in electoral contests themselves. Vast amounts of resources and leaders are diverted to electoral competitions. As a result, grassroots mobilization in general and mobilization for local environmental issues in particular decline as electoral campaigns grow. Local environmental problems now become more an opportunity for politicians to gain media exposure than a chance to mobilize the grassroots. In cases where media attention is unlikely to follow or the issues are too sensitive, local protests often do not receive much support from external personalities or groups.

The situation is no better in the countryside. Most rural villages are indigenous villages and have close-knit community structures controlled tightly by a small group of rural elites who benefit from local economic development and, unwittingly, the environmental deterioration coming with it. Consequently, grassroots mobilizations for the environment, especially those initiated by outsiders such as social workers, are difficult and easily pacified by the elite (Chiu and Hung 1997). This perhaps explains why rural grassroots struggles for the environment are so rare, and why they rarely spread to other localities or are not sustained for long.

Cultural and Ideological Processes

A third set of factors shaping the development of environmental movements is primarily cultural and ideological, that is, environmental groups' (or their leaders') perceptions and framing of environmental problems, and their articulation of the possible solutions. Environmentalists often cite a simple answer, a socio-cultural one, to the questions of why consensual strategies better serve the environment than confrontation, and why so far these strategies have not succeeded in mobilizing popular support. In this view, consciousness of environmental protection is largely a by-product of societal modernization and affluence. The postmaterialism thesis, for example, suggests that society will turn to environmental protection after a protracted period of affluence and the solving of basic issues of survival. Environmental consciousness is thus part and parcel of the rise of a postmaterialist culture, which in turn determines societal support of environmental movements and other efforts toward environmental protection. As Chau (1993: 12, our translation) suggests, "[e]nvironmentalism largely appeals to people's senses of righteousness, morality, and altruism." That is why environmental movements prefer an earth-centered green philosophy to people-centered environmentalism.

We believe, however, that the process of social construction, by which local environmentalists conceive and define environmental issues, is also critical. Different NGOs in fact developed different "frames" in the interpretation of environmental problems. These cultural or ideological frames sensitized them to certain problems at the expense of others, and also highlighted the viability of certain means of resolving them as well as the futility of others. As such, they were also responsible for shaping the developmental trajectories of the environmental movement in Hong Kong.

Contrasting with the left-libertarian tradition of green political groups in Europe and mass movement–oriented and militant environmental groups in certain other Asian countries, Hong Kong's environmental NGOs, their leadership, and active members show no trace of leftist political ideology and no interest in developing a mass movement. While it is not uncommon for community groups and environmental NGOs to work together in environmental education, they appear to be separated on other environmental and social issues and types of actions. Part of the reason seems to lie in their assumptions and perceptions about the general public. There is a perception among Hong Kong's NGOs that the general public does not like confrontation and is not likely to participate in confrontations over the environment. One environmentalist said that they had no aversion to taking the issues to the masses and mobilizing the public for confrontation, but one simple reason for their not doing so was that they strongly believed the masses would not respond to their calls. For them, there are not too many issues like the Daya Bay that can arouse public involvement. Some organizations like CA have also gone through a more radical phase, which did not seem too effective.

Yet more important in accounting for the consensual approach is the NGOs' own definition of the nature of environmental problems. One environmentalist pointed out during our interview that environmental problems were different from other social problems. "Most [environmental] problems are incremental. Pollution may not kill you at once, but it will eat you gradually. Without an imminent threat, many people would not even notice them. When you say we should protest over these issues, they respond why not tomorrow? When you try to mobilize the masses they just don't share the sense of urgency."

For green groups, the particular nature of the environmental problem "dictates" their mode of operation; the best way is to take a long-term strategy through a non-confrontational approach rather than the use of radical means without a mass base, becoming discredited and marginalized. FoE also shared this view when it explained the split with FoE International: "We take the view that, while confrontation may have been the only posture available to environmentalists in the 1970s, times are changing and industrial attitudes along with them. We have therefore sought to establish a relationship with industry which is suited to the present." The result is "a more honest, courteous and fruitful relationship [with business]" (*One Earth* 1991 [spring & summer]: 11). Under the "incremental" conception of environmental problems, it is much easier to work not only with business, but government as well. Green groups are not demanding overnight wholesale changes in the government's policy; they can accept incremental solutions. GP, especially under Simon Chau, argues for radical "holistic" changes in society and politics, but also frames that as the result of a long-term gradual cultural transformation rather than of popular mobilization for political and protest actions (see Chau 1993).

The NGOs often framed the environmental problem as a technical one, the alleviation of which made their professional inputs essential. Their lobbying efforts, for example, are often couched in terms of technically and scientifically sound reasoning. Often viewing the environmental question as a non-zero-sum problem, they believe that adverse impacts on the environment can be avoided by better planning and implementation. They are confident that with their professional training and experience in environmental issues, they could persuade and guide the government toward a better environmental policy and in avoiding blunders. Man (1996: 2) called this the "management approach to the environment," which includes a tendency to "technologize" environmental problems: "all of them are taken as issues concerning which 'optimal decisions' can be secured and expert knowledge can offer the ultimate guidance." As a result, for example, NGOs stress the need to maintain their "independence" in environmental issues. An environmentalist said this during our interview: "We hope to use our professional knowledge to analyze problems in a calm, objective manner. If we simply take sides and follow the masses, it will affect our [professional] credentials; they [the government and the society] will think we are unprofessional."

Man (1996: 12) also argues that the management approach often excludes issues related to conflicts of interest, justice, and democratic rights, since these are regarded as unscientific and value-laden. For example, one reason why CA did not take part in the Tsing Yi struggle against the oil depot was that there was a feeling that the residents were fighting more for their own vested interests than simply for the environment. The depot was there before the residents of Mayfair Garden moved in, and the latter still took advantage of the low housing price. This and other examples convinced environmentalists that they should be wary of attempts to jack up property values disguised as environmental struggles. This also means, however, they are often hesitant or react slowly to local conflicts.

Following this interpretive frame, environmentalists also perceive ways to deal with environmental problems within the existing institutional framework of government. While they clearly recognize the political dimension of environmental problems and harshly criticize the shortcomings or inadequacies of government policies or the structure of environmental administration, they still hope that the government can be persuaded to solve environmental problems. Committed to a consensual approach and cooperation with the powers-that-be, green groups believe that compromise is a rule of the game, and that if they wish to continue playing the game, they need to accept its limitations. Had they seen the environmental problem differently (as some European and other Asian ecologists have done), it would have been impossible for them to work toward incremental solutions.

In a sense, the life-style and consensual approach was highly successful, as it was adopted by most environmental groups, the government, and even the business sector. "Green consumerism" becomes a predominant interpretive frame of the environment or within the environmental movement. Yet, the effect of this framing of the environmental problem is to produce a rift in the minds of the grassroots between the environment and their livelihood. Environmentalists' arguments are sometimes perceived as foreign to their livelihood or even threatened by it (Hung 1996). For example, in the aforementioned survey on public support of environmental protection, a majority of respondents agreed or strongly agreed that "environmentalists care more about the state of the natural environment than the livelihood of fellow citizens" (61.6 percent), while only 24.8 percent contested the statement. Moreover, Hong Kong also ranked third highest among forty countries and regions with 39 percent of the respondents agreeing with the statement that "the environmental pollution problems in Hong Kong are not as urgent as suggested by environmentalists" (Lee, Chiu, and Hung 1997: 21). We do not want to dispute that the ways in which common people earn their living are sometimes a main source of waste and pollution, but in these cases the precept of a green life-style, by framing environmental problems as individual moral failures, largely shifted the burden of environmental protection to the grassroots, leading paradoxically to confrontation rather than communication.

The popularization of "green ideas" is thus still largely confined to the middle classes, and conflicts between environmentalists and other social groups abound. For example, in cases of grassroots mobilization against the government and the business sector, against the degradation of their immediate environment, like the cases of Sham Tsang mentioned earlier, the assistance of established NGOs is not sought. Now all too often in cases when tenant farmers were evicted by landlords with government approval to turn their land into development projects, green groups have not taken the initiative in articulating a united front with these farmers against greedy landlords and developers and have not lent a helping hand to the resistance.

When the less educated, lower-income people get the impression that green groups seem remote from their problems of livelihood or survival and their material-cum-environmental grievances are being ignored, they naturally develop a sense of distrust toward green groups. They sometimes even see themselves as "victims" of environmentalism while the NGOs work with, rather than attack, larger environmental culprits like the government or big business. The failure to forge a cultural frame that bonds together livelihood problems at the grass roots and broader environmental issues thus sticks like a thorn in the flesh of the local environmental movement, hampering its effort to generate a new and environment-friendly societal consensus.

Conclusion

In this chapter, we presented an overview of environmental movements and their actions since the 1980s. A brief assessment of their achievements precedes some interpretations regarding their outstanding characteristics and developmental trajectories. Overall, we want to affirm the achievements made by environmental groups, both at the communitywide and the local levels, in contributing to the mitigation of environmental problems in Hong Kong. The limitations of the environment movement we identified are not directed toward particular persons or individual organizations. Instead, we detected problems for the movement as a whole. We can compare the local environmental movement as a habitat in which we found a diversity of species (groups). Individually, they have their own niches and operate smoothly, at least in the case of the established NGOs. Each made a good contribution to the cause of environmental improvement in Hong Kong. Yet when we look at the habitat as a whole, there are significant lapses. For one thing, the niches of the communitywide groups appear to overlap with each other (with a focus on the middle-class educated strata), resulting in competition for resources and, in some cases, duplication of efforts. Furthermore, the more marginal groups (the local confrontational type) have so far received little support from the more dynamic groups. It is this disarticulation that explains why environmentalism has not made major inroads into the grassroots of society. If bio-diversity is something ecologists value, we also hope that a greater diversity of organizational forms and action repertories can develop in Hong Kong.

This is a short chapter for such a big topic. There are still many things we do not know about the environmental movement. We need more case studies of individual groups and how they operate. We need to know more about how they perceive and construct the environmental problem. We also need to know more about how the public, especially the grass roots, perceives the environment and green groups' activities. Our chapter only makes a modest effort in comprehending all these questions; it would be a success if we could stimulate more reflection on the state of the environmental movement in Hong Kong.

In the near future, the economic and political integration with mainland China will have a contradictory effect on Hong Kong's environmental movements. On the political front, it is unlikely that confrontational politics will flourish in Hong Kong under Chinese sovereignty. The history of mobilization against the Daya Bay nuclear plant and its aftermath reminds us of the difficulties in pursuing environmental movements against a national agenda of economic development. In a sense, the Chinese government is even more pro-development than the colonial administration. Under such circumstances, it is not surprising that the consensual approach will continue to develop among Hong Kong's environmental groups. Grassroots environmental mobilization will likely be further weakened, and the agenda for the environmental movement will be channeled toward an emphasis on individual life-styles, conservation, and education.

However, on the economic front, although industrial relocation of manufacturing and other polluting industries to mainland China may have cut down Hong Kong's community grievances against pollution in the short run, industrial relocation also has the potential to strengthen community mobilization against cross-border pollution. In 1996, some record-breaking episodes of air pollution in Hong Kong occurred under the influence of light northerly winds. It seems that air pollutants imported from Guangdong and Shenzhen factories have contributed to the buildup of the pollution level in Hong Kong. The dumping of industrial wastes by mainland factories in the Pearl River Delta has also threatened the livelihood of the farmers and fishermen in the New Territories of Hong Kong. Needless to say, the April 1995 shut down for major inspections of the Daya Bay Nuclear Power Station, situated across the border in Shenzhen, has aroused the concern of the Hong Kong community.

Facing the pro-developmental policy of the Chinese government and the growing threat of pollution across its border, how to work within a politically acceptable framework but transcend its limitations is the challenge facing Hong Kong's environmentalists in the next century.

References

Chang, Fiona. 1993. "Tackling Environmental Pollution in Sham Tseng." In *Limited Gains: Grassroots Mobilization and the Environment in Hong Kong,* edited by Peter Hills and Cecilia Chan, pp. 149–160. Hong Kong: Centre of Urban Planning and Environmental Management (HKU).

Chau, Simon S.-C. 1990. "The Environment." In *The Other Hong Kong Report— 1990,* edited by Richard Y.C. Wong and Joseph Y.S. Cheng, pp. 491– 505. Hong Kong: The Chinese University Press.

———. 1992. *Letters to Activators of the Green Power Limited.* 10 November. Unpublished.

———. 1993. "Green Power: Yesterday, Today and Tomorrow." *Green Produce* 53: 12–39. (In Chinese).

Chau, Simon Sui-cheong, and Kam-kong Fung. 1990. "Ancient Wisdom and Sustainable Development from a Chinese Perspective." In *Ethics of Environment and Development: Global Challenge, International Response,* edited by Ronald Engel and Joan Gibb, pp. 222–231. London: Belhaven.

Cheng, Wai Ling, Mei Kei Lam, and Wing Han Ng. 1995. *Green Consumption— A New Phase of Consumerism.* Unpublished project report, Department of Sociology, The Chinese University of Hong Kong.

Chiu, Stephen W.K., and Ho-Fung Hung. 1997. "The Paradox of Stability Revisited: Colonial Development and State Building in Rural Hong Kong." *China Information* 12: 66–96.

Chui, Wing-Tak, and On-Kwok Lai. 1994. *Patterns of Social Conflicts in Hong Kong in the Period 1980–1991.* Monograph No.1, Department of Applied Social Studies, The Hong Kong Polytechnic University.

Commissioner for Administrative Complaints of Hong Kong (COMAC). 1994. *The Sixth Annual Report of the COMAC.* Hong Kong: Hong Kong Government Printer.

Environmental Protection Department (EPD). 1996. *Environment: Hong Kong 1996.* Hong Kong: Hong Kong Government Printer.

Fung, Kam-Kwong. 1994. *Draft on the Environmentalists' Profile in Hong Kong.* Unpublished.

Green Productivity. 1990. "The Private Sector Committee on the Environment—A Private Sector Approach to Environmental Issues." *Green Productivity* 4: 10–12.

Hoi, Sing (Hung Ho-fung). 1994. "How the Greens Cannot Become a Power: A History About the Abortion of the Grassroots Ecology Movement in Hong Kong." In *Grassroots Social Movements in Hong Kong: An Alternative Viewpoint.* Hong Kong: Radical Press.

Hong Kong Council of Social Service (HKCSS)—Editorial Board of the *Quarterly*. 1991. "A Situation Report on Voluntary Agencies' Environmental Protection Activities." *HKCSS Quarterly* 18: 11–18.

Hong Kong Council of Social Service (HKCSS)—Resource Group on Town Planning. 1992. *Case Analysis on Building a Golf Course at Sha Lo Tung*. Hong Kong: HKCSS.

Hung, Ho-fung. 1996. "Much Worse than Indifference: On Anti-Grassroots Ethos of Hong Kong Environmental Groups." *The Centre for Environmental Studies Newsletter* (The Chinese University of Hong Kong) 5 (no. 2): 4–5.

Hung, Wing-Tat. 1994. "The Environment." In *The Other Hong Kong Report—1994*, edited by Donald H. McMillen and Si-Wai Man, pp. 253–264. Hong Kong: The Chinese University Press.

————. 1995. "The Environment." In *The Other Hong Kong Report—1995*, edited by Stephen Y.L. Cheng and Stephen M.H. Sze, pp. 343–360. Hong Kong: The Chinese University Press.

King, Ambrose Y.C. 1981. "Administrative Absorption of Politics: Emphasis on the Grassroots Level." In *Social Life and Development in Hong Kong*, edited by Ambrose King and Rance P.L. Lee. Hong Kong: The Chinese University Press.

Kwok, Ngai-Kuen. 1994. "Political Exchange Network of Kwai Tsing District Board." M.Phil. thesis, Department of Sociology, The Chinese University of Hong Kong.

Lai, On-Kwok. 1992. *Opinion Survey Report on Environmental Problem in Kwai Chung & Tsing Yi*. Unpublished report to the Kwai Chung & Tsing Yi District Board.

————. 1997. "Community, Environment, and Sustainable Development." In *Community Mobilization and the Environment in Hong Kong*, edited by Peter Hills and Cecilia Chan. Hong Kong: Centre of Urban Planning & Environmental Management, University of Hong Kong.

Lai, Wing-Hoi. 1993. "Environmental Education in Social Welfare Agency." MSW dissertation, Department of Social Work and Social Administration, University of Hong Kong.

Lam, Kin-Che. 1989. "The Environment." In *The Other Hong Kong Report—1989*, edited by T.L. Tsim and Bernard H.K. Luk, pp. 333–367. Hong Kong: The Chinese University Press.

Lee, Yok-Shiu F., Stephen W.K. Chiu, and Ho-fung Hung. 1997. "Public Support for Environmental Protection in Hong Kong: Final Report." Mimeograph.

Lui, Tai-Lok, and Stephen W.K. Chiu. 1997. "The Structuring of Social Movements in Contemporary Hong Kong." *China Information* 12: 97–113.

McAdam, Doug, John McCarthy, and Mayer Zald. 1996. "Introduction: Opportunities, Mobilizing Structure, and Framing Processes." In *Comparative Perspectives on Social Movements*, edited by Doug McAdam, John McCarthy, and Mayer Zald, pp. 1–20. Cambridge: Cambridge University Press.

Man, Si-Wai. 1995a. "Too Soft—Lashing the Greens." *One Earth* [Quarterly of the FoE] (Hong Kong) summer: 35.

————. 1995b. "In Search of Community: The Breakthrough of the Discussion on Public and Private." In *Public and Private: The Development of Human Rights and Civic Society*, edited by Si-Wai Man and Chan-Fai Cheung, pp. 3–22. Hong Kong: Humanities Press.

————. 1996. "De-constructing the Management Approach to the Environment." *The Centre for Environmental Studies Newsletter* (The Chinese University of Hong Kong) 5 (no. 2): 1–7.

Ng, Cho-Nam, and Ting-Leung Ng. 1992. "The Environment," In *The Other Hong Kong Report—1992,* edited by Joseph Y.S. Cheng and Paul C.K. Kwong, pp. 365–382. Hong Kong: The Chinese University Press.

Ng, Mei. 1997. "Environmental Education in Hong Kong." In *Community Mobilization and the Environment in Hong Kong,* edited by Peter Hills and Cecilia Chan. Hong Kong: Centre of Urban Planning & Environmental Management, University of Hong Kong.

One Earth (official magazine of Friends of the Earth, Hong Kong). Various issues.

Siddall, Linda. 1991. "The Environment." In *The Other Hong Kong Report— 1991,* edited by Yun-Wing Sung and Ming-Kwan Lee, pp. 403–419. Hong Kong: The Chinese University Press.

Sing, Ming. Forthcoming. "Mobilization for Political Change—The Pro-Democracy Movement in Hong Kong, 1980s–1994." In *Social Movements in Hong Kong,* edited by Tai-Lok Lui and Stephen W.K. Chiu. Hong Kong: Hong Kong University Press.

Wong, Koon-Kwai. 1996. "The Environment: Heading toward Sustainability?" In *The Other Hong Kong Report—1996,* edited by Mee-kau Myaw and Si-ming Li, pp. 367–387. Hong Kong: The Chinese University Press.

4

Environmental Movements in South Korea

Su-Hoon Lee

Acronyms

GLM	Green Life Movement	KEPSA	Korean Environmental and Pollution Studies Association
KAPCMC	Korean Anti-Pollution Civilian Movement Council	KFEM	Korean Federation for Environmental Movement
KAPMA	Korean Anti-Pollution Movement Association	KPRI	Korea Pollution Research Institute
KAPMC	Korean Anti-Pollution Movement Council	NGOs	Non-Governmental Organizations
KAPMYC	Korean Anti-Pollution Movement Youth Council	NIMBY	Not-In-My-Backyard
KCIA	Korean Central Intelligence Agency	SGP	Study Group of Pollution
KEPCO	Korean Electric Power Company	UNCED	United Nations' Conference on Environment and Development

Dark smoke arising from factories is symbolic of our nation's growth and prosperity.

—*Park Chung Hee, Ulsan, 1962*

Pollution is a phenomenon that appears when the contradictions of capitalism, with the sole objective of pursuing profits, reach extremes.

—*Korea Pollution Research Institute, 1982*

... to realize the importance of the ecosystem, to respect life,
to protect the environmental rights of each individual ...

—Korean Federation of Environmental Movements, 1993

Environmentalism: Creation of the "Korean Miracle"

Since the early 1960s, South Korea has undergone one of the most
dramatic capitalist growth processes with the average annual GNP
growth rate at approximately 10 percent. At least until the crash of
1997–98, many Western scholars—particularly Americans—have described this economic growth as a "miracle," suggesting that the Korean model should be adopted by other less developed Third World
economies.

However, the much lauded high-speed industrialization of South
Korea has brought about devastating consequences. One such negative
consequence is the irrevocable damage to the environment, which is
nothing short of an environmental crisis. Many people refuse to recognize the ugly and dirty side of high-speed industrialization. Korean
government technocrats assume, perhaps with the tacit consent of the
populace, that some environmental damage is the unavoidable by-
product of rapid economic growth. In recent decades, however, many
people have come to realize the severity of environmental problems
and the high price for such growth in the destruction of nature and the
environment. Since the late 1980s, the Korean people began to question the growth-, achievement-, and target-oriented models of development that the Korean government has pursued. Koreans not only
questioned, but also began to take concrete actions to stop further
damage to the environment and reverse ever-increasing pollution.
They did so in organized ways, signaling the emergence of the environmental movement in South Korea.

In a sense, Korea's environmental movement was created by the
"Korean miracle," that is, the very high-speed industrialization that
South Korea pursued and achieved during the past thirty years or so.
The distinctive pattern of national development, based on rapid growth
of export industries, inevitably paid less attention to the natural environment. The outcome was the massive, widespread destruction of
nature and the environment. As speed was critical to the Korean
growth model, the speed of environmental destruction was likewise

devastating. The speed of growth was the underlying force that reveals three defining characteristics of environmental degradation in Korea: (1) it is nationwide—every single individual is affected to a greater or lesser degree; (2) pollution unfolds rapidly; (3) pollution is highly malignant (Korea Pollution Research Institute 1986: 36–39). Needless to say, damage to the environment is hazardous to human health, and destruction of the ecosystem will have long-term negative effects on the quality of human life. Today the "environmental crisis" that South Korea faces is widely discerned by the public and admitted by the government.

Environmental movements in South Korea emerged as a result of the environmental crisis that was a product of the high-speed, export-oriented industrialization strategy. Lee and Smith (1991) sketched the history of the Korean environmental movements of the 1980s from the viewpoint of the anti-systemic movement. In doing so, they high-lighted issues, tasks, and prospects. Smith (1994) paid attention to an anti-systemic role in the contemporary world economy played by environmentalists who critically examine basic assumptions of capitalist growth and development, and who organize and act on that basis.

This chapter examines the origins and transformation of the South Korean environmental movements over the past two decades. Following an abbreviated history of Korea's environmental movements of the 1980s and 1990s, with a focus on anti-pollution and anti-nuclear movements, it explores the relationship between democratization and environmental movements. It then considers the strategies and impact of environmental movements in Korea. The discussion focuses on the largest, most active, and most representative movements.

The discussion in this chapter relies upon (1) interviews with environmental activists, and (2) pamphlets, leaflets, newsletters, and other materials published by various environmental organizations.

Emergence of Environmental Movements in the 1980s

Environmental groups have existed in Korea since the 1970s. For the most part, however, these groups were small and connected with churches or based in universities. The primary activities of these small, isolated groups were designed to heighten the environmental consciousness of the citizenry.

The very first recognized environmental group was the Study Group on Pollution (SGP). A small non-public organization with comparatively little activity, the SGP nevertheless signaled the blossoming of organized environmental movements in the 1980s (Lee 1990). The key members of this group were primarily concerned with scientific and technological advances/improvement. They were concerned with such issues as the social meaning of science and technology, the role of scientists and engineers, and the need to recast the existing image of scientists. Students involved in this group were mostly science or engineering majors rather than social sciences or humanities majors. The latter groups were usually more active forces in student movements, compared to science and engineering majors.

Anti-Pollution Movements

In 1982, through the initiatives of church leaders, the Korea Pollution Research Institute (KPRI) was founded. The KPRI was the first organized environmental movement group, in the sense that it had staff, office space, and other resources required to operate an organization. Choi Yul, a founding member of KPRI who was also its associate director of research, is now the most active and perhaps most widely recognized environmental movement leader in Korea. Choi is currently secretary-general of the Korea Federation for Environmental Movement (KFEM)—the largest and most active environmental organization in Korea today.

Under the frozen political circumstances of the Chun Doo Hwan dictatorship, the KPRI carried out significant, albeit limited, activities. The Church provided the group with a protective shield. By supporting the activities of small environmental groups, the KPRI provided a link among those isolated environmental groups. At the same time, it did fieldwork in polluted areas and helped local residents promote their own programs to reduce pollution damage. It also held pollution-related counseling and open lectures to promote awareness among the populace.

The successful fieldwork at the Onsan Industrial Complex (located on the southeastern coast near Ulsan)—the site of non-iron heavy metal industries—may be singled out among the numerous achievements of the KPRI. In 1985, the KPRI issued a series of reports, the major finding of which was the epidemiology of "Onsan illness," which had struck about five hundred Onsan residents as of 1985 (KPRI 1986: 86–119). The number has increased each year, and sufferers now number more than one thousand. "Onsan illness" was confirmed by a Japanese scientist who identified it as a Korean version of Japan's well-known "Itai-itai illness." The cause of "Onsan illness" was the contamination of the majority of the Onsan residents with heavy metal elements such as cadmium.

The KPRI's reports were well covered by the press. Subsequently, the organization succeeded in publicizing not only the Onsan incident, but the potential for pollution-related illnesses everywhere. This was the hottest social issue in 1985 and became known overseas as well. Mounting public pressure forced the Agency of the Environment to conduct an epidemiological survey of the alleged sufferers of the "Onsan illness." After the hurried survey—which took only one week to complete (KPRI 1986: 108–109)—the government publicly declared that the density level of heavy metal in the blood and urine of Onsan residents was "normal." Eventually, however, the government was forced to move the residents of Onsan, yielding to the struggles of residents and environmental activists. About forty thousand residents have been resettled, enacting an "exodus from pollution" (Cho 1990: 209).

In 1984, various small groups—including campus clubs, groups of white-collar workers, and so on—the most notable of which was the SGP, formed the Korea Anti-Pollution Movement Council (KAPMC 1990) in hopes that the movement would become more systematic if links were established. However, this attempt failed because the Council could not operate without the strong support of each member group. The radical subgroup became the driving force in forming the Korea Anti-Pollution Movement Youth Council (KAPMYC) in 1987, while the moderate subgroup, which emphasized technical and theoretical expertise, was absorbed into the Korea Environment and Pollution Studies Association (KEPSA) founded in 1989. Some left the movement to find regular jobs, but continue to express their earlier concerns in their individual occupational fields such as journalism, academia, households, and so forth.

In 1986, in the midst of popular pressure for democratization, the formation of the Korea Anti-Pollution Civilian Movement Council (KAPCMC) became a significant milestone. In the following year, the above-mentioned KAPMYC was formed as a version of the earlier KAPMC with a more open and public posture. The significance of these organizations was that they broadened the support base of Korea's environmental movements during a nascent stage.

In 1988, the Korea Anti-Pollution Movement Association (KAPMA) was formed by merging the earlier KAPCMC and KAPMYC. At that time KAPMA was a mass-based Korean environmental movement, with the largest organization and most diverse anti-pollution and anti-nuclear activities. With a membership of more than 1,300 as of early 1991, it published and distributed a monthly newsletter called *Survival and Peace*. In February 1991, it held its fourth General Assembly, where it reconstituted its organs to accommodate young professionals such as professors, medical doctors, lawyers, and journalists. Even though all these environmental organizations formed in the 1980s were nominally nationwide organizations, in reality they were all Seoul-based and their activities limited in that regard. Nevertheless, the Korean environmental movement in the 1980s also saw the activation of environmental movements in local areas, particularly late in the decade.

The origins of the more organized environmental movements of the 1980s lie in the anti-pollution struggles waged by local residents who were direct victims of Korea's environmental destruction (KPRI 1986: 263). Therefore, we must not underestimate various resident-level (primarily farmers and fishermen) movements taking place in major industrial complexes such as Ulsan, Pusan, and Yeocheon. Despite the fact that those movements took place in isolation and that their economic objective was the right to survive, they were often the roots of more organized local anti-pollution movement associations.

In 1987, in the southwestern coastal area, the Mokpo Green Movement Council was formed under the leadership of a local medical doctor. This group evolved from an earlier, loosely organized nature preservation group—the Association to Preserve Youngsan Lake. This association is famous among Korean environmentalists because of its successful campaign in 1983 to stop the government from approving the construction of a Jinro Alcohol Plant—the maker of Jinro Soju (Korean whiskey)—near Youngsan Lake, a reservoir providing tap water for the city of Mokpo.

In 1989, a number of important local organizations were founded: the Pusan Anti-Pollution Civilian Movement Council, the Kwangju Environment and Pollution Movement Association, and the Mokpo Youth Association Against Pollution and Nuclear Plants. In an area near Mokpo where four nuclear plants were either in operation or under construction, the Youngkwang Anti–Nuclear Plant Movement Association was established. In the same year, the Ulsan Anti-Pollution Movement Association was formed. As is well known, Ulsan is an industrial city designated by the government as a site to accommodate petrochemical industries in the 1960s and 1970s and later as the site of Hyundai's shipyard and automobile assembly lines.

These local environmental movement organizations were mostly independent and isolated, although some linkage and support from Seoul-based organizations did exist. Apparently, a close personal relationship between local movement leaders and Seoul activists continued.

In the 1980s, even the terminology was distinct. Movement groups used the term "anti-pollution" rather than "environmental protection." Their slogans and goals were the "elimination of pollution" or "anti-pollution," rather than protection of the environment or control of the environmental crisis. They resisted, opposed, and struggled. They also drew a clear line between polluters and victims, and considered the capitalist system the primary cause of pollution.

Anti-Nuclear Movements

South Korean anti-nuclear movements constituted one of the main currents of Korean environmental movements from the very beginning of these environmental movements.

To sustain high-speed, export-oriented industrial growth, electricity is at the center of Korea's economic development. The Korean government opted for the nuclear path to supply electric power. Once the South Korean government chose this path, the structural interests of international nuclear industries, primarily from the United States, technocratic government elites, and local conglomerates converged to promote the nuclear power industry in South Korea. The declining U.S. nuclear industry saw a business opportunity in South Korea, whose leader at the time, President Park Chung Hee, entertained ambitions of nuclear weapons development.

After the South Korean government pursued thirty years of a vigorous nuclear energy development program, eleven commercial nuclear power plants were in operation as of 1996, with five under various stages of construction. All together, fifty-five more nuclear plants are scheduled to be built by the year 2031. From a pro-nuclear energy viewpoint, South Korea today can be regarded as quite an impressive achiever.

But South Korea today is a nation suffering from a deep nuclear crisis. Out of the eleven plants already in operation, 193 accidents have halted operations in seven plants (Bello and Rosenfeld 1990: 108–109). All ongoing nuclear power plant construction meets with vehement resistance from local residents. The country also faces a nuclear waste storage crisis. Each on-site temporary spent fuel repository is reaching capacity. The country desperately needs a long-term site for storing nuclear wastes, but the omnipresent NIMBY—Not-in-My-Backyard—phenomenon is at work in South Korea too.

Obviously, the nation is torn by nuclear conflict. The basic position of the government remains unchanged. The general public mistrusts the government when it comes to nuclear issues. Construction projects worth billions of dollars are pending without any progress in either direction. Nuclear wastes pile up, but no permanent site(s) for storage is foreseen. Not only is there a lack of consensus between the government and the general public, but the gap continues to widen.

South Korea has one of the highest levels of nuclear dependence in the world. In the 1980s, South Korea relied on nuclear power to supply more than 50 percent of its electricity (Bello and Rosenfeld 1990: 103; Hart-Landsberg 1993: 268). At present, the ratio stands at more than one-third.

However, since the mid-1980s, the populace began to show serious concern over the government's firm and ever-ambitious nuclear power generation program. This concern was perhaps a result of the numerous nuclear plant accidents coupled with the political liberalization of the time. The nuclear issue, taboo under the authoritarian regimes up to the mid-1980s, emerged in the public debate arena during the late 1980s. The debate questioned the efficiency of nuclear power, and, more important, the safety of nuclear plants. As the public debate heated, the government fought back by citing successful nuclear programs in select Western countries, while ignoring the worldwide trend toward ultimate termination of nuclear energy programs.

South Korea as a nation today faces a grave dilemma. On one hand, giving up the nuclear development program is too costly from a short-term point of view. On the other hand, negative perceptions of nuclear energy by the general public are too high to be silenced. As time passes, negative perceptions are most likely to increase, despite continued costly efforts by the government. This dilemma is one of the origins of Korea's anti-nuclear movements.

The history of South Korean anti-nuclear movements begins in 1987. In that year, local residents living in the county of Youngkwang—the site of Korea Nuclear No. 7, No. 8 (both already in operation), No. 11, and No. 12 (both under construction)—launched a campaign calling for compensation for losses to fisheries. In 1988, the National Assembly took up the issue of the pending construction of Korea Nuclear No. 11 and No. 12 in Youngkwang. A heated debate between the government and anti-nuclear forces ensued both inside and outside the National Assembly. The major issue at stake was safety, perhaps reflecting the impact of the Chernobyl incident. Environmental movement leaders launched a major campaign against the construction of the two plants. They organized mass rallies and obtained signatures from citizens. They also published a newsletter called *Anti–Nuclear Plants*. The objectives of this campaign were to create a national consensus against nuclear power plants and consolidate existing resident-level movements.

In the spring of 1989, twenty-one environmental and other (pharmacists, medical doctors, and so on) social movement organizations formed the National Headquarters for the Nuclear Power Eradication Movement (Cho 1990: 190). This was originally an ad-hoc organization, drawing together the scattered, nascent anti-nuclear movements that previously existed. Resident-level anti–nuclear power plant movements provided a major impetus for the formation of the National Headquarters. The National Headquarters was established for more organized and effective campaigns. Even though the Korean government eventually completed Korea Nuclear No. 11 and No. 12, this campaign, conducted under the guidance of the Headquarters, became a critical turning point in the history of Korea's anti-nuclear movements in the sense that it succeeded in raising public awareness to a significant extent.

We must not overlook the issue of nuclear weapons on the Headquarters' agenda and its importance within the South Korean anti-nuclear movement. It was "an open secret" that a sizable number of nuclear warheads were placed in South Korea; North Korea consistently raised this issue against Seoul and Washington.

In the late 1980s, nuclear weapons became the object of public debate. Therefore, when we refer to "anti-nuclear movements in South Korea," these clearly include the issue of nuclear weapons in addition to nuclear plants. But, due in part to the anti-nuclear movements and in larger part to the progress made between the two Koreas, South Korea became "non-nuclearized" as of December 1991, when the historic "Non-nuclearization Declaration" was officially announced by Seoul and Pyongyang: neither side would store or process nuclear weapons, nor have the means to produce them. The declaration also stated the two parties' commitment to establishing an inspectorate to verify the absence of such weapons and facilities by mutual observation (Cotton 1993: 291–292). Nuclear warheads known to be scattered around South Korea were retrieved. As a result of this, nuclear weapons per se are not on the agendas of Korean anti-nuclear movements today. However, this does not imply that Koreans close their eyes toward global nuclear weaponry.

In many ways, 1989 is the turning point not only in terms of the public debate over nuclear energy issues, but also over nuclear weapons issues (Cho 1990: 183). Existing resident-level movements focused on illegal nuclear waste disposal. They waged protests to invoke public awareness of the potential damage nuclear plants may cause. In addition, there was the external shock of the disastrous Chernobyl incident in 1986.

Among the populace, the dangers of nuclear plants were no longer regarded as remote. With nine nuclear plants in operation as of 1988, a mishap similar to Chernobyl could occur at any time on the Korean peninsula—an area smaller than the state of Ohio. In addition to the pending construction of Korea Nuclear No. 11 and No. 12, the government announced disturbing nuclear energy plans: (1) by the year 2001, five more nuclear plants are to be built; and (2) by the year 2031, 55 more (Cho 1990: 184).

While preventing new nuclear plant construction is a goal of Korean anti-nuclear movements, another major issue is the location of a permanent site for nuclear waste. Indeed, in the 1990s, Korean anti-nuclear movements gained crucial strength from struggles against the government's plan for a permanent and centralized nuclear waste repository site.

Like other countries with nuclear power plants, Korea faces the problem of storing or depositing spent nuclear fuel. So far, spent fuel has been stored in pools at each reactor site. However, these temporary sites apparently reached their limits during the mid-1990s, although there were variations across different reactor sites. Yet the South Korean government found difficulty in locating a long-term waste storage site for spent fuel and other waste nuclear materials. There have been several reported incidents of the dumping of other radioactive wastes such as rubber gloves and vinyl shoe covers. There have also been reported cases of leukemia near nuclear plants (Bello and Rosenfeld

1990: 108). As a result of these reports, public fears have risen, perhaps coupled with the memory of the Chernobyl disaster in 1986.

For nearly ten years, the country has experienced a battle between the government and the opposition over the issue of long-term storage of nuclear waste. In 1988, the government proposed a long-term storage site on South Korea's southeast coast. Three possible sites were selected: Uljin, Youngil, and Youngduk (counties or towns not distant from one another, and very near several existing nuclear plants). However, when the sites were announced, anti-nuclear activists and local residents organized protests and blockaded major highways with tractors. After months of confrontational protests, the government had to cancel its plan. This stand-off between the government and the opposition was not nationally publicized at the time, but it was not an isolated episode. From then on, the struggle became nationwide, making control by the government much more difficult and reducing its bargaining power.

Another episode followed less than two years later. In 1990, anti-nuclear activists grew aware that the government had secretly identified Anmyondo (a remote island off the west coast of the peninsula in Chungnam Province) as a proposed site for a permanent nuclear waste repository. The islanders, assisted by a coalition of environmental associations, launched protests against the yet-unannounced project. What really angered the islanders was the deceptive government announcement that the island was chosen as a research complex site, not a nuclear waste disposal site. The response of residents across the entire island was explosive when they found out the truth. Police and public buildings were attacked and several set on fire. Shops were looted. Many people were injured. Parents refused to send children to school, and children joined the riots. As the uprising showed no sign of subduing, the Minister of Science and Technology (Dr. Chung Kun Mo, a prominent scientist) appeared on national television's evening news to announce his resignation. The government was forced to withdraw its plan and look for another site. The Anmyondo uprising and its success are recorded as "a great victory" in the history of the Korean anti-nuclear movement.

In 1994, the cycle repeated itself once again when the Korean government announced an alternative site to be the town of Uljin (a small town on the southeast coast of Kyungbuk Province, already the site of two commercial nuclear plants). Violent protests and demonstrations followed; roads were blockaded with burning tires; firebombs were thrown. A sizable police force had to be called in to quell the tensions. Once again, the Ministry of Science and Technology was forced to withdraw the plan.

Immediately after that episode, the government hurriedly announced its proposal to designate Kulupdo (a tiny island about fifty miles off the west coast, near the famous port city of Inchon) as an alternative storage site. The island only had ten residents, who, according to the government, agreed to accept compensation for their properties. But by now public awareness was high as a consequence of previous episodes. Environmentalists objected to the government's selection. This time, they raised questions about its suitability on the grounds that the island could be geologically vulnerable. They began to organize the islanders and the people of neighboring Dukjok Island. Local residents quickly turned their backs to the government. Residents simply stated that they would never move from their homes no matter what monetary rewards were offered. Their homelands, where their ancestors rest and where they will rest upon death, should not be an object of bargaining.

These episodes clearly document that the government, unlike in the past, cannot implement its policy without consent from the population to be affected by such a policy. Therefore, the Korean government has a serious problem. It must find a place for a permanent nuclear waste repository because the capacity at each reactor, which is itself temporary, is reaching its ceiling. However, no locale is willing to become the site for dangerous wastes. NIMBY is at work here. Democracy in Korea is too new to handle this phenomenon in a "mature" way. The root cause of this problem can be found in the non-democratic (often clandestine), bureaucracy-centered, and authoritarian policymaking and administration of the government.

South Korean anti-nuclear movements should build solidarity between local residents and concerned citizens in cities, particularly cities not too distant from nuclear plants. As consumers of power, city-dwellers are also potential victims of nuclear disasters or minor radioactivity. Public hearings, debates, and exhibits in these cities are instrumental to promoting solidarity. In order to activate anti-nuclear movements in urban areas, campaigns like Help Children of Chernobyl and Develop Alternative Energy Programs should persist.

At the center of the Korean nuclear crisis lies the government-run electric power industry's monopoly (in production and distribution), the

Korea Electric Power Company (KEPCO). The industry should be liberalized. Calls for the liberalization of KEPCO's monopoly are timely because liberalization is the Korean government's policy toward state enterprises. Pluralistic power production and distribution will create market mechanisms through which progressive ideas (e.g., alternative forms of power generation) can be implemented. The revision of existing energy-related laws and measures should be instituted.

The defining traits of the Korean environmental movement in the 1980s were anti-pollution and anti-nuclear movements. During the first half of the 1980s, the major issue was the various types of pollution produced as a consequence of rapid industrialization. In the second half of the decade, more weight was given to anti-nuclear issues, although this does not mean that pollution is no longer a key issue within the environmental movement.

Consolidation and Expansion of Environmental Movements in the 1990s

In the 1990s, environmental movements experienced significant transformations under different structural contexts. Qualitative changes also took place under the altered political mapping.

In the early 1990s, more ecologically oriented green organizations emerged. The reconstitution or reorganization of existing environmental groups also took place. In terms of activities and membership, two organizations deserve our attention. The first is the Korea Federation for Environmental Movement (KFEM), which I will discuss later. The second is Green Korea. Green Korea is the result of a merger of two existing organizations in 1993: the Baedal Eco Club, a research group of professionals, which was founded in 1991; and the Civic Association for Recovering Green Korea, which was also founded in 1991. As the term "green" in its title implies, Green Korea tends to be more ecologically oriented. This ecological orientation was evident in the words of its secretary-general, Jang Won: "recycling, diversity, coexistence, networks, ecosystems. . . . "

Among the many green organizations, groups, and even a political party (the Green Party of Korea) that emerged in the late 1980s and early 1990s, only KFEM and Green Korea had memberships of more than 1,000. This may indicate how nascent environmental movements in Korea were, in spite of the quantitative expansion of environmental movements during this period.

Table 4.1

Trends in the Organizational Expansion of Environmental Movements

Year	1985	1986	1987	1988	1989	1990	1991	1992
Number	none	2	3	6	11	8	19	18

Source: Ku (1994: 114).

Domestic Structural Contexts

The consolidation and expansion of environmental movements started in the last years of the 1980s (refer to Table 4.1). The following factors were critical in consolidating and expanding environmental movements: (1) the 1987 June uprising and the ensuing June 29 Declaration (see Lee 1993 for a detailed account); (2) a series of tap water contamination incidents in 1989 and 1990; and (3) the role of mass media. In addition to these, the activities of environmental movements in the early 1980s provided a crucial impetus for later developments.

The 1987 political scene provided environmental activists with a windfall opportunity to consolidate and expand their movements. It signaled a democratic transition from an authoritarian regime to a civilian government. It also signaled the activation of civil society (Lee 1993). The participation of urban, white-collar groups in the Great Uprising—a nationwide, anti–Chun regime uprising—had enormous implications on environmental movements. The implications were various in respect to movement ideology, the composition of movement membership, and movement organizational expansion. Precisely because of their critical role in the watershed of Korea's political development, this group, the "new middle stratum," began to appear as a central force in leading diverse social movements in the 1990s.

In the summer of 1989, tap water in Seoul was reported to be contaminated by heavy metals such as cadmium and mercury. Major newspapers carried news of this shocking incident. People's reactions were enormous, providing a major stimulus for promoting public awareness of Korea's greatly deteriorated environment. Until then, for the majority of the public, anti-pollution was "their" issue, not "my" problem. The contamination of the city's water supply shook the entire citizenry. Exactly one year later, in the summer of 1990, a second incident involving tap water contamination occurred. Reportedly, tap water in Seoul contained the cancer-causing chemical element THM. Once again, the incident received a great deal of media attention. People responded with anger, but more important, they began to question the reliability of the government and to listen to what environmental activists were saying.

In the spring of 1991, about half a year after the second shock, yet another major incident occurred, this time even more disastrous. "Doosan Electronics"—a semiconductor-chip manufacturing plant—dumped a large amount of phenol into the upper Nakdong River, which fed the reservoir supplying tap water to the southeast region. This incident was reported in newspapers and televised nationally, invoking nationwide anger and frustration. This caused the "environmental crisis" to be perceived as real. Residents of the major cities located in the southeast (Taegu, Pusan, Masan, Changwon) demonstrated sentiments of extreme anger and betrayal toward the government. The chairman of the Doosan Group announced that the Group would pay 50 billion won (about 60 million U.S. dollars) to the city of Taegu in compensation for the damages caused by the incident. He also stepped down from his position.

Ku (1994: 55–58) underscored the positive role that the mass media played from 1987 in the growth of environmental movements in his analysis of the coverage of environmental issues by Seoul-based major daily newspapers. In Table 4.2, the coverage of environmental issues in newspapers increased greatly from 1987. Compared to the previous year, in 1987 alone the coverage doubled, and thereafter increased significantly.

Equally telling statistics indicate an increase of mass media concerns, as seen in the number of editorials related to environmental issues carried in the six major daily newspapers (*Chosun, Dong-Ah, Hankook, Choongang, Kyunghyang*, and *Seoul*). According to Table 4.3, the number of environment-related editorials increased from 1988, with a notable increase in 1989. Although there was a minor reduction in the following year, the trend appears to persist. Editorials do not simply represent public opinion, they also influence it. They often place considerable pressure on the government and business, and provide a morale boost to environmental activists.

Additionally, environmental newspapers came into being during this period. They cover only environmental issues and problems, and are

Table 4.2

Newspaper Coverage of Environmental Issues

Year	Number	% increase
1982	479	
1983	406	−15%
1984	369	−9%
1985	299	−19%
1986	433	45%
1987	873	102%
1988	1,313	50%
1989	3,250	148%
1990	5,331	64%
1991	6,464	21%
1992	8,884	37%

Source: Ku (1994: 56).

mostly weekly with a limited circulation. As of August 1995, more than twenty such weekly papers were registered with the Ministry of Information. How seriously they are taken by the public, and how influential they are over the government and their readers, is unknown. Nevertheless, the very fact that environmental newspapers emerged reveals the blossoming of public concern and the importance of the environment in Korea.

In sum, the positive role that the mass media played during this time is indisputable. But the question is, why during this period? This must be examined in the context of the political situation after the 1987 Great Uprising and the June 29 Declaration. The mass media were under tight control during Chun Doo Hwan's rule; agents of the National Security resided in newspaper companies; censorship was practiced; and "pollution," and the environment in general, were topics still perceived as part of the opposition's discourse.

But with the changing tides of the time, the environment became a popular issue. When the words "environment" (*hwankyung*) and "environmental protection" (*hwankyungboho*) no longer carried any nuance of opposition and/or militancy, they became the subject matter of daily life, introduced into everyday discourse and concerning everyone. Even the government began to take a pro-environmental posture, while business sensed enormous implications that could impact profit-seeking behavior after the Rio Conference on Environment and Develop-

Table 4.3

Newspaper Editorials

Year	1987	1988	1989	1990	1991
Number	42	58	91	81	101

Source: Ku (1994: 56).

ment (UNCED). Thus, the business sector too began, at least in gestures and rhetoric, to appear pro-environmental. The mass media also reacted to these new developments by increasing their coverage of environmental issues. Some newspapers even organized or acted as sponsors to environmental organizations. The *Dongah Ilbo,* a prestigious newspaper in Seoul, sponsored the "Green Scout" campaign, which enlisted the support of 17,435 individual members, five kindergartens, 78 elementary schools, 66 secondary schools, 11 universities, and 656 other organizations as its members (Cho 1995: 294–296).

World-Historic Context: The 1992 Rio Conference

The 1992 UNCED held in Rio gave Korean environmental movements significant momentum. During the several months prior to the Conference, all sorts of preparatory activities took place. Seminars organized by either the government, environmental organizations, or the business sector were held almost daily. The topics were diverse: how to deal with the Summit Meeting, the changing strategies of the business sector, the role of NGOs in the Conference, and so forth. The business sector released its "Businessmen's Environmental Declaration" in May, and the government announced a "Declaration for Environmental Protection" during the celebration events of Earth Day. In the past, neither the government nor the business sector had shown any interest in the Earth Day events. They had to change their positions because the world-historic context forced them to do so. With the Korean economy so deeply dependent upon the world market, they had little choice but to respond.

Through these activities, contacts between green activists, the government, and the business sector became frequent. This meant a lot because in the past, environmental activists generally held a hostile posture toward both the government and the business sector. Preparatory activities created a platform on which these different actors, facing common challenges—albeit with different implications—could interact. The environmental crisis was indeed real and something to be dealt with properly, not to be avoided or ignored.

In the midst of this preparation, the "Korean Commission for the Rio Conference" was formed by the environmental organizations' initiatives. Initially, the membership of the Commission was to be limited to NGOs only. But later, representatives of the business sector joined the Commission, or, more accurately, the NGOs allowed them to join. This was possible in part due to the frequent contacts they had through the preparatory activities. The business sector not only sponsored some of the NGOs' activities—including those of environmental organizations like KAPMA—but also covered the travel expenses of NGO representatives to Rio. This stirred infighting within environmental organizations, eventually leading to KAPMA losing its more radical, non-conciliatory membership and eventually transforming its basic characteristics, such that, after the Rio Conference, KAPMA began to take a more moderate stance than in the past.

An equally important impact of the Rio Conference was the broadening of the concerns of Korea's environmental movements. Prior to their participation in the Rio Conference, they tended to place their attention on domestic environmental issues. Contacts with international green organizations or with organizations in other countries were isolated and minimal. After the Conference, however, they became more global. They came to realize the global nature of environmental problems and the importance of global solidarity in tackling environmental issues.

The Democratization Movement: The Root of Environmental Movements

Student movements in South Korea have a long and prestigious history, recording remarkable achievements and far-reaching impacts on the lives of Koreans in modern times. These movements also led and dominated famous Korean democratization movements.

Democratization movements overthrew the authoritarian Syngman Rhee in 1960, and were also responsible for the fatal pressure on Park Chung Hee's eighteen-year bureaucratic-authoritarian regime, which

collapsed after the assassination of the dictator by one of his confi-
dants, the KCIA chief, in 1979. When the military government led by
General Chun Doo Hwan came to power, students resisted it vehe-
mently and consistently. And when Chun transferred power to his
longtime friend, ex-general Roh Tae Woo—who took off the uniform
but nonetheless took power through his participation in the 1979
military coup—students continued to resist the pseudo-civilian government. As President Roh Tae Woo's regime underwent the trying periods of "democratization," student movements still stood strong. Even
under the civilian government of President Kim Young Sam, student
movements were highly visible, although their social impact was comparatively reduced.

There are no apparent connections or organized ties between student
movements and the environmental movement. This is not to say that
students, as individuals, do not participate in environmental movements, or similarly, that on-campus environmental groups do not exist.
In both instances, they do, and actually some do very actively (for a brief
account, see *Sisa Journal* 1990: 62). One example is the University Students Association under the umbrella of the KFEM. This Association is
by no means inactive. However, the core strands of the two movements
have never worked together in a systematic or organized manner. In that
sense, the relationship between the two movements is still ambiguous.

Nevertheless, an indirect linkage between student movements and the
environmental movement exists in the sense that the former produced
many key environmental activists and the origins of today's diverse environmental organizations can be traced back to the campuses of the 1970s.
In that sense, the roots of Korean environmental movements are the democratization movements dominated by university students.

In the first instance, many environmental movement leaders today
are former democratization movement activists. Let us take the KFEM,
the largest and most active environmental movement organization in
Korea, as a case in point. Choi Yul, KFEM's secretary-general, is a
former democratization movement activist. Choi was imprisoned for
six years during Park Chung Hee's authoritarian regime. In addition, at
least half of the eight-man Executive Committee of the aforementioned
KAPMA—which, before transforming into the KFEM used to be the
highest day-to-day decision-making organ of KAPMA—were active in
democratization movements. Besides Choi, there was a medical doctor
who also served a prison term, a theatrical director, and a medical

school professor, all known to have been very active in democratization movements.

In the second instance, the discussion in the previous section on scattered campus environmental groups and "circles" is quite relevant. The transformatory history of the SGP is most notable. Student participants in the scientific technological movement played crucial roles in giving birth to environmental movement organizations. By occupying middle-level support positions, they constantly provided a driving energy to all the organizations.

In the 1980s, anti-pollution movements considered themselves a part or a subsidiary of the democratization movement. They asserted that anti-pollution was only one of the many arenas to be "liberated" at the end of the military dictatorship. Anti-pollution was one of many ways in which democratization movement forces could attack the military government. Since pollution was the product of business monopolies, political oppression, and the peninsula's north–south division—all crystallized into the military-ruled authoritarian regime—an end to this regime was the most appropriate path to stop worsening pollution. There was definitely a solid link between the solutions to ever-increasing and life-threatening levels of pollution and democratization.

In a sense, the democratization movement was not simply the root of Korea's environmental movements. Environmental movements in Korea in the 1980s were equal to democratization movements. Until 1987, environmental movements could not be properly approached outside the contours of democratization movements. During the first half of the 1980s, environmental movements—more correctly "anti-pollution" movements—were deeply influenced or perhaps dominated by the prevailing tide of democratization. They were influenced by the dominating *Minjung* (masses') discourse of the time. Like other movements, anti-pollution movements in the 1980s were radicalized, resistant, and hostile.

The Korea Federation for Environmental Movements: A Case Analysis

Formation of the KFEM

In 1993, the Seoul-based KAPMA and its eight local chapters formed the KFEM, a national, unified organization. By the end of 1994, its membership numbered about 13,000, and as of December 1996, it numbered approximately 25,000 (interview with Kyung Sook Lee, in charge of membership management of KFEM, January 22, 1997). This increase was due to a determined drive to expand its membership. It should be pointed out that the drive was successful because the projected image of the KFEM was more moderate.

The KFEM discarded some distinctive characteristics of the original KAPMA: hostility toward big business and the state, radicalism, and "anti-pollution." It softened its tone and modified its strategy. Although it is difficult to say that it lost its basic focus, a notable shift took place. It began to emphasize popularity and technical expertise as critical elements of a successful movement. Grassroots participation was underscored. The KFEM's motto at its inception was "environment is life." This alone reveals a lot about the transformation from the KAPMA to the KFEM.

Headquartered in Seoul, the KFEM had twenty-seven local chapters under its umbrella as of January 1997. More local chapters are expected to be founded in the future. The KFEM headquarters runs a think-tank called the "Center for Citizens' Environment." In addition, in order to provide legal advice on cases relevant to pollution, it runs the "Center for Legal Counsel." University professors and lawyers play major roles in carrying out these activities. It also runs the "Center for Information," whose main purpose is to collect all forms of information and disseminate them to the public. In 1996, the Center opened a world wide web home page (called "Korean Environmental Information") on the internet. Local chapters are already connected, and international sources of environmental information will be connected in the future. Users have easy access to all internet information—domestic and international—thanks to this service.

In a similar vein, environmental activists underscore the importance of education for future generations. The KFEM made efforts to promote such education. They demanded that the government include subjects related to the environment in primary and secondary school textbooks. They also developed their own programs, such as summer camps, night lectures, and a taxi-drivers' environmental monitorship program. As environmental education is increasingly emphasized as a long-term vehicle for promoting public awareness, the Citizens' Environment School has become a crucial organ of the KFEM. The school offers a month-long program open to the general public. Students pay a nominal fee and, as of the end of 1996, sixteen programs have been conducted. In 1995, the KFEM opened a facility for educational purposes in Hongcheon, Kangwon Province, and currently is raising funds to construct a headquarters office building.

Activities of the KFEM

Environmental issues are in part manifested in KFEM's monthly newsletters and its magazine titled *Hwankyungundong* (Environmental Movement). They include anti-nuclear activities—struggles against nuclear plant construction and the construction of nuclear waste disposal sites. KAPMA's legacy of putting a great deal of energy into anti-nuclear activities continues. One example of this discussed earlier was the successful struggle waged by local residents and the KFEM against the government's plan to designate Anmyondo and Kulupdo as permanent nuclear waste disposal sites.

Conventional issues of environmental degradation, including water and air pollution, are also major battles to be fought. In fact, in 1994, the KFEM centered on "water" as the focus of its activities with the catch phrase "water is life." Major rivers that supplied reservoirs for tap water were closely monitored. The Ministry of Environment was pressed for the tighter regulation of rivers and improved management of tap-water-processing plants. In spite of these efforts, the quality of tap water has not improved, indicating that rivers are not adequately controlled or managed. For instance, in 1996 a bitter and angry struggle was waged by the residents of Pusan and the province of Kyungnam, who rely upon the Nakdong River for their tap water (this river is used as the reservoir for tap water in the southeast region). They were opposed to the plan to designate Wicheon—situated alongside the river, and located on the outskirts of the city of Taegu—as the site for a new industrial complex. The city government of Taegu claims that the complex will revive the rapidly declining industrial activities in and around the city. However, constructing an industrial complex near the river will have devastating implications in terms of the water quality of the Nakdong River, the water quality of which has already been severely degraded. This plan met with enormous opposition not only from the residents of Pusan and of Kyungnam Province, but also from local governments.

This quickly became a political issue. The opposition argued that the Kim Young Sam government was begging for votes from Taegu and the province of Kyungbuk, which would benefit from the complex, for the 1997 presidential election. Residents of Taegu and Kyungbuk Province believe that the new complex will revive their regional economies and argue that it should not be canceled. The Seoul government has said that strict environmental regulations, even after the development of the complex, will prevent the further degradation of the Nakdong River. The opposition flatly rejects such an idea. Newspapers in Pusan carried editorials and followed the issue on the front page on an almost daily basis. The opposition was all-out. As the issue became politicized, cleavages began to emerge between the residents of the two regions. As of the end of 1998, the issue remained unresolved.

In 1995, the KFEM made "air" the focus of its activities. This time, to deal with the issue more systematically and popularly, the KFEM created a subunit, called the Green Life Movement (GLM), which was intended to focus upon air pollution and clean air. One of the major daily newspapers, *Hankook Ilbo,* housed the GLM and sponsored its activities. An outstanding achievement of the GLM was the production of a national map of air pollution. A team of scientists, activists, local green movement groups, and other pro-environmental civic associations conducted a nationwide survey (measuring about 12,000 locations) of the levels of NO_2 in the air, from which a sophisticated air pollution map was produced (GLM 1995).

The destruction of nature due to the construction of golf courses has also been a focal point attracting a good deal of energy from the KFEM in the 1990s. Toward the end of Roh Tae Woo's presidency, permission to construct a large number of golf courses was issued to the extent that the Sixth Republic was often referred to as the "golf republic." Mountainous areas, in particular the province of Kyonggi, which is physically annexed to Seoul, were the preferred sites for new golf courses. Golf course development is "a very lucrative business" involving speculation and windfall profits (Han 1994: 231). Almost every single golf course construction site met with strong opposition from local residents. The central KFEM or its local chapters were involved in supporting the opposition. Golf courses present nearby residents with no benefits, but rather losses, such as land price increases. The construction process alone is an enormous nuisance, with noise, traffic, dust, and lost soil. Golf courses also offer almost no job opportunities to local residents. Instead, they bring about a whole range of environmental problems, such as the destruction of surrounding habitats, potential surface soil inflow to agricultural fields (landslides and crop damages), pesticide pollution, and a sense of relative deprivation.

When the civilian president, Kim Young Sam, was sworn into office in February 1993, the general public and the environmental movement had high hopes for a much better environment. President Kim even declared himself an "environmental president" in 1996. But his government's policy and performance unfolded in the opposite direction. It loosened the tightly controlled "Green Belt" regulations by formulating a deregulatory policy. The implications of this policy posture are enormous in terms of development versus preservation. It implies development over preservation and severe damage to the ecosystem. The would-be profit makers responded as if this were what they had been waiting for. They took actions to loosen up the constraining "Natural Park Law" and demanded the legislation of environmental deregulation. A series of development-oriented legislations ensued. For instance, bills that allow the development of hot springs and underground drinking water were passed. Environmental movement organizations, including the KFEM, took counter-actions, submitting a petition opposing such legislation, implementation of which was consequently put on hold. But once the government's position was set, it was difficult to reverse, regardless of how strong the opposition was. Like other semiperipheral states, the Kim Young Sam government was under "pressure to maintain global industrial competitiveness, with local and multinational business interests pushing the state to minimize costs, including relaxing environmental vigilance" (Smith 1994:21).

In 1995, local elections were held for heads of local governments. This was significant in the history of Korean political development, because since 1961 these heads had been appointed by the president. Relevant to our subject was the direct and aggressive participation of the KFEM in the elections, which solicited and supported "environmental candidates" to run for multilayered positions. There were 46 such candidates, out of which 32 won. Among those, two won mayoral positions (interview with Chi Beom Lee, the deputy secretary-general, November 20, 1995). This was a major victory, since it meant that the victors would be, to say the least, pro-environmental in their capacities. Perhaps it would be meaningful to put "the environment" on a political platform and publicize it through campaigns.

Strategies and Impacts of the KFEM

The KFEM does not appear to have identifiable or distinctive long-term strategies. It employs and adopts all kinds of activities: demonstrations, protest rallies, sit-ins, public hearings, seminars, conferences, lectures, cultural events (performances), fund-raising events, education and training, and the acquisition of space. These do not constitute a clear set of strategies, but are the activities, means, or perhaps methods of movements. The activists use these methods differently, depending upon the nature of the issues they fight for or against. The methods or activities of other organizations are not very different from those adopted by the KFEM, although the KFEM tends to be less moderate than others.

In spite of the short history of Korea's environmental movements, the impact has been far-reaching. Many environmental NGOs now exist, active and well-organized, and the membership of some of the representative organizations has steadily increased. The composition of their membership is also broad-ranging. Perhaps as a result of this, the public's awareness has risen. The mass media have tended to be sympathetic toward environmental NGOs, covering their activities and waging a wide range of environmental campaigns themselves. Obviously, this too has had a positive impact in promoting public awareness.

Political leaders have shown serious interest in environmental issues. Some selected environmentalists as their policy advisers or full-time aides; some even run research centers. Others have sponsored conferences on environmental issues, and there are a few politicians who maintain close personal ties with environmental activists. Politicians are generally the patrons of environmental organizations. During the elections, the environment becomes a popular issue with almost every candidate; everyone is pro-environment. This may point to the alleviation of the public consciousness about the environment. How politicians actually stand once they are elected to office is quite another issue, but in order to attract votes, candidates must address environmental issues.

The government tends to listen to the demands of environmental organizations, although its sincerity is questionable. After the 1992 Rio Conference, the government appeared to change its environmental policy on the grounds that unless the entire economy turns into a pro-environmental system, it will be difficult to compete in the world market.

The government emphasized development of green technology by the business sector. Otherwise, according to the government, Korean products will lose out on the world market, which is responsive to developments in green technology. In 1994, the government upgraded the erstwhile Agency of Environment to the Ministry of Environment and expanded its size and budget. It is difficult to determine whether this upgrading was a result of environmental movements, or of an external stimulus such as the Rio Conference.

The business sector has generally shown signs of change in its attitude toward environmental movements. A good number of big business groups now declare a pro-environmental posture. Clean technology is now emphasized, and some firms volunteer to sponsor environmental movements. Yet, the sincerity of the would-be pro-environmental business sector is also questionable. No environmental organization is so naive as to place a deep trust in what the business sector says and does. The profit motive is inherent and strong. Once monitoring is loosened, the business sector can change its attitude overnight.

Perhaps the most significant, real impact of Korea's environmental movements, particularly the KFEM, is on the word "environment" itself. This may mean an elevation of public awareness or the activation of environmental movements. In any case, "environment" is omnipresent in Korea today. Everyone speaks about the environment; everyone is pro-environment. This is a positive trajectory in terms of environmental protection. However, some analysts and activists express concern for this very fact. They worry that the environment may become "commodified," in the sense that it will be used as an issue or matter of concern only when needed. Of course they worry that environmental movements may become "functionalized," such that certain characteristics of the environment are invoked to mobilize support to achieve particular goals when they are deemed useful by certain social groups and organizations (see Lee 1995). Such groups may include business firms, political parties, newspaper companies, and civic associations.

Despite these positive impacts and achievements of Korea's environmental movements, the environment in general unfortunately has not improved over past years. If environmental movements aspire to alleviate and ultimately eliminate pollution, Korea's environmental movements are far from this goal. In spite of "booming" environmental movements, the environment itself shows no notable signs of improvement. The quality of water and air in cities has not improved, the destruction of nature as a result of diverse development projects (e.g., golf course construction) continues, and the country's nuclear policy, in essence, remains intact. From this angle, Korea's environmental movements have recorded no successes.

It is difficult to explain this paradox—while Korea's environmental movements are booming, the environment has not improved. People are now more conscious of environmental problems than in the past; issues that received little attention from environmentalists are now very prominent. The paradox is a subjective phenomenon. Information about the environment is more open than before, and access to information is easier. Mass media coverage of environmental problems has increased rapidly. Yet, the state and big business have succeeded in containing environmental movements, in part by laying claims themselves to being pro-environment. The government allows environmental organizations to act, but only within the confines of the larger system. It responds to certain demands by environmental movements, but only to the degree that they do not represent a major barrier to the smooth operation of the national economy. The business sector responds to certain demands, but only to the extent that they do not conflict with the sector's fundamental interests. Such notions are only speculative and need to be verified through more systematic analysis.

Concluding Remarks

After thirty years of high-speed industrial growth in South Korea, the price of rising industrial strength is an extreme environmental crisis. In 1996 alone, major incidents related to pollution or environmental deterioration included the illegal release of water from the contaminated Siwha Lake, incidents of pollution illness reported in the Yeocheon petrochemical industrial complex, dead fish in major rivers, and summertime ozone-related smog in Seoul. These incidents defy the government's claim that pollution has been tamed.

The environmental crisis gave birth to environmental movements in the late 1980s. Prior to the mid-1980s, because of military authoritarian regimes, the environmental crisis was considered taboo. Raising questions about pollution was perceived as a challenge to national goals, and thereby an opposition to be suppressed. But as the liberalization of the political regime took place, the environmental problem together with many other issues became public. Movements whose main concerns and goals were the reversal of pollution and the protection of nature have emerged.

From the beginning of the environmental movements in South Korea, two issues have been central: pollution (or degradation of the environment) and the nuclear issue. High-speed industrialization has produced all kinds of pollution—air pollution, water pollution, noise, dust, the destruction of nature. From the late 1980s, when environmental movements began in South Korea, anti-pollution movements were generally at the center of environmental movements. Air and water quality are two issues that have persisted within the movements.

Anti-nuclear movements have also been at the center of South Korean environmental movements. So long as the South Korean government maintains its nuclear energy policy position—continuing to operate multiple nuclear plants while constructing many more—anti-nuclear movements, whose ultimate goal is the closure of the nuclear industry, will be a major current in environmental movements in South Korea. Given the fact that the Korean economy is structurally dependent upon nuclear power, the tasks before South Korea's anti- nuclear movement are enormous. But their success relies on the participation of ordinary people. "A Nuclear-Free Twenty-first Century" may be a dream, but it is a dream to which the movements must aspire.

Only in recent years have environmental movements in South Korea become the subject of serious investigation. Therefore, much more research on the topic needs to be done. For example, is the ideology (or philosophy) of environmental movements in South Korea anti-systemic, reformist, or green alternative? Is there any ideology at all? What are the main strategies adopted by organizations? Are those strategies more militant or more moderate than in the past? Are they state-oriented (e.g., policy change) or life-world-oriented (e.g., change in individual life-styles) in terms of their impact? What is the relationship between environmental movements and other social movements? What is the linkage between environmental movement organizations (in particular their leaders) and institutional politics? Do environmental movements function as vehicles for activists to ultimately enter institutional politics? How local or global are the movements? Is the international solidarity to which everyone aspires making any substantive progress? What are the main barriers preventing such solidarity?

References

Bello, Walden, and Stephanie Rosenfeld. 1990. *Dragons in Distress: Asia's Miracle Economies in Crisis.* San Francisco: Food First.

Cho, Dae Yup. 1995. "A Study of Korean Social Movements and Changes in Their Organization Types." Ph.D. Dissertation, Department of Sociology, Korea University (in Korean).

Cho, Hong-Sup. 1990. "A Debate on Nuclear Energy: Technological Orientation or Ecological Orientation?" *Society and Thoughts.* 1990: A special issue (in Korean), pp. 183–191.

Cotton, James, ed. 1993. *Korea Under Roh Tae-Woo.* Canberra: Allen and Unwin.

Eder, Norman. 1996. *Poisoned Prosperity.* Armonk: M.E. Sharpe.

GLM (Green Life Movement of Korea). 1995. *A Report of a Nation-wide Air Pollution: Dreaming the Green Wind.* Seoul: GLM (in Korean).

Han, Do Hyun. 1994. "Environmental Movements Against Golf Course Development Since the Late 1980s in Korea." In *Environment and Development,* edited by Korean Sociological Association, pp. 231–246. Seoul: Seoul Press.

Hart-Landsberg, Martin. 1993. *Rush to Development.* New York: Monthly Review Press.

KAPMC (Korea Anti-Pollution Movement Association). 1990. *Compendium in Commemoration of 1990 Earth Day: For This Earth, for This Sky, and for All of Us.* Seoul: Korea Anti-Pollution Movement Association (in Korean).

KFEM (Korea Federation for Environmental Movement). 1993–97. Monthly. *Hwankyungundong* (Environmental Movement). Seoul: KFEM (in Korean).

KPRI (Korea Pollution Research Institute). 1986. *Pollution Map in South Korea.* Seoul: Ilwolseogak (in Korean).

Ku, Do-wan. 1994. "The History and Characteristics of Environmental Movements in Korea." Ph.D. Dissertation, Department of Sociology, Seoul National University (in Korean).

Lee, Deuk-Yeon. 1990. *Evolution of the Korean Environmental Movement in the 1980s.* Unpublished paper (in Korean).

Lee, Su-Hoon. 1993. "Transitional Politics of Korea, 1987–1992: Activation of Civil Society." *Pacific Affairs,* vol. 66, no. 3, pp. 315–367.

Lee, Su-Hoon, and David A. Smith. 1991. "Antisystemic Movements in South Korea: The Rise of Environmental Activism." Paper prepared for the 15th PEWS Conference, University of Hawaii, March 28–30.

Lee, Yok-shiu. 1995. "Understanding Contemporary Environmental Movements in Asia." Paper presented at the First Workshop on Asia's Environmental Movements in Comparative Perspective, East-West Center, University of Hawaii, November 29.

Ministry of Environment. Annual. *Yearbook of the Korean Environment.* Seoul: Ministry of Environment (in Korean).

Park, Jae-Mook. 1995. "Locally Based Anti-nuclear Movements and Citizens' Participation." Ph.D. Dissertation, Department of Sociology, Seoul National University (in Korean).

Sisa Journal. 1990. November 15 issue, pp. 69–72 (in Korean).

Smith, David A. 1994. "Uneven Development and Environment: Notes on a World-System Approach." In *Environment and Development,* edited by Korean Sociological Association, pp. 3–26. Seoul: Seoul Press.

5

Environmental Movements in Thailand

Alvin Y. So and Yok-shiu F. Lee

Acronyms

EGAT	Electricity Generating Authority of Thailand	TBCSD	Thailand Business Council for Sustainable Development
MOSTE	Ministry of Science, Technology, and Environment	TEDNET	Thailand Environment and Development Network
NEB	National Environment Board		
NGOs	Non-Governmental Organizations	TEI	Thailand Environment Institute
PER	Project for Ecological Recovery	TEMCO	Thailand Exploration and Mining Corporation
PP21	People's Plan for the 21st Century		

The rapid economic growth in Thailand was mainly due to the explosive development of manufacturing industries, tourism, and direct foreign investment over the past few decades. However, the haphazard and opportunistic industrialization not only has produced many adverse social and economic effects, but also has had dramatic environmental costs, many of which are unfortunately irreversible. According to Komin (1993), Thailand's environmental problems are very serious, including all sorts of pollution from industrial wastes, widespread deforestation, depletion of mineral resources, and encroachment on national parks and wildlife.

In Bangkok, air, noise, and water pollution have far exceeded standard acceptable levels. There are at least two million vehicles moving around Bangkok, 800,000 of which are motorcycles. They emit dangerous gases as well as smoke and dust that contain lead and carbon. In 1989, some 900,000 people suffered from respiratory illnesses. Doctors have also found lead in the umbilical cords of newborn babies (Siriyuvasak 1994).

The major source of dangerous environmental problems stems from Thailand's estimated 100,000 factories. Wastes discharged from these factories in the form of air pollutants, waste water, and chemical waste directly invade the bodies of the people, taking their toll in both short-term and long-term effects. Thailand's rivers are contaminated with all kinds of filth and garbage, industrial wastes, chemicals, plastics, human waste, and disease-contaminated garbage from hospitals. *Matichon* (23 March 1989), for example, reported that two hundred farmers and residents living near a dye factory marched to the provincial hall in Nakhon Pathom Province, where they called on government officials to stop the factory from discharging untreated water into the river, which was polluting the water needed for their farms and household use. Contaminated water had flooded the whole area, killing fruit trees and causing people to become ill. When the situation remained unchanged, 400 farmers rallied in front of the factory seven months later, resulting in a confrontation.

Despite Thailand's rapid economic development, the majority of Thais live in rural areas and their livelihood depends on the rural resource economy. Over the past two decades, they have been drawn into political conflict over the environment by the mounting pressure that so-called "resource-intensive" development exerts on the sources of their sustenance (Hirsch and Lohmann 1989: 439). For example, since the late 1970s, Thailand has suffered considerable loss of fertile crop land and forest as industrialists and developers have turned such land into industrial sites, resorts, golf courses, and condominiums. Thailand's forest areas have shrunk by almost half since 1961, from 53 percent of the total land area in 1961 to only 28 percent in 1988 (Komin 1993).

In the North, logging and encroachment into upland forests have motivated farmers to take action to protect the watersheds that feed their fields. Farmers' protests against timber-cutting in more than ten provinces in the North were important components of the rising environmentalist pressure that resulted in the banning of all logging nationwide in 1989 (Hirsch and Lohmann 1989).

In the South, the level of degradation as a result of deforestation was brought to public attention by the tragic November 1988 mudslide and flood in which a heavy rain brought down thousands of legal and illegal logs from the forest, killing 300 villagers and destroying a number of villages overnight in several provinces (Hirsch and Lohmann 1989). The situation in the East has been aggravated since 1981 by the promotion of the Eastern Seaboard industrial zone. The Gulf of Siam is heavily contaminated with industrial waste from 1,647 plants located at the Laem Chabang and Mab Taphud areas in the eastern province of Rayong. Among them, 494 are chemical-producing plants, 40 are large chemical users, and 21 are in the petrochemical industry (Siriyuvasak 1994).

In the Northeast, illegal rocksalt mining has polluted one of the region's major rivers, the Nam Siew (Siew River). Rocksalt is used in the export-oriented soda ash and glass-making industries. Extensive mining in the 1970s and the 1980s has resulted in rapid land erosion and destruction of the Nam Siew and its aquatic life. The river is now twice as salty as sea water. The livelihood of 300,000 people in 500 villages along the banks of the river is badly affected (Siriyuvasak 1994). Finally, many foreign companies see Thailand as a polluter's haven because of a lack of enforcement of anti-pollution regulations. A good illustration is provided by the practice of dumping tons of toxic chemical wastes from foreign countries at the Port Authority area; this went on for years, until the waste exploded accidentally in 1990 (Komin 1993).

Similar to other developing countries, environmental degradation in Thailand has led to the emergence of environmental movements over the past three decades. In the 1970s and the 1980s, there was a fairly robust environmental movement from below organized by the non-governmental organizations (NGOs) to protect the livelihood and welfare of the local populations. However, by the 1990s, the thrust of Thailand's environmental movement has shifted to a form that can be called an "environmental movement from above" organized by big businesses and state bureaucrats to address life-style and "cosmetic" issues. This chapter will first discuss the environmental movements from below in the 1970s and the 1980s, then explain how big businesses and state bureaucrats were able to usurp the environmental movements from above. Finally, this chapter will discuss the future contour of Thailand's environmental movements in the twenty-first century.

The Origins of Thailand's Environmental Movements in the 1970s

As Quigley (1996) points out, prior to the 1970s there were virtually no environmental organizations in Thailand. However, by the early 1970s, there was a loose network of student-organized ecological clubs. These clubs had some influence in expressing students' anger regarding the environmental policies of the military government of Thanom.

Thailand has been under military rule since 1932. In Thai's military-dominated system, coups d'etat (eleven between 1932 and 1973) became an institutionalized means for military generals to alternate in power while at the same time suppress the emergence of civil society (Paribatra 1993). In this respect, the ecological club made history in 1973 when they exposed a hunting scandal of the military government. Following a helicopter crash on May 1, 1973, it became clear that government officials had been hunting in a restricted reserve at Thung Yai Naresuan Wildlife Sanctuary in western Thailand. Students at Ramkhamhaeng University published a satirical account of this incident, for which nine of them were expelled. The scandal led to demands for a government investigation, increased interest in conservation among youth and the general public, and to the establishment of the Royal Forestry Department's Wildlife Conservation Division (Hirsch and Lohmann 1989).

In addition, this scandal is cited as one of the catalysts for the student-led rebellion in 1973. In October 1973, a march of 30,000 students against the military government snarled Bangkok traffic for two days. Oppositional forces to the military government then used this opportunity to press for a new constitution, leading to an "open politics" period between 1973 and 1976 (Heinze 1974).

The most sustained environmentally oriented political battle during this period was the so-called TEMCO movement of 1974–75. The surging student movement at this time succeeded on March 14, 1975, in forcing the government to withdraw extremely profitable (and illegal) mining concessions in southern Thailand that had been granted by a few shareholding high government officials to the Union Carbide–dominated Thailand Exploration and Mining Corporation (TEMCO). This campaign epitomized the use of environmental issues by students to highlight abuses of power by government officials and to build popular support (Hirsch and Lohmann 1989).

As a result of the success of the TEMCO movement, environmental groups proliferated during this open politics period. However, they were the focus of the crackdown following the 1976 coup that returned Thailand to authoritarianism under Prime Minister Thanin. Student leaders fled to the forest, as it came to be associated with refuge for the disaffected and a source of opposition to the authoritarian regime. Other than the forest, there was little space for open opposition to the military government, and students were barred from activism in rural areas (Hirsch and Lohmann 1989). Although the period of "open politics" was brief, it signaled the end of the unchallengeable supremacy of the military's right to rule Thailand.

Environmental Movements from Below in the 1980s

Favorable Conditions

Just a few years after the 1976 coup, environmental movements rose up in Thailand again. Quigley (1996) has identified the following factors for the growth of environmental movements in the 1980s. First, there was mounting evidence that unbridled development was degrading the environment. Particular concerns, including water pollution, deforestation, and dam building, began to emerge in the 1980s. The degradation of natural resources, previously protected by their inaccessibility, had accelerated rapidly during the late 1970s under strict military rule. Thus, Hirsch and Lohmann (1989) estimate that Thailand's forests are being destroyed at an amazing rate of approximately 2,500 square kilometers, or 1.6 percent of remaining forest area, per year.

Second, there was a rapid expansion of the middle class as a result of economic development in Thailand. Paribatra (1993) suggests that the size of the middle class in Thailand has grown from 178,000 in 1960 to 1,800,000 in 1986. The middle-class members were mostly young (ages 25–35), well educated (bachelor's degrees or the equivalent), exposed to Western culture, and employed in professional and managerial occupations. Members of the middle class, especially in Bangkok, did not have to look far to see ample evidence of environmental degradation. Their concerns about the deteriorating environment and their dissatisfaction with the state's failure to address these problems motivated middle-class professionals to form NGOs in order to change government policy toward the environment.

Third, the military government began to adopt a more tolerant policy toward dissent after the collapse of the communist insurgency in Thailand in the early 1980s. The military granted an amnesty policy that encouraged many radical students to return from the forests (Maisrikrod 1997). Thus, civil society organizations that were interested in influencing public policy on environmental issues found an opening. Political activists tended to focus on environmental issues because they had more room to maneuver these issues than with democracy issues. On the other hand, government officials who had previously been suspicious of environmental organizations began to pay them some credence. For example, the mass demonstrations protesting the proposed Nam Choan Dam in Kanchanaburi from 1982 to 1984 are considered to be the first events where political activists could publicly express themselves after the 1976 coup.

Finally, Thai environmental movements were helped by the global environmental movements in the 1980s. Global linkages provided both an umbrella and some financial resources for Thailand's new environmental organizations to harness growing dissatisfaction with the government's poor environmental record. For example, the Wildlife Fund in Thailand received significant backing from the World Wildlife Fund, and the Project for Ecological Recovery was established with funding from Germany.

Environmental Activities

The first major environmental issue that erupted in this period was the proposed Nam Choan Dam on the Khwae Yai River in Kanchanaburi. In Hirsch and Lohmann's (1989) account, as the cabinet was considering whether to go ahead with the dam in early 1982, a storm of protest arose following a campaign by students in thirteen university environmental clubs. The Nam Choan Dam project was then shelved for several years. When the Thai cabinet tried to revive the project in the spring of 1986, another wave of protest erupted. Students, NGOs, university scientists, and dozens of foreign environmental organizations joined hands to challenge the government's ministers, technocrats, military leaders, and big corporations. Rallies, marches, and concerts were held, and posters were put up all over the province to denounce the project. The protests were energized by the participation of a leading popular singer (Ad Carabao), a revered abbot (Phra Buddhadhasa

Bhikku of Suan Moke Temple of Surat Thani), and the ascetic governor of Bangkok (Major General Chamlong Srimuang). Fearing that the anti-dam movement might topple the eight-year-old government of Prem Tinsulanonda, political parties in both the government coalition and the opposition began to come out against the dam in March 1988, finally leading to the shelving of the dam project.

Another major environmental protest activity in this period involved the politics of the planting of the fast-growing eucalyptus for the wood chips and paper-pulp industry. Growth in Japanese wood chips and paper pulp led to the eucalyptus boom in Thailand in the 1980s, as a Japanese-Thai joint venture, called Thai Eucalyptus Resources, promoted the planting of 2,000 square kilometers of eucalyptus to produce chips for export. The Thai state enthusiastically supports the tree plantation companies because it can be seen as discharging its responsibility to "reforest the country" after years of logging. However, expansive eucalyptus plantations have few of the characteristics of natural forests and can reduce the water table and damage neighboring crops and village agro-systems. Villagers complain that eucalyptus allows little intercropping; it is useless for fodder, damages local soil and water regimes in ways villagers are sensitive to, and supplies little firewood to the community. Every five or six years, eucalyptus is harvested just like any other export crop, leaving the ground temporarily exposed to soil erosion and mudslide. In addition, a eucalyptus plantation requires use of land currently under cultivation and owned by the villagers. Displacement from such land is increasingly common. Protesting against the eucalyptus companies, small-scale farmers are weathering the contempt of bureaucrats, standing up to assassination threats, and arranging meetings with villagers from other areas. They are holding rallies, speaking out at seminars, blocking roads, marching on government offices, singing songs composed for the occasion. Where other means fail and they are well enough organized, they are ripping out eucalyptus seedlings, chopping down eucalyptus trees, stopping bulldozers, and burning nurseries and equipment. Many villagers are planting fruit, rubber, and native forest trees to preempt or replace eucalyptus (Lohmann 1991).

In February 1990, at the Environment 90 seminar attended by more than 950 participants, an alternative development plan to the government's was proposed. It strongly suggested a fairer measure of economic distribution and sustainable growth instead of the trickle-down approach that has been used throughout the previous six economic plans (1963–1990). It stressed that the goal of economic development must be reconsidered, taking into account the costs of natural resources and the cost to the environment, in order to provide for a balanced and humane social and economic development (Siriyuvasak 1994). The alternative development strategy was further spelled out in the People's Plan for the 21st Century (PP21) in the "1991 People's Forum." PP21 declares that "promoting alternative development is to share alternative development approaches, which is economically self-reliant, politically just, and environmentally sustainable. To enhance people's control of the development direction and their natural resources is the agenda for the approaching century" (People's Plan 1992: 6).

In August 1990, Seub Nakhasathien, a leading conservationist, took his own life as an act of protest in order to safeguard Thailand's national parks and wildlife reserves. The budget allocated for the Huay Kha Khaeng National Wildlife Sanctuary, for instance, was one baht (US$0.04) per 50 square kilometers. Clearly, the foot patrol of wildlife conservationists is simply no match in deterring those with more modern technology felling trees. Seub Nakhasathien's tragic death raised public awareness about the plight of the national forest reserve and spurred the conservation movement to step up its campaign (Siriyuvasak 1994).

By the 1990s, of the approximately 12,000 NGOs in Thailand, some 200 are environmentally related organizations. Of these environmental organizations, the great majority focus on improving the local environment, while some 15 to 20 of these address broad issues of national environmental policy. The NGOs are a highly diversified group, and differ greatly in terms of ideology, strategy, and organization. The Project for Ecological Recovery (PER) is one of the most successful grassroots-oriented NGOs in contesting government environmental decisions.

Project for Ecological Recovery (PER)

Quigley (1996: 15–18) has provided a lucid account of the social origins, the mission and program, the strategy, and organization of PER. Founded in 1985 by Witoon Permpongascharoen, a community development activist from rural Kanchanaburi, PER grew out of an environmental coalition formed during the protests over the proposed construction of Nam Choan Dam. This coalition involved a variety of social forces, including Buddhadhasa Bhikkhu (one of Thailand's most revered monks), grassroots NGOs, students, rural residents, as well as sympathetic governmental officials.

The mission of PER is to mobilize people to address specific environmental problems that affect their livelihood. PER aims to give people a greater say in how the problems of the environment are addressed. Consequently, the principal activities of PER involve training of and advocacy for local groups. These activities aim to promote local solutions to environmental problems, such as empowering citizens to have a role in the selection of dam sites. Thus, PER advocates an anti-bureaucratic, egalitarian ideology born of opposition to the mainstream development path that has marginalized the less privileged sector of society and done so much to damage Thailand's natural resources (Hirsch 1994).

In its advocacy work, PER will not hesitate to adopt a confrontational strategy if needed. Since its inception, it has been highly visible in contesting some of Thailand's most well-known environmental flash points, such as deforestation, logging, and dam controversies. For example, PER has called for the shelving of forest-affecting commercially oriented projects such as resorts; it suggests that unoccupied or unused forests, whether degraded or not, be protected from commercial plantations (Lohmann 1993). Thus, PER has given voice to the concerns of local rural people who were not previously involved with the government's decisions on major hydroelectric dam projects and other vital environmental issues.

PER has a small permanent staff of ten and a modest annual budget of US$100,000, consisting primarily of grants from international agencies and overseas organizations. PER was founded with assistance from the German government and has received support from numerous overseas foundations such as Ashoka Fellowship and the Ford Foundation.

Weaknesses of the NGOs

Despite the success of PER and the proliferation of other environmental organizations, Quigley (1996) points out that Thailand's environmental NGOs face the following structural constraints. First, most of the local NGOs are not well financed, and they are dependent upon foreign financing. For many environmental organizations, external support averages between 80 and 90 percent of their operating budgets. By the 1990s, a reduced level of funding from overseas donors has become a major constraint on their operations and led them to look for new funding sources, including those originating from both the government and the business sector (*Thai Development Newsletter* 1995, No. 29). However, in order to apply for funding from the government and the business sector, the NGOs have to change their strategy from confrontation to cooperation. Thus, Decha Premrudeelert, chairperson of NGO-COD's Northeastern Chapter, remarks, "NGOs will have to experiment more in marketing, community business and fund-raising activities. Thus, they need to adapt their personality and attitudes toward people in other sectors, such as the middle class and various socially committed groups which include government officers, business people and consumers in general" (*Thai Development Newsletter* 1995, No. 29: 40).

Second, many local environmental organizations do not have long-term staffs who are professionally trained. They do not network well and tend to live and die with their leaders. Their leaders, for the most part, are young and do not have experience in government offices. They focus on local issues and single events and generally lack a strategic view. As Srisawang Phuavongphaet, chairperson of NGO-COD, remarks, "We have to admit that NGOs are not good at management. Their way of working has not required them to be strictly organized" (*Thai Development Newsletter* 1995, No. 29: 38). When funding became a serious problem in the 1990s, it affected the quality of NGO staff as well. Phra (monk) Phasian Wisalo explains, NGOs "can't go on paying higher and higher salary to their staff whose expectations and family needs will increase all the time. But once the organizations reach their budget ceiling, disappointed workers would leave for other better-paying jobs. Disruption of work resulted" (*Thai Development Newsletter* 1995, No. 29: 44).

Third, the NGOs are highly diversified. There are many different kinds of NGOs, with their concerns ranging from environment, rural development, human rights, indigenous people, and so on. Karunan (1995: 5, 7) laments that while the mushrooming of numerous NGOs signifies the diversification of NGO approaches and methods of work, "it also resulted in increasing fragmentation of community work and the inevitable polarization of conflicting orientations in development work ... It has often been difficult for NGOs to come together and present a viable and sustainable alternative to mainstream development programmes and parliamentary politics in Thai society. Thus, while strong community linkages and organizational network continue to prevail at local and provincial levels, Thai NGOs still have a long way to go in terms of developing effective cross-sectional alliances and national network."

Fourth, although environmental organizations have had some success in attracting media attention around specific projects, they still have underdeveloped media and public relations capacity. Thailand's electronic media are still under government control. For example, all of the more than 300 radio broadcast bands are controlled by the military or military-related organizations, and they are licensed on a one-year contract to private operators. Given these short leases, station operators are wary about having their leases renewed, so they are quite circumspect in what they say about the government. In fact, in the government-controlled mass media, environmental organizations have been criticized as being agents of foreign governments, as trouble makers who aroused the public to create problems for the government, and as agents impeding Thailand's developmental process. As Dej Phoomkhacha, director of Thai Volunteer Service, remarks, "Time and again, grassroots people and their allies have asked for justice, proposed alternatives, and even organized protest rallies. Instead of rendering sympathy and compassion, Thai society as a whole tends to treat these people as trouble-making rebels" (*Thai Development Newsletter* 1995, No. 29: 39).

Finally, environmental organizations are under close supervision by the government through licensing. Aside from the general bureaucratic obstacles to registration with government (such as time-consuming, cumbersome, and expensive registration procedures), environmental organizations have to go through checking by the police, the cultural ministry, and the tax authorities. Government registration is a political means to keep the environmental organizations in conformity with governmental policies, so they will not become too rebellious.

Given the number of the environmental organizations and the broad scope of their activities, coupled with some international support, it was difficult for the state to suppress the Thai environmental movements from below completely. Nevertheless, given the considerable constraints—such as weak financial base, lack of organization, fragmentation, poor mass media image, and close government supervision—faced by the NGOs, the Thai state and big businesses grasped a golden opportunity to appropriate the environmental movements from above.

Business's Environmental Movement

The Ascendence of Business in Thai Politics

During the period of liberalization in the 1980s, General Prem broadened his social basis of support through sharing some power with the business community. Since most leaders of major parties were businesspeople, almost half of Prem's cabinet members were persons with a business background (Laothamatas 1992). Through political parties, businesses were able to develop close relations with the government at the national, provincial, and local levels. This further facilitated the permeation of business elites into the government circles, money politics, and patronage. Paribatra (1993) remarks that the relentlessly growing nexus between political parties, big business, and government officials strengthened the propensity toward the pursuit of self-interest in the discharge of political responsibilities, as manifested in the widespread corruption and cynical jockeying for cabinet portfolios.

The business community seems to have the ability to sustain its power, irrespective of the military coup d'etat of February 1991 or the massive demonstration in May 1992. Even when the military dissolved the parliament and imposed martial law in 1991, it appointed Anand Panyarachun, a diplomat-turned-businessman, as prime minister to form an interim government. Anand was allowed to choose most members of his technocrat-dominated cabinet (Paribatra 1993). When a massive demonstration by the students, NGO leaders, former bureaucrats, and politicians forced the military to relinquish some power in May 1992, a caretaker government under Anand Panyarachun was again set up to prepare for elections in September 1992. The second Anand government merely transferred the top members of the junta to inactive posts; it has made no attempt to tackle the deep-rooted linkages between the military and the business sector (Bell 1997).

Business's Environmental Initiatives

In response to the grassroots-oriented environmental movement from below, Thailand's big business has waged its own mode of environmental movement from above. In the 1980s, businesses were accused by the grassroots social movements of being the chief villains in matters of environmental degradation. In the 1990s, business groups and individuals have fought back against this negative image and they have taken environmentalist stands of one sort or another in recent years.

Among the best known of the business environmentalists is Sophon Suphaphong, president of Bangchak Petroleum and an important supporter of the Thailand Environment Institute (TEI). Sophon made a strong impact on Thailand's environmental movement through his influence on environmental policies at the national level. Bangchak Petroleum helped set up the Thailand Environment and Development Network (TEDNET), whose objectives were to coordinate environmental activities put forth by government agencies and NGOs. In addition, since 1995, Bangchak Petroleum became the major organizer of the Annual Environmental Conference, which in the early 1990s was organized solely by the NGOs. The taking over of the Annual Environmental Conference by Bangchak Petroleum symbolically represents the ascendance of business environmentalism over NGO's grassroots environmentalism.

Khunying Chodchoy Sophonpanich, daughter of Bangkok Bank founder, took a stand against skytrain, claiming that the aesthetics of the Bangkok streetscape lie at the center of her concern. However, critics of Chodchoy charge that her stand is related to her family's business interests (e.g., real estate to be devalued by the proposed overhead rail; releasing the Bank from commitments to finance the system). Aside from being the founder of the Magic Eyes environmental organization, she is also a member of the Environmental Impact Assessment Study Committee, an adviser to the Environment Committee of the National Council of Women of Thailand, and an adviser to the Environmental Lawyer Association of Thailand.

Pornthep Pornprapha, founder of "Think Earth," is another prominent business personality associated with environmental activities. As president of Siam Motors, Pornthep is involved with the automobile industry, an industry that is itself heavily implicated in the country's pollution problems.

Other prominent business initiatives included the Regent Hotel, which sought the assistance of the Faculty of Environmental and Resource Studies at Mahidol University to develop an environmentally sound "master plan" for its Cha-am hotel resort site in southern Thailand (Hirsch 1994). Likewise, the Hotel Association of Thailand encouraged hotel operators nationwide to become members of the "Green Hotel" project and participate in the Energy Concern and Waste Treatment Scheme. For instance, by joining the Green Building Project introduced by the Electricity Generating Authority of Thailand (EGAT), corporate participants could receive a 10 percent discount on electricity bills (*Manager Newspaper*, January 13–14, 1996).

Finally, there is the Thailand Business Council for Sustainable Development (TBCSD), comprising more than fifty big corporations in Thailand. The Council's activities are coordinated by the Thailand Environment Institute, which is administered under the chairmanship of Anand Panyarachun, a former prime minister of Thailand. Among the many roles of TBCSD is the promotion of ISO14000 registration and the Green Label in Thailand. The launch of the Green Label project in 1993, for instance, provided added incentives to the business sector to produce environmentally friendly products, such as natural products marketed by the Oriental Princess company.

Aside from fighting back the environmental offensive from the grass-roots NGOs, there are also market considerations that prompt businesses to adopt an environmental stand. First, corporations want to appeal to middle-class consumers who are increasingly environmentally concerned. Second, in the 1990s, the government began to enact more stringent environmental protection laws and regulations that the business sector must comply with. Third, requirements stemming from international trade and international organizations such as the World Trade Organization and the European Union shaped the environmental behavior of Thailand's export-oriented businesses. Finally, multinational corporations that operate in Thailand, by complying with environmental practices initiated by their headquarter offices, set examples for local businesses to follow in enhancing the latter's environmental record.

In order to illustrate the activities of the business environmental movement, the following discussion will focus on Magic Eyes, one of the largest and most visible environmental organizations in Thailand in the 1990s.

Magic Eyes: A Typical Business Environmental Organization

Governance

The Thai Environmental and Community Development Association, Samakom Sangsun Thai—better known as "Magic Eyes" because of its trademark pair of watchful eyes—is a typical example of the business environmental movement. The following account draws heavily upon Quigley (1996: 10–15).

Magic Eyes was founded in 1984. It was formally registered in 1986 by Khunying Chodchoy, a dynamic entrepreneurial member of one of Thailand's better-known business families. Unlike other local NGOs, Magic Eyes uses a business association membership model, which requires an annual meeting with presentation of an annual budget and statement of expenditures that has been reviewed by a qualified accountant.

Magic Eyes is governed by a board of trustees, which has 21 representatives from among its 36 corporate members. These members include some of Thailand's most well-known corporations, including Thai Airlines, the Bangkok Bank, Siam Cement, and Shell of Thailand. It is this board of trustees and a full-time paid staff of twenty that provide Magic Eyes with a stable organizational structure that most local NGOs lack. Needless to say, businesspeople have dominated the board of trustees, and grassroots people from local NGOs are not represented on the board.

Mission and Program

Khunying Chodchoy (1997: 30) explains the goal of Magic Eyes as follows: "What I have been trying to do since I started the Magic Eyes programme 13 years ago is to look at the positive issues and try to come up with ways and alternatives that can be beneficial to the industrial and business sectors." The Magic Eyes mission is to enhance cooperation among businesses, government, and citizens in improving the quality of the environment. It seeks to accomplish this goal by creating a popular awareness that encourages people to assume civic responsibility by becoming engaged in small-scale projects that can appreciably improve the quality of the environment.

Magic Eyes has four general program areas: (1) cleanups, (2) waste reduction, (3) environmental appreciation, and (4) special initiatives. One of the most visible examples of waste was styrofoam in the country's waterways. Hoping to reach millions in an educational campaign, Magic Eyes targeted the Loy Krathong festival, through which Thai people seek to evoke good fortune by placing small floats on the country's myriad waterways. Since the 1990s, these floats had increasingly been made of styrofoam rather than of traditional biodegradable materials such as banana leaves. Magic Eyes launched a major public education campaign to encourage a return to traditional float materials and sponsored competitions to promote innovative designs. The campaign was a major success in reducing styrofoam waste in the waterways. In the 1996 festival, 90 percent of the floats were made of biodegradable products. Magic Eyes also spoke with various supermarkets and food centers that use styrofoam to pack food. Magic Eyes asked them to use plastics or containers that can be recycled.

Starting as a public education civic environmental organization to conduct cleanup campaigns, over time Magic Eyes has become increasingly engaged in a range of environmental policy issues. For example, Magic Eyes held discussions with Bangkok's Metropolitan Authority about how to expand sanitation services and to change its policies on waste collection and disposal.

Strategy

Different from many grassroots NGOs, which do not hesitate to adopt a confrontational strategy if needed, Magic Eyes maintains a cooperative attitude with business and government. Magic Eyes does not want to get involved in environmental flash points. Its leadership believes that to accomplish something you must work effectively with both business and the state.

Recognizing that environmental problems are complex, Magic Eyes seeks to involve a cross-section of Thai society, including entrepreneurial problem-solvers from the state and the business sectors, as well as university professors, scientists, and responsible citizens. Therefore, Magic Eyes's projects generally involve an outreach or advertising component, an educational dimension, and cooperation with other solution-oriented individuals and institutions.

Strengths

Compared to small local NGOs, Magic Eyes is far superior in terms of economic, symbolic, and political power. First, as a business environmental organization, Magic Eyes is full of resources. It is the largest environmental organization in Thailand; with twenty full-time staff and an annual operating budget of US$360,000. Magic Eyes's funds come primarily from its corporate members, with modest contributions from overseas agencies such as the Asia Foundation. This budget does not include the significant value of in-kind contributions such as the office space provided by Thailand's largest bank, the Bangkok Bank, and the public service announcements by Thailand's major television channels.

Second, Magic Eyes is influential because it is adept at working with the mass media. Magic Eyes originally conducted anti-litter campaigns by means of advertising on television, radio, and billboards, as well as by placing its trademark watchful eyes on garbage containers. Given that most of its thirty-six board members are marketing executives from many of Thailand's leading corporations, it is understandable that initially Magic Eyes focused on advertising campaigns. In addition, Magic Eyes's outreach capacity is considerable since all of the major television stations have representatives on its board. Therefore, Magic Eyes's activities are frequently featured on television, making it perhaps the best known environmental organization in Thailand.

Finally, Magic Eyes is well connected to the state. It has a small advisory board of eight to ten prominent current or former government officials, including the former government spokesperson from the prime minister's office, the permanent secretary of the Ministry of Science, Technology, and Energy, and the director of the Department of Social Welfare of the Bangkok Metropolitan Administration, which is responsible for registering NGOs in the Bangkok area. Magic Eyes representatives also serve on numerous governmental committees at the national and local levels. These official and corporate links provide Magic Eyes with considerable access to bureaucratic power.

Statist Environmental Movement

Appropriating the Environmental Discourse

During the 1980s, the environmental movements can be seen as an "anti-state" activity because movement activists were highly skeptical of the Thai state. The state was seen as being controlled by a group of military officials who were undemocratic, and the state had promoted a set of growth-first policies that led to the degradation of the environment in Thailand.

However, by the late 1980s, the technocrats in the Thai government had jumped upon the "environment bandwagon" and began to embrace many of the discourses and areas of action that were once the purview of grassroots environmental movements. Rigg (1995) points out that forest loss, land erosion and degradation, pollution, congestion in Bangkok, national parks, and endangered fauna have all become the common currency of government planning and rhetoric. The National Economic and Social Development Board has stressed increasingly the importance of targeting less advantaged areas and population groups; with reference to grassroots development, the Board has also aimed to give greater responsibility and power to those at the local level. The Sixth National Economic and Social Development Plan, for instance, aims to encourage the public to find solutions to their own problems on the basis of self-reliance; local organizations at the village level will be strengthened; local resources will be mobilized; and people will be encouraged to solve their own and community problems (Rigg 1991). In addition, the Thai government also put forward the following environmental initiatives.

Bureaucratic Initiatives

In the 1990s, an important bureaucratic reform has been the changed role of the National Environment Board (NEB). The NEB was established in connection with the "open politics" initiative in 1975 under the first National Environment Quality Act. However, the NEB had little enforcement power and a limited bureaucratic role. In 1992, there was the enactment of a new Enhancement and Conservation of the National Environmental Quality Act, which aims to strengthen and enhance the role of certain government agencies in dealing with environmental issues. Through this 1992 Environmental Quality Act, the Ministry of Science, Technology, and Environment (MOSTE) was created, with three new departments specifically concerned with the environment added to the old Ministry of Science and Technology (Hirsch 1994).

In addition, the Thai government established an Environment Fund to support projects concerned with environmental protection and natural resource conservation. The Fund, set up under the Seventh National Economic and Social Development Plan (1992–96), is designed to provide grants to government agencies and local administrations to pay for the operation of wastewater treatment plants and waste disposal facilities. State agencies and privately owned enterprises, as well as environmental NGOs that are registered, can submit funding proposals to this Fund. The government considers the Fund the primary mechanism to draw the business sector into a joint effort to resolve the nation's environmental problems. However, while many environmental NGOs were interested in getting some kind of support from this Fund, they were deterred by the complicated procedures for submitting and winning approval from the Fund committee. Since the establishment of the Fund, only sixteen NGOs have been granted support for their proposals in the mid-1990s.

There has also been a push for a move away from the old "command and control" approach to environmental legislation and standards toward a more market-oriented approach such as adopting the polluter pays principle that relies on business self-interest. Of course, for the market approach to work, an effective monitoring system is vital. However, little has been achieved thus far in instituting an adequate monitoring and enforcement mechanism (Hirsch 1994).

In order to assist policymaking, several think-tanks were created by the Thai government. Two of the most significant ones are the Thailand Development Research Institute and the Thailand Environment Institute (which have environment at the center of their policy and research agendas). Similar to other bureaucratic organizations, the professional orientation of these two think-tanks is characterized (Hirsch 1994: 9) as "technocratic/rationalist." In the environmental arena, this means development of policy that makes for more sound environmental management from a technocratic viewpoint. Grassroots concerns about citizen participation and environmental politics are seldom taken into account in the technocratic mode of thinking.

Aside from a technocratic mode of thinking, the government also promotes the value of harmony and cooperation on its environmental policy. As Somchet Thinaphong, the governor of the Industrial Estate Authority of Thailand, explains, it is important to devise a strategy for development that is in harmony with the environment. This concept of harmony implies that any technology chosen should satisfy many stringent environmentally friendly criteria. For example, a clean technology is energy-efficient technology whose waste products can be recycled. Another concept is cooperation. In order for the process of development to be effective, it must involve cooperative action by the public and private sectors as well as the general populace and the world community (*Business in Thailand,* December 1991).

The Future Prospects for Thailand's Environmental Movements

Thailand's environmental movements represent a very complicated phenomenon because two different forms of environmentalism have intersected with one another since the 1980s. On the one hand, there is a grassroots environmental movement from below waged by the rural poor, students, and NGOs against business and the state's deforestation, dam construction, mining, and high-growth policy. Rallies, demonstrations, and confrontations are some of the strategies used by the grassroots environmental movements to protect the livelihood and welfare of the poor and indigenous people. On the other hand, there is an environmental movement from above organized by big corporations and government officials in order to pacify the protest activities of the environmental groups. Big business and state officials emphasize the importance of maintaining the harmony of different interests and the need for cooperation. They promote "a green life-style" and the use of ecologically friendly consumer products among the Thai citizens as well as the adoption of technical solutions to clean up Bangkok. In the 1990s, it seems that big business and the state have, so far, successfully contained the grassroots environmental movements through funding, new environmental policy, and mass media support.

However, it is unlikely that the business sector and the Thai government will be able to contain the grassroots environmental movements from below for long. Despite the "cosmetic" initiatives of the business community to beautify the environment, and despite the government's new environmental initiatives, the following issues indicate that Thailand's environmental problems will get worse in the next century.

First, the Thai government is known for its inability to carry out its promise to protect the environment because of bureaucratic problems. Although the government promulgated a new Environmental Quality Act in 1992, the fact that ministers and ministries can, and do, ignore environmental plans remains an important constraint limiting the effectiveness of environmental management. Thai ministries tend to operate as "kingdoms," answering only to themselves; they compete with one another for funds and influence, and they rarely cooperate with one another in a coherent fashion (Rigg 1991, 1995). The National Environmental Board (NEB) has no direct administrative authority for managing the environment. Moreover, agencies with such authority are numerous and their actions are largely uncoordinated. For example, there are about twenty government agencies with responsibilities related to the problems of water pollution. The common practice adopted in response to these problems is to set up additional agencies or committees and to draft additional regulations that are destined to be ineffective. Many government agencies have made no commitment to enforce environmental regulations. Ministries can ignore planning objectives presented by the National Economic and Social Development Board and pursue policies of their own. It is significant that national development plans lack statutory enforcement power and are not binding in terms of budget allocation (Rigg 1991). Thus, the Thai government has been impotent in enforcing anti-pollution law (Komin 1993).

Second, the Thai government has been unable to fully implement its environmental policies due to political problems. No government official has been able and willing to put the interests of the public above the economic interests of powerful corporations. As Komin (1993: 271) points out,

> [the Thai] government is dominated by those who determine and change regulations to fit their own vested interests, ignoring calls for curbing corruption and caring little for environment protection. Politicians who have bought their way into office seek to recoup their losses after the election. Such a political system, with its rampant corruption and profit orientation, has served to promote the worsening of environmental problems in the country by fostering poor management of environment, inadequate implementation of existing policies, and lax law enforcement.

Third, after a period of rapid economic development, the business sector is willing to start a few environmental initiatives and provide some environmental funding in order to pacify the grassroots environmental movements from below. However, in the late 1990s, as the economic crisis deepens in Thailand, there is reason to believe that Thailand's environmental problems will get worse, not better. As Thailand is burdened by an enormous foreign debt, its stock market and currency falling sharply, its unemployment rate approaching double-digit figures, economic growth will become the number one priority of the Thai government and big corporations at the expense of environmental integrity.

In his discussion of the economic crisis in Thailand, Bello (1998: 10–11) sadly conjures to the following environmental nightmare:

> According to government statistics, only 17 percent of the country's land area remains covered by forest, and this is probably an overestimation. The great Chao Phraya River that runs through Bangkok is biologically dead to its lower reaches. Only 50,000 of the 3.5 million metric tons of hazardous waste produced in the country each year are treated, the rest being disposed of in ways that gravely threaten public health, like being dumped in shallow underground pits where seepage can contaminate aquifers. So unhealthy is Bangkok's air that, a few years ago, a University of Hawaii team measuring air pollution reportedly refused to return to the city.

However, as Thai's environmental conditions worsen, the environmental struggles against deforestation, dam construction, community lands, fishing rights, and air and water pollution will intensify. The rural poor will fight for local control and subsistence security, Bangkok residents will fight for clean air and water, and they will be backed by a wide variety of groups—students, intellectuals, and NGOs—who share a similar environmental agenda. As such, it seems that, as the country embarks into the twenty-first century, the grassroots environmental movements from below could be empowered and revived in Thailand.

References

Bell, David. 1997. "A Review of *Interpreting Development: Capitalism, Democracy, and the Middle Class in Thailand.*" *Crossroads* 11: 135–138.

Bello, Walden. 1998. "The End of a 'Miracle': Speculation, Foreign Capital Dependence and the Collapse of the Southeast Asian Economics." *Multinational Monitor* 19 (1–2): 1–11.

Business in Thailand. Various issues.

Chodchoy, Khunying. 1997. "Industrialization and Environmental Preservation." *Business in Thailand* 28: 28–32.

Heinze, Ruth-Inge. 1974. "Ten Days in October—Students versus the Military: An Account of the Student Uprisings in Thailand." *Asian Survey* 14: 491–508.

Hirsch, Philip. 1994. "Where Are the Roots of Thai Environmentalism?" *TEI Quarterly Environment Journal* 2 (2): 5–15.

Hirsch, Philip, and Larry Lohmann. 1989. "The Contemporary Politics of Environment in Thailand." *Asian Survey* 29: 439–451.

Karunan, Victor P. 1995. "Introduction." In *Thai NGOs,* edited by Jaturong Boonyarattanasoontorn and Gawin Chutima, p. 408. Bangkok: NGO Support Project.

Komin, Suntaree. 1993. "A Social Analysis of the Environmental Problems in Thailand." In *Asia's Environmental Crises,* edited by Michael C. Howard, pp. 257–274. Boulder: Westview Press.

Laothamatas, Anek. 1992. *Business Associations and the New Political Economy of Thailand.* Boulder: Westview Press.

Lohmann, Larry. 1991. "Peasants, Plantations, and Pulp: The Politics of Eucalyptus in Thailand." *Bulletin of Concerned Asian Scholars* 23 (4): 3–17.

————. 1993. "Land, Power, and Forest Colonization in Thailand." *Global Ecology and Biogeography Letters* 3: 180–191.

Maisrikrod, Surin. 1997. "The Making of Thai Democracy." In *Democratization in Southeast and East Asia,* edited by Anek Laothamatas, pp. 141–166. Singapore: Institute of Southeast Asian Studies.

Manager Newspaper. Various issues.

Matichon. Various issues.

Nicro, Somrudee. 1997. "Environmental Movements in Thailand." Paper presented to the conference entitled Asia's Environmental Movement in Comparative Perspective, University of Hong Kong, February.

Paribatra, Sukhumbhand. 1993. "State and Society in Thailand." *Asian Survey* 33: 879–893.

People's Plan (People's Plan for the 21st Century). 1992. *Experiences of Hope: Reaching for the 21st Century.* Bangkok: NGO-Coordinating Committee on Rural Development.

Quigley, Kevin. 1996. "Environmental Organizations and Democratic Consolidation in Thailand." *Crossroads* 9 (2): 1–29.

Rigg, Jonathan. 1991. "Grass-Roots Development in Rural Development: A Lost Cause?" *World Development* 18: 199–211.

————. 1995. "Counting the Costs: Economic Growth and Environmental Change in Thailand." In *Counting the Costs,* edited by Jonathan Rigg, pp. 3–24. Singapore: Institute of Southeast Asian Studies.

Siriyuvasak, Ubonrat. 1994. "The Environment and Popular Culture in Thailand." *Thai Development Newsletter* 26: 64–69.

Thai Development Newsletter. Various issues.

6

Environmental Movements in the Philippines

Francisco A. Magno

Acronyms

ACES	Agency for Community Educational Services	FSS	Foundation for a Sustainable Society
APEC	Asia-Pacific Economic Cooperation	IAP	Individual Action Plan
		IPAF	Integrated Protected Area Fund
BCCs	Basic Christian Communities	LC	Local Community
CADI	Center for Alternative Development Initiatives	LGUs	Local Government Units
		LRT	Light Rail Transit
CALM	Cagayan Anti-Logging Movement	MABINI	Movement of Attorneys for Brotherhood, Integrity, and Nationalism, Inc.
CPAR	Congress for People's Agrarian Reform		
		MCCBI	Movement of Concerned Citizens of Bolinao, Inc.
DENR	Department of Environment and Natural Resources	MPFA	Manila People's Forum on APEC
DFA	Department of Foreign Affairs	NACFAR	National Coalition of Fisher-folks for Aquatic Reforms
ECC	Environmental Compliance Certificate	NGOs	Non-Governmental Organizations
EISs	Environmental Impact Statements	NIPA	NGOs for Integrated Protected Areas
EOI	Export-Oriented Industrialization		
		PAP	Philippine Aid Plan
EPZs	Export Processing Zones	PBE	Philippine Business for the Environment, Inc.
FDC	Freedom from Debt Coalition		
		PCC	Pangasinan Cement Corporation
FPE	Foundation for the Philippine Environment	PCSD	Philippine Council for Sustainable Development

PDF	Philippine Development Forum	SRDDP	Sustainable Rural District Development Program
PFEC	Philippine Federation for Environmental Concerns	SUSDEVAPI	Sustainable Development: Asia-Pacific Initiatives
PHILIDHRRA	Philippine Partnership for the Development of Human Resources in Rural Areas	TRIPUD	Tripartite Partnership for Upland Development
POs	People's Organizations	UNCED	United Nations Conference on Environment and Development
PRRM	Philippine Rural Reconstruction Movement	WAND	Women's Action Network for Development
RDDP	Rural Development and Democratization Program	WB-GEF	World Bank—Global Environment Facilities
SIBS	Social Infrastructure Building and Strengthening	WHO	World Health Organization

Introduction

In August 1996, the Department of Environment and Natural Resources (DENR) through its review committee reaffirmed an earlier decision to deny the application of the Pangasinan Cement Corporation (PCC) for an Environmental Compliance Certificate (ECC) to build a giant cement plant, worth 1.3 billion pesos ($50 million), in the coastal town of Bolinao, Pangasinan, in the northwestern part of the Philippines. An earlier attempt by the PCC to acquire official approval for the project failed when the DENR in October 1995 ruled against the construction of the plant due to unresolved issues pertaining to land use, social acceptability, and pollution mitigation. The government's decision came on the heels of a vigorous campaign by environmental activists to mobilize public sentiment against the cement complex on grounds that its construction will not only foster marine destruction, biodiversity loss, river siltation, and geological disturbances, but will threaten as well the health and security of local residents.

The resistance to the cement project, displayed in numerous mass rallies and public hearings, was spearheaded by the local group Movement of Concerned Citizens of Bolinao, Inc. (MCCBI). MCCBI garnered support from the Marine Science Institute of the University of the Philippines, the Lingayen Gulf Coastal Area Management Commission, municipal and provincial officials, non-government organizations (NGOs), and mass media practitioners. On the other side of the fence, strong lobbying efforts were mounted by the PCC and its business partners, which included Japan's Marubeni and Nihon Corporation and Taiwan's Tuntex Group of Companies. They were able to enlist members of the Bolinao Fishermen and Fish Dealers Association as allies in their campaign based on the promise of alternative incomes to be generated by the project in the face of dwindling fish stocks in the Lingayen Gulf. In the end, however, the anti-cement crusade prevailed.

The impressive display of citizen activism in Bolinao marks an important episode in the evolving story of environmentalism in the Philippines. While local actions to defend the environment against outside agents have been a characteristic feature of the environmental movement, what is striking in this case is the manner in which environmental collaborations were forged across the public–private divide. The joint participation of local citizen groups, national NGOs, academics, public officials, and media people in the Bolinao campaign signifies environmentalization spilling into various social institutions (Buttel 1993). Indicative of such a process were the numerous pressures brought to bear on government institutions by the green movement in fostering the integration of environmental concerns into development planning. In the aftermath of the cement project's rejection, the Department of Trade and Industry decided to constitute an environmental unit within the Board of Investments which would cooperate with the DENR in ensuring the transparency of the process governing the issuance of ECCs.

Within the context of the severe ecological crisis confronting the Philippines, this study will assess the nature and character of the environmental movement and evaluate its strategic role and impact in society. In the first part of this study, a survey of the critical ecological problems engulfing the Philippines is presented. The following section unearths the origins and dynamics of the environmental movement and frames them within the context of changing political structures, development policies, and civil society formations. This is followed by a critical assessment of the key players, issues, and orientations within the environmental movement, and examination of the movement's relationship with other social organizations. Next will be an examination of the impact of environmental activism on policy orientations, governance processes, corporate accountability, and citizen empowerment. Finally, this study identifies the strategic challenges facing the environmental movement and probes into its potential directions amid the swift pace of societal and ecological transitions.

Environmental Problems

Partly as a concession to a burgeoning civil society and partly in response to an emerging green trade market, the Ramos administration announced that Philippine Agenda 21, the individual action plan (IAP) submitted to the 1996 Asia-Pacific Economic Cooperation (APEC) summit meeting in Manila, would help position the country as a "green tiger" in twenty-first century Asia, deeply committed to the attainment of economic progress without sacrificing the environment. Nevertheless, the constraints to be overcome are great; the development policymaking in the Philippines has been guided, since colonial times, by the overwhelming pursuit of short-term economic gains at the expense of long-term social and environmental costs. Past state failure to adequately regulate resource users and tax polluters, and apply equity and efficiency criteria in the distribution of resource rights, contributed immensely to the speedy deterioration of the environment.

The gravity of Philippine environmental problems is typified by the highly degraded state of its forests, fisheries, and crop lands in the countryside, and the deteriorating quality of the air, water, and sanitation services in the cities. Rapid deforestation rates, caused by overlogging, agricultural expansion, and upland migration, reduced the forest cover to only 5.7 million hectares, or slightly less than 20 percent of the country's total land area. From 1969 to 1993, a total of 4.8 million hectares of forest cover was eradicated, equivalent to an average forest loss of 200,000 hectares per annum (Asian Development Bank 1994). From being a major world exporter of logs from the 1950s to the early 1980s, the Philippines is now a net importer of wood in the 1990s.

The negative impact of forest denuding extends far beyond the decline of timber resources; it also induces biodiversity loss, watershed degradation, soil erosion, and siltation. Forest degradation deprives wildlife of their natural habitat. An estimated 46 of the 1,657 existing wildlife species in the Philippines are under severe threat of extinction. Soil erosion affects 100,000 hectares every year and results in the tremendous loss of fertile top soil, as well as the siltation·and sedimentation of rivers, lakes, and waterways. Watershed degradation increases the incidence of flooding disasters, threatens water supply, and decreases the productive life span of irrigation canals and dams (Sajise et al. 1992).

Fish production declined in recent years due to the environmental effects of overfishing, especially of small pelagic fish, certain species of juvenile tuna, nearshore demersal stocks, and municipal fish stocks. The sustainability and potential for future regeneration of fishery resources are also threatened by marine habitat destruction traceable to pollution, sedimentation, coral reef destruction, and mangrove clearing. Siltation resulting from forest degradation and mine tailings buries corals under huge sediment loads. In Bacuit Bay, Palawan, sediment deposits caused by logging generated a 50 percent loss of coral cover during a one-year period on reefs close to the outlet of a small river. Dynamite fishing and the underwater use of sodium cyanide by tropical fish collectors, likewise, put corals under extreme stress (World Bank 1989).

It is estimated that a large portion of the country's coral reefs have been destroyed, while mangrove areas were converted into fish ponds and prawn farms at a brisk pace. Similar to the downward trend in marine productivity, the decline in crop productivity was influenced by drastic environmental changes. The degradation of crop lands through soil erosion, pollution, and the conversion of farmlands into residential and industrial estates, generate negative consequences on crop production levels as agricultural lands become scarcer and poorer in quality. Soil erosion is now a major problem in 36 of the nation's 75 provinces. The heavy use of chemical fertilizers and pesticides decreases the humus content and affects the infiltration and water-holding capacities of large portions of agricultural land which are rapidly becoming acidic. Mine tailings and industrial wastes pollute valuable crop lands. For example, the sedimentation of agricultural lands and rivers in the Ilocos region contributes to the loss of 208 million pesos ($8 million) per year in rice production (Sajise et al. 1992).

In the cities, the intensification of environmental problems like inadequate water and sanitation services, lack of wastewater disposal facilities, ambient air pollution, and uncollected solid and hazardous wastes accompanied the tremendous growth in the urban population over the last few years. Metro Manila, which ranks as the sixteenth largest city in the world with an estimated population of 10 million, grows at a rate of 2.9 percent annually and already has a population density of 12,467 persons per square kilometer. The attendant ecological pressures are enormous. The unavailability of affordable housing pushed urban poor people to establish slum settlements on open-access public and private lands, river banks, and in flood-prone areas where exposures to health risks are abundant, while access to clean water and sanitation services are in short supply.

In Metro Manila, Cebu, and Davao, only 16.7 percent of households can access direct water supplies. There is still high dependency on artesian wells, public faucets, and open wells, which makes people vulnerable to gastrointestinal diseases. A mere 14 percent of Metro Manila's population benefits from the use of sewage systems, while the rest are served by individual septic tanks that directly discharge into rivers and waterways, leaving 70 percent of biodegradable pollutants flowing into the various river systems. Untreated or partially treated industrial wastes, toxic substances from hospitals, and solid wastes are also released into these rivers, where levels of dissolved oxygen are severely reduced such that the waterways have become biologically dead (Sajise et al. 1992).

Urban air pollution is most severe in Metro Manila with its high concentration of motor vehicles and factories. In 1994, air pollution in the city exceeded the tolerable limits jointly set by the Philippine government and the World Health Organization (WHO) by 500 percent. Given the absence of a mass transport system and considering that the completion of the expanded light rail transit (LRT) system is not expected until the late 1990s, at best, rising passenger demand and vehicle population growth will further heighten traffic congestion and gas emission levels even more in a city where unleaded fuels are not yet widely used. Philippine Motorist Association data indicate that the volume of vehicles in Metro Manila, currently pegged at 1.5 million, climbed 10 percent annually from 1990 to 1993. On the other hand, even as the DENR upgraded the country's air quality standards in 1993, weak enforcement of pollution regulations enables industries to continue spewing toxic effluent into the sky.

Historical Review of the Environmental Movement

An analytical review of the genesis and transformation of the environmental movement in the Philippines can be divided into three phases. The first phase (1978–85) was a period of active environmental defense, where issue-specific coalitions were established to support local communities in resisting the ecological destruction posed by the giant infrastructure and development projects of the Marcos martial law regime. Environmental issues during this time were normally subsumed within the broad demands of the democratic movement. On the other hand, the second phase (1986–91) was a period where environmental groups, freed from the urgencies of overthrowing a dictatorship, started clarifying the basis of their identity and unity. Ecologically sound development alternatives were seriously proposed, studied, and pursued through the involvement of NGOs in community-based resource management initiatives in various parts of the country. In the third phase (1992–97), the environmental movement continued to push the frontiers of environmental governance further as the advocacy of sustainable development policies moved across the public–private divide. Within a span of three decades, tremendous transformations occurred in the Philippine environmental movement.

Environmental Defense Phase (1978–1985)

In the early phase of its development in the late 1970s, Philippine environmental activism was fueled by threats to local people and nature generated by environmentally high-impact projects such as the Chico River Dam in Kalinga-Apayao and Mountain Province; the Cellophil Pulp and Paper Plant in Abra; the Philippine Nuclear Power Plant in Morong, Bataan; the Copper Smelter Plant in San Juan, Batangas; and the Kawasaki Sintering Plant in Cagayan de Oro, Misamis Occidental. The Marcos government deemed these economic ventures vital to the pursuit of an export-oriented industrialization (EOI) strategy. In particular, the building of power infrastructures, like the Chico hydroelectric dam and the Morong nuclear plant, was considered key to policy efforts to entice foreign firms to set up shop in the export-processing zones (EPZs) of Baguio City and Bataan. Labeled as national priority concerns, huge development projects were often allowed to proceed even without the preparation of social and environmental impact assessments.

Coercive measures were habitually employed by the Marcos regime and its business allies, especially after the imposition of martial law in 1972, to silence opposition to their development policies. Thus, the early environmental struggles were simultaneously understood as human rights issues (Sachs 1995). Similar to circumstances in other developing countries, local people occupying places where strategic natural resources could be found are usually branded as development obstacles and, in most cases, subject to involuntary relocation (Johnston 1995). In the World Bank–funded Chico Project, an estimated 100,000 Kalinga and Bontoc tribal people from six towns in the Mountain Province and four towns in Kalinga-Apayao faced massive dislocation with the expected inundation of their villages and centuries-old rice terraces. The determined resistance of the indigenous people to the dam, however, led to the withdrawal of the World Bank from the project, and it was subsequently canceled. The success of this environmental campaign, nevertheless, did not come easily. It exacted a heavy toll in terms of human suffering, with the incarceration of numerous protesters and the killing of Kalinga leader Macli-ing Dulag during the height of the anti-dam struggle.

Environmental protest actions, exemplified in the vigorous opposition to the Chico Dam, became part of a broad democratic struggle waged in the 1970s and 1980s, as activists from national political formations undertook organizational work in the local sites of environmental conflicts to expand the range and scope of the anti-dictatorship movement. The face of Macli-ing Dulag appeared together with those of slain opposition figures, like Senator Benigno Aquino, Jr., in large mural paintings paraded through Manila's streets during the huge anti-Marcos rallies of the 1980s. The environmental activism emerging during the martial law period was influenced by the values and agenda of the democratic movement and highlighted the negative relationship between environmental protection and authoritarianism. Indeed, the environmental movement was formed in opposition to the ecological abuses that arose from the exclusion of public participation in development planning, the concentration of resources in a few hands, and the intolerance to alternative development strategies fostered under undemocratic political and economic structures.

Given the historical predominance of rent capitalism in the Philippines, economic protection provided by the state became the principal pathway for business elites to accumulate private wealth. Under a rent-seeking economic regime, mere ownership of property rights assures access to revenues acquired through the operations of the state which circumscribe the assignment of economic advantages (Montes 1988). Considering that privileged access to economic benefits are largely politically determined, rent capitalism may ultimately thrive on the plunder of state machinery by powerful economic interests (Hutchcroft 1994). This plunder was translated into the plunder of the environment when logging licenses, mining concessions, and fishing permits were indiscriminately issued on the basis of patronage ties rather than on efficiency, sustainability, and equity grounds. This indicates weak state capacity in asserting autonomy over dominant economic interests. During the martial law period, the Cellophil Resources Corporation, owned by Marcos crony Herminio Disini, was awarded timber concessions amounting to almost 200,000 hectares in three Northern Luzon provinces. Cellophil built a pulp and paper plant and ravaged the forests of Abra so intensely that members of the Tingguian tribe fought their displacement from their ancestral land by joining the armed communist rebellion during the height of the environmental conflict.

Aside from the rise of single-issue coalition groups that opposed the ecologically destructive development projects of the state and its business allies, the authoritarian period also witnessed initial steps to bring together various organizations with environment-related interests under an umbrella organization. In 1979, the First Philippine Environmental Congress was convened and released a Declaration of Environmental Concern arguing that "at the root of environmental problems are social, economic, and political systems imposed upon this nation which allow greed and exploitation to predominate over a proper respect for the well-being of present and future generations. These same systems also foster the inequitable distribution of the benefits of the resources and allow the rich to dominate the poor." Out of this meeting emerged the Philippine Federation for Environmental Concerns (PFEC). With a style of environmentalism rooted in a critical awareness of the interconnection between ecological degradation and social, economic, and political inequities, the PFEC vigorously participated in the activities of the anti-dictatorship movement (Ganapin 1989).

The political environmentalism of PFEC, while eschewed by more traditional conservation groups which sought to divorce nature-based concerns from raging social conflicts, was embraced in the 1980s by previously apolitical environmental NGOs like the Haribon Foundation for the Conservation of Natural Resources, Inc. (Haribon). Originally founded in 1972 as a birdwatching society by personnel from the Asian Development Bank and the American embassy in Manila, Haribon launched its Philippine eagle and tamaraw preservation project in 1978, and formally became a conservation foundation interested in environmental research, education, and advocacy in 1984. It was during Celso Roque's presidency that the organization started to grapple with the challenge to draw connections between environmental destruction and structural infirmities in society. In an essay published under the Haribon White Paper Series, Celso Roque pointed out that "poverty and the distorted distributional effects of the political economy have grave ecological consequences" in developing countries (Rush 1991). Haribon's transformation from an exclusive club of nature lovers in the 1970s into an organization of socially informed green activists in the 1980s led to its widening strategic horizon, once narrowly focused on wildlife conservation efforts, through involvement in advocacy campaigns geared toward the protection of marine and forest resources and the preservation of indigenous culture.

Identity-Making Phase (1986–1991)

The identity-making phase was ushered in by the dramatic removal of Marcos from power and the installation of Corazon Aquino to the Philippine presidency in 1986. Capturing power on the heels of massive citizen activism, the new government recognized the legitimate role of NGOs and people's organizations (POs) in social change, in contrast to the antagonistic attitude of the previous government. The new Constitution approved in 1987 emphasized that the state should encourage non-governmental organizations and community-based or sectoral organizations that promote national welfare. It should be noted that during the twilight years of martial law, many donor agencies started sending development funds directly to NGOs, instead of coursing them through the public bureaucracy. Private and official donor agencies, distrustful of the authoritarian administration, decided to channel food and relief aid not to official social welfare agencies, but to development NGOs and church-based groups for distribution to poor communities in the rural areas. NGOs were thus favorably perceived as having the legitimacy, accountability, and flexibility required in the successful delivery of social services and the effective implementation of development programs.

Under the Aquino government, the former Ministry of Natural Resources was restructured into the Department of Environment and Natural Resources (DENR). The National Environment Protection Council and the National Pollution Control Commission were merged into the Environmental Management Bureau, which became a staff bureau of the new DENR (Ganapin 1989). The powers of the Bureau of Forest Development, a mini-fiefdom overseeing the distribution of vast timber concessions to politically connected oligarchic families, were curtailed. It was renamed the Forest Management Bureau and reduced into a staff organization of the DENR. Fulgencio Factoran, Jr., a member of the Movement of Attorneys for Brotherhood, Integrity, and Nationalism, Inc. (MABINI), which handled high-profile human rights cases against the martial law regime, was appointed in 1987 to lead the reconstitution of the Department into an effective environmental agency. He brought with him a management team consisting of a lively combination of development technocrats and NGO veterans, which steered the expansion of the DENR's community-based resource management programs (Ganapin 1994). To facilitate NGO participation in such innovative programs, an NGO desk was created as part of the Department's Special Concerns Office, which was placed under the direct supervision of the Office of the Secretary. Regional NGO desks were also set up in various parts of the country (Factoran 1992).

Reform measures within the environmental bureaucracy, mixed with international demands for environmental aid to developing countries, led to an avalanche of foreign loans, grants, and technical assistance to the DENR (Korten 1993). As environmental funds poured into the country, NGOs were tapped by government and donor agencies to participate in the implementation of environmental projects. Many NGOs, confined to research and advocacy work in the past, expanded their activities by incorporating into their agendas the task of mobilizing local communities for the protection of the environment.

In 1989, the Haribon Foundation established its Community-Based Resource Management Program. Alex Anzula, a longtime community organizer, was recruited from the Agency for Community Educational Services (ACES), a rural development NGO, to coordinate Haribon's immersion in field intervention activities. The program's mission was to empower target communities within a five-year period to enable them to manage their productive resources. Haribon's organizing strategy involved the fielding of a community organizer and a research specialist to work with local leaders in planning and undertaking environmental education and resource management training sessions in fishing and forest communities. Moreover, the group's implementation of projects in community forest management, marine conservation, and marine sanctuary establishment, which include sites in the provinces of

Zambales, Quezon, Batangas, and Palawan, was closely linked with the pursuit of appropriate livelihood schemes (Anzula 1993).

Aside from the diversification of environmental NGO activities into community resource endeavors, the post-Marcos period was also characterized by the decision of prominent development NGOs, like the Philippine Rural Reconstruction Movement (PRRM), to integrate environmental concerns into their strategic programs. Founded in the 1950s, the PRRM was revitalized in the 1980s under the leadership of popular democratic activists Horacio Morales and Isagani Serrano, with the strengthening of the organization's poverty-eradication and people empowerment goals. This was reflected in the forging of its Rural Development and Democratization Program (RDDP), which sought to promote principles of self-governance, socioeconomic development, and health security through the pursuit of projects falling under the following major components: (1) organizing and leadership formation, (2) livelihood enterprise development, (3) savings and credit, and (4) health service delivery. Addressing the need to be sensitive to issues of environmental change and geographical scale, the PRRM revised the RDDP into the Sustainable Rural District Development Program (SRDDP) in 1990. Under the new program, sustainable development and empowerment intervention schemes are to be implemented on the scale of a district or small province. The SRDDP's areas of operation include the provinces of Bataan, Nueva Ecija, Ifugao, Camarines Sur, and Cotobato (Morales 1992).

While big NGOs such as Haribon and PRRM were involved in a host of environmental issues ranging from community forestry to marine protection, smaller NGOs became environmentally active in the late 1980s, such as the Tambuyog Development Center and the Kapwa Upliftment Foundation, Inc., whose development interventions were sectorally specific. For instance, the Tambuyog Development Center renders training and organizational assistance to fishing communities. In its community organizing work, the Center helps build the institutional capacity of local fishers not only in response to environmental threats posed by trawl fishing in municipal waters, cyanide fishing practices, and mangrove conversion, but also in cultivating alternative livelihood options. Founded in 1984, Tambuyog's foray into environmentalism was facilitated by a rise in concerns among fishing communities over the impact of marine resource degradation on their means of livelihood. It undertook coastal resource management projects in the provinces of Zambales, Mindoro, Iloilo, and South Cotobato (Perez 1993; Anonuevo 1996).

Patterns indicating the transformation of many NGO activists into environmentalists were also visible among social activists in church-based institutions in the Philippines. Touched by the social teachings of the Vatican II, social action centers and Basic Christian Communities (BCCs) were widely organized in the 1960s and 1970s by religious activists promoting social justice, human rights, and development initiatives for the poor. As environmental degradation increasingly jeopardized the livelihoods of poor communities, local church activists in the 1980s became active participants in ecological campaigns. Human rights desks in socially active Catholic dioceses were converted into environment desks (Walpole 1994). The Lingkod Tao Kalikasan (which literally means "Service to People and Nature"), an environmental advocacy group headed by Sister Aida Velasquez, was established by members of the Order of St. Benedict in 1986. The organization assisted the local fishers of Marinduque to pressure the DENR in 1988 to stop Marcopper Mining Corporation's operations dumping mine tailings into Calancan Bay. Unfortunately, this was later reversed by the Office of the President.

In the Cagayan Valley region, where some of the last old-growth forests in the Philippines can be found, the Cagayan Anti-Logging Movement (CALM), based in the social action center of the Tuguegarao Archdiocese, is spearheaded by Father Gary Agcaoili. In Midsalip, Zamboanga del Sur, the Parish Pastoral Council was heavily involved in the campaign to stop the illegal logging activities of Sunville Timber Products, which was responsible for the severe soil erosion, siltation, and irrigation failures experienced by the town. Sustained protests led to the suspension of Sunville's logging permit in 1988.

The active defense campaigns characteristic of the first phase of the environmental movement's development spilled over into the second phase and even proliferated with the widening of the democratic space. During the Aquino administration, among the prominent ecological defense actions waged by civil society formations, were the anti-logging struggles of local people in San Fernando, Gabaldon, and Midsalip, the Lingkod Tao Kalikasan's effort to stop Marcopper from polluting Marinduque's fishing zones, and the "Save Palawan" campaign of Haribon, which petitioned the state to ban timber and wildlife trade in the province of Palawan. However, the greater amount of freedom afforded to environmentalists in organizing people should not be seen in absolute terms. Political risks to social activists persisted in the post-Marcos period, as reflected in the 1991 assassination of Catholic priest Nerlito Satura a few months after orchestrating the confiscation of illegally cut logs in Bukidnon, as well as the detention of fourteen members of Haribon charged with subversion following the group's allegations of military complicity in log-smuggling in Palawan the same year. Nevertheless, it is safe to say that under the restored democratic system, there was a rapid expansion of environmental and development NGOs throughout the country. Furthermore, the oppositional brand of ecological advocacy carried over from the early phase of the environmental movement flourished into a more alternative-oriented type of activism in the second phase.

The search for a coherent set of developmental alternatives with an ecological vision found expression in efforts at environmental networking on a nationwide basis. Political engagement was raised to a higher level in the late 1980s, as fresh initiatives built a broad environmental front, primed not only to resist the bearers of ecological degradation, but to reinvent the developmental wheel itself. In 1989, the United States launched a multilateral aid initiative aimed at helping the Philippines in its economic recovery. The Aquino government outlined how to use the funds in the Philippine Aid Plan (PAP), which it submitted to the American government. The plan, however, was criticized by members of the U.S. Senate for its failure to incorporate environmental components. Environmental NGOs in the Philippines were then requested to prepare a report to PAP. Subsequently, a delegation of leaders from ten NGOs was invited to Washington to meet with their American counterparts. The Philippine NGOs represented in the meeting included Haribon, PRRM, and the Philippine Partnership for the Development of Human Resources in Rural Areas (PHILDHRRA). The members of the Philippine NGO mission, following their return from the United States, convened the Green Forum.

In 1989, the Green Forum, with more than 200 NGOs, grassroots organizations, and church groups, was the biggest environmental coalition in the country. In its sustainable development agenda, the Green Forum sought to promote: (1) the cultural identity and ethnic heritage of Filipinos and their spiritual and ecological solidarity with other peoples of the planet, (2) social equity and justice in the custodianship of natural resources and democratizing access to technology and financial services, (3) ecologically sound economic activities primarily benefiting poor families and communities, and (4) authentic participation in governance and social transformation through popular empowerment. With a program of action aimed at creating a communications network to facilitate people's participation in development, empowering communities through technology transfer for sustainable resource management, and developing a constituency for sustainable development programs, the Green Forum strove to build, expand, and consolidate the capacity of environmental activists and their organizations to affect policy directions (Hipolito 1990; Green Forum—Philippines 1991; Kalaw 1991a).

Strategic Engagement Phase (1992–1997)

In the strategic engagement phase, the environmental movement showed vigor and confidence in intervening in the process of governance. In 1992, Fidel Ramos became the new president of the Philippines. After a successful campaign to reject the prospective appointment of a politician with past links to big logging companies as the DENR chief, leading environmental NGOs pushed for the nomination of Angel Alcala, then president of Siliman University and a board director of Haribon Foundation, for the vacant position. The NGO lobby paid off as Alcala became the first DENR secretary to be chosen from the ranks of environmentalists in 1992.

The growth in the environmental movement's capacity to influence policy directions in the 1990s was facilitated through the entry of environmentalists in government and the expansion of participatory modes of governance. Under the 1991 Local Government Code, basic services performed by the central bureaucracy in the policy areas of health, education, public works, tourism, social welfare, housing, agriculture, and the environment were devolved to local governments. The law broadened the administrative authority of local government units (LGUs) and encouraged the representation of NGOs in decision-making bodies such as local development councils and resource management councils.

The application of the Code, however, remains uneven, given the wide variations in the revenue base, technical capacity, and policy thrust among municipal and provincial governments. Nevertheless, the Code's recognition of NGO legitimacy in local governance fosters creative efforts aimed at pushing ecological collaboration across the public–private divide. Illustrative of this synergy is the Tripartite Partnership for Upland Development (TRIPUD) program, launched by the Partnership for the Development of Human Resources in the Rural Areas (PHILDHRRA), a national network of fifty-nine development NGOs. The program is geared toward uplifting the quality of life of upland farmers by increasing their productivity through the application of ecologically sound agroforestry technology, the improvement of their land tenure claims, and the development of their capacities as natural resource managers. Under the Social Infrastructure Building and Strengthening (SIBS) component of the program, a PHILDHRRA-affiliated NGO is expected to organize local POs and conduct training sessions with local leaders to enable them to work with local government structures and national government agencies in ensuring the effective delivery of public services to local communities. A tripartite body consisting of representatives from the NGO, PO, and LGU sectors is formed at the community and provincial levels to facilitate technical support for the program. TRIPUD pilot projects are now undertaken in the provinces of Davao, Sorsogon, and Leyte.

NGOs also became important agents in the direct management of environmental funds provided by donor governments, private foundations, and multilateral institutions. The active participation of NGOs in the joint management of these funds was reflected in the creation of several innovative funding mechanisms in the 1990s. With an initial endowment generated from a debt-for-nature swap in 1991, the Foundation for the Philippine Environment (FPE) was established to render financial support to NGOs and POs in the pursuit of multi-year integrated projects in the areas of community-based resource management and biodiversity conservation. A similar body is the NGOs for Integrated Protected Areas (NIPA), which received a $16 million grant from the World Bank—Global Environment Facility (WB-GEF) to fund environmental management efforts in high-priority protected areas. NIPA served as the secretariat of the Integrated Protected Areas Fund (IPAF) board, chaired by the DENR secretary and composed of government, NGO, and indigenous people's representatives. The WB-GEF grant is intended to support alternative livelihood projects for local residents in protected areas.

Meanwhile, a 1995 debt-for-development swap arranged by the Federal Office for Economic Affairs of Switzerland and the Department of Finance of the Philippines led to the endowment of $18.6

million to the Foundation for a Sustainable Society (FSS) to provide financial assistance to environment-friendly and sustainable production activities in agriculture, fisheries, and small industry. FSS is governed by a board of trustees consisting of six NGO leaders, one non-voting representative from the Department of Finance, and an observer from the Swiss embassy (Gonzales 1995).

Critical Issues

Major Streams of Environmental Activism

Environmental advocacy campaigns in the Philippines have been waged along nature conservation, pollution, and nuclear energy issues. It is around these concerns that the three major streams of environmental activism developed. They are not mutually exclusive, however, considering the dynamic interface of environmental issues and the overlapping membership of individuals and groups in various types of ecological activism. The green movement is thus characterized by a lively mix of players and a diverse collection of strategic responses to ecological conflicts. On the other hand, the movement's multi-sectoral orientation enabled it to develop strong linkages with various civil society formations.

The nature conservation stream is by far the most active among the principal types of Philippine environmentalism. In contrast to Western nature conservation, which revolves around the provision of state protection over natural parks and wildlife reserves in isolation from human activities, the nature conservation thrust in the Philippines is linked to the demand for state recognition of local community rights to the control and management of resources. In this sense, the conservation of nature through people, rather than the protection of nature from people, is emphasized. Such a viewpoint is anchored in a "politics of place," where local communities that dynamically coexist with their natural ecosystems and weave livelihood systems heavily dependent on the sustainability of the resource base are often the most intensely predisposed toward preserving nature (Kemmins 1990). Natural conservation issues are thus simultaneously conceived as livelihood concerns.

In many instances, when influential outside agents secure state-conferred rights to engage in high-impact resource extraction and production activities in ecologically sensitive forest, cropland, and coastal areas, local communities and their supporters are pushed to undertake collective action directed toward the joint defense of nature and livelihood (Friedmann and Rangan 1993). With natural resource conflicts often embedded in inequitable structures of power and resource distribution, nature conservation campaigns are transformed into struggles to democratize access to resources. Hence, nature conservation is pursued together with demands for equity, livelihood, and community resource rights.

The anti-pollution stream of the environmental movement is manifested in numerous cases of citizens' resistance to pollution-causing industrial projects, such as the construction of coal-fired thermal facilities, copper smelter plants, geothermal power facilities, and cement plants. Organized dissent is channeled against negative externalities generated by development activities, such as toxic emissions destroying natural habitats and endangering the health security of local residents. Anti-pollution protests also seek to protect nature-based livelihood systems. For example, in the campaign against the Masinloc Coal-Fired Thermal Plant in Zambales in the early 1990s, environmental groups indicated that thermal pollution would damage the marine ecosystem and disrupt the flow of income benefits local people derive from fishing. Since the Masinloc power plant threatens the life support systems of the local community, it was recommended that clean and sustainable energy sources should instead be explored, and the protection and rehabilitation of critical watersheds be intensified to maximize the productivity and lifespan of existing hydroelectric plants (Task Force Masinloc 1991). The anti-nuclear movement developed around the twin demands to stop construction of nuclear power facilities and terminate the presence of American military bases, which were believed to harbor nuclear weapons, on Philippine soil. Anti-nuclear protest actions were led by such groups as the Nuclear-Free Philippines Coalition and the No Nukes Philippines. A focal point of citizen mobilization in the late 1970s and the 1980s was the $2.2 billion contract awarded to Westinghouse Corporation by the Marcos government in 1976 to build two nuclear reactors in Morong, Bataan. The project was criticized not only for the threat it posed to public health, considering the inadequacy of the safety features in the plant's design and its location in an earthquake zone, but also for the anomalies involved in fashioning the deal. Hiring the services of crony capitalist Herminio Disini as its special sales representative, Westinghouse won an "overpriced" contract to undertake the power project without going through normal public bidding procedures. From an initial price of $500 million for two nuclear plants in 1974, the cost for one reactor astronomically jumped up to $1.1 billion in 1975. Despite the heavy cloud of suspicion surrounding the appropriateness of the project's price tag and the government's failure to open the project to public bidding and auditing procedures, a huge commercial loan was packaged by a consortium of banks led by Citicorp, with the first wave of loans guaranteed by the U.S. Export–Import Bank, to fund the project. The unfinished nuclear facility was "mothballed" by the Aquino government when it assumed power in 1986.

As the country continued to pay the bank loans incurred by the Westinghouse project, the interest alone amounting to $130 million annually, the 250–organization Freedom from Debt Coalition (FDC) launched a campaign to repudiate these loans, which it considered as used for fraudulent purposes. The demand for public accountability was a major theme in anti-nuclear campaigns, as a thick wall of secrecy often shrouds the development of nuclear energy programs in many countries. On the other hand, the demand of the anti-nuclear movement for the removal of American military facilities and their nuclear weapons culminated in the 1991 rejection by the Philippine Senate of the proposed treaty extending the tenure of U.S. bases in the country. Earlier, an anti-nuclear weapons provision was placed in the 1987 Constitution. With tons of toxic wastes left behind in the former baselands, anti-nuclear activists, NGOs, and community groups decided to establish the People's Task Force for Bases' Cleanup in 1994, which forged links with the U.S. Working Group for Philippine Bases' Cleanup in pressuring the U.S. government to take moral responsibility in providing financial and technical assistance for the bases' cleanup.

Key Players

Membership in the environmental movement is marked by a mix of players with varying organizational features and levels of engagement. The key participants fall into three major clusters: (1) a non-government organization (NGO) cluster, (2) a people's organization (PO) cluster, and (3) a local community (LC) cluster. These are not exactly exclusive of one another, as numerous alliances and collaborative efforts are often forged across the various clusters

The most active members in the NGO cluster can be categorized, based on their organizational history, either as environmental NGOs that became development-oriented, or as development NGOs that turned environmentally sensitive. The first category involves the transition of a conservation NGO like the Haribon Foundation into a leading advocate for local community control over natural resources. The second category is represented in the creation of the Convergence for Community-Centered Area Development (Convergence), an alliance of eighteen development NGOs that declared their commitment to a community-centered area approach in the propagation of economic self-reliance, popular empowerment, and ecological sustainability. The marriage of environmental protection and developmental goals in the strategic agenda of these two sets of groups transformed them into what we may refer to as sustainable development NGOs. These play an important role in providing organizational, educational, and technical support to POs and local communities in negotiating resource rights, conducting resource inventories, crafting livelihood programs, fighting ecological plunderers, and protecting nature.

Included in the PO (People's Organization) cluster are sectoral groups and mass organizations which, under authoritarian rule, were routinely mobilized for human rights and social justice campaigns. In recent years, the traditional clamor of POs for social redistribution policies in the agricultural and fishery sectors were laced by sustainable development demands. Farmers' groups in the Congress for a People's Agrarian Reform program (CPAR) are exploring regenerative agricultural strategies, while fishers' groups belonging to the National Coalition of Fisherfolks for Aquatic Reforms (NACFAR) collaborate with NGOs in the application of coastal resource management programs.

The LC (Local Community) cluster is represented by the various instances of environmental protests launched by informally organized local residents and the church. Unlike POs, which may also be community-based, LCs are not necessarily organized in terms of having well-defined programs of action or formalized membership structures. In this sense, local acts of resistance may best be seen as expressions of a victim activism possibly difficult to sustain (Hsiao, Milbrath, and Weller 1995). Collective energies dissipate in the long run when left unchanneled into more organized patterns of engagement. Nevertheless, protest activities undertaken by small Philippine communities and the church have, in the past, served as springboards for larger campaigns.

The dynamic creation of environmental task forces and coalitions that slice through sectoral boundaries and organizational clusters led to thickening webs of interdependence among ecologically concerned NGOs, POs, and LCs. Such a process is vital, not only in sustaining citizens' participation in environmental activities, but also in building trust and cooperation among different groups by enabling them to engage in the joint enterprise of formulating a coherent agenda and a strategy for sustainable development.

Strategy and Identity

The changing phases of the environmental movement can be attributed to transformations in state–civil society relations. Under authoritarian rule, the environmental movement functioned largely as a partner of the democratic movement in clamoring for political liberalization. In general, environmental movements and democratic movements share a common distaste for non-participatory modes of governance and development planning practiced by authoritarian states. Within the context of the democratic struggles of the 1970s and 1980s in the Philippines, local communities displaced by ecologically damaging economic activities were often seen as human rights victims and organized in large measure to resist the repressive regime and its development policies. Since the reinstitution of democratic processes under the Aquino government, however, environmental activism emerged out of the shadows of the democratic movement and actively asserted its collective identity as a distinct social movement.

Through the use of identity-oriented strategies, the environmental movement seeks to articulate new development values, societal visions, and political spaces anchored in the construction of new relationships between the state, the economy, and civil society, including the creation of a renewed synthesis between the public and private spheres (Piccolomini 1996). The establishment of sustainable development alliances like the Green Forum and Convergence exemplify such innovative identity-making efforts. While the environmental movement places substantial emphasis on social equity in the allocation of natural resource benefits, the movement goes beyond the social redistribution agenda of older social movements like the labor movement through its advocacy of community-based approaches to sustainable development, challenging the politics of space and identity of traditional governance structures and market relations (Kitschelt 1993). Green Forum, for instance, promotes a life-flow, culture-centered, community-based model that recognizes a structure of relational values incorporating ecology into economics and integrates nature and society. The realization of environmental protection and social equity—the twin factors in sustaining a community—is facilitated through the devolution of power from the state to the people, and the shift in the base of authority from ideology to ecology (Kalaw 1991b).

There also is convergence over the need to shape a new politics of space, by offering an area-development framework for development. According to the coalition's leaders, alternative development planning should transcend traditional, political boundaries of provinces or regions by focusing on ecological zones of several municipalities that share environmental, social, economic, and political features (Broad with Cavanagh 1993). Deriving a politics of appropriate size and scale to match community and regional needs is now a key factor in sustainable development (Thomashow 1995).

Aside from pursuing identity-oriented strategies, the environmental movement is also employing power-oriented strategies aimed at influencing policy directions. Power-oriented strategies are particularly applicable in conflict-ridden situations in which the movement had to negotiate, pressure, and confront opponents, in order to affect the balance of power (Rucht 1990). Such a strategic stance was taken by the Green Forum when it launched an initiative to organize a green electoral bloc in 1991 to influence the outcome of the 1992 elections. The impetus for the Earthvote Philippines Project was summed up in the following response made by politicians to Haribon president and Green Forum convenor Maximo Kalaw, Jr., when the latter attempted to convince them to push for environmental protection policies: "It is hard to listen to you. The trees don't vote and the fish don't vote. The farmers have a coalition; the fishermen have a coalition; labor has a coalition; but you don't have any. So why should I vote for the forest?" (Kalaw 1991a). The immediate impact of the project was realized when the leading presidential candidates in 1992 began addressing nature-based issues in their campaign speeches. In this case, environmental issues gained recognition as important public concerns (Alario 1995).

Civil Society Linkages

The multi-sectoral character of the environmental movement enables it to develop strong ties with groups and coalitions belonging to the peasant, fisherfolk, and women's sectors. Although in its early stages, the environmental movement is likewise forging links with the labor movement. Farmers and fishers are natural allies of environmental activists in nature conservation activities. Not surprisingly, the major farmers' coalition fighting for agrarian reform (CPAR) and the fishers' alliance struggling for aquatic reform (NACFAR) are active members of Green Forum. Ostensibly, the nature-based livelihoods of workers in the agricultural and fishing sectors are most vulnerable to environmental changes. Many local initiatives demanding a halt to logging activities were led by peasant communities who were often caught at the receiving end of crop-damaging floods and droughts induced by deforestation. A growing number of farmers' groups and cooperatives are also attempting to move away from agricultural technologies highly dependent on chemical fertilizers by experimenting on regenerative and organic-based cropping methods. Meanwhile, upland farming communities are assisted by NGOs in negotiating land tenure certificates and preparing community resource management programs. Fisherfolk, on the other hand, became environmentally active as their catch dwindled due to overfishing and marine degradation. A number of NGOs assist organizations of fishers to strengthen their community-organizing capabilities in order to fight for equitable fishing rights and undertake coastal resource management, livelihood, credit, and health programs.

The *inang kalikasan* (mother earth) is a prominent symbolic code in Philippine culture adopted by the environmental movement. It signifies women's nurturing, caring, and non-domineering attitude—precisely how nature should be treated. Living up to this ecological symbolism, women's organizations are active in collaborating with the environmental movement in the pursuit of joint actions. The Ugnayan ng Kababaihan sa Pulitika (literally meaning "Union of Women in Politics") is a member of Task Force Zero Waste, which aims to develop an alternative solid waste management program. Community organizing is a key component of this program, which uses an integrated approach and gives priority to recycling and waste reduction at its source. The program seeks to encourage households to separate biodegradable from non-biodegradable waste and establish resource recovery centers. On the other hand, the Women's Action Network for Development (WAND), an alliance of more than 120 women's NGOs and POs, occupies one of the NGO seats in the Philippine Council for Sustainable Development as the representative of the women's sector.

While the Philippine labor and environmental movements share an understanding of the importance of social redistribution policies, their perspectives on the role of environmental protection in development may not exactly exist in unison. At the height of the energy crisis in the country in the early 1990s, trade unions and environmental groups were divided on the strategic move to block the construction of pollution-generating power plants. Union members were worried that prolonged power outages might force their factories to close up shop, while environmental activists were concerned about the environmental impact of power projects. Nevertheless, dialogues allow for the cross-fertilization of ideas between the two groups, with environmentalists proposing that future collective bargaining agreements should contain an ecological clause stipulating that the mismanagement of natural resources, which adversely affects the community's welfare, could serve as grounds for a strike (Kalaw 1991a).

Strategic linkages between the environmental movement and sympathetic mass media practitioners led to substantial ecological gains. For example, mass media coverage contributed significantly to the success of anti-logging campaigns in San Fernando and Midsalip. In addition, the adept use of strategic modes of information dissemination through the media by environmental groups such as the Center for Alternative Development Initiatives (CADI), the Haribon Foundation, and Luntiang Alyansa para sa Bundok Banahaw (literally, "Green Alliance for Mt. Banahaw") alerted the public and increased policy concerns over the harmful effects of pesticides, the highly degraded state of the forest, and the imperatives of rescuing Mt. Banahaw from ecological decline.

Local–Global Partnerships

Environmental partnerships are being forged, not only across society, but beyond borders. This stems from the recognition that in a globalizing economic context, the strategic pursuit of sustainable development is facilitated through the cultivation of ties with transnational allies. A good example is the collaborative efforts of Philippine NGOs and their American counterparts to inject ecological sustainability criteria into the provision of official U.S. development assistance to the Philippines. Such cooperative endeavors were institutionalized through the establishment of groups such as the Philippine Development Forum (PDF), an alliance of NGOs in the United States concerned with sustainable development issues in the Philippines. PDF held its first membership conference in Washington, D.C. in 1991 with leading Philippine NGOs in attendance. In Canada, more than a third of the government's development assistance to the Philippines is channeled directly to major NGO networks as a result of the aggressive lobbying efforts by citizen groups (Broad with Cavanagh 1993).

Another instance of ecological collaboration across the global–local divide was the creation of the People's Task Force for Bases' Cleanup and the U.S. Working Group for Philippine Bases' Cleanup in 1994. They demand that the American government shoulder the costs of the cleanup of toxic wastes left behind by former U.S. military bases. Earlier, the Pentagon was pressured, through joint Philippine-American NGO action, to release to the Philippine government two reports naming dozens of sites at Subic Bay and Clark Air Base where toxic dumping, accidental spills, and ecologically harmful practices occurred. On the other hand, public awareness and concern regarding the global trade in toxic waste is increasing with linkages between Greenpeace and local environmentalists. Already, opposition was raised against the dumping of used lead batteries on Philippine soil from the United States, Britain, Canada, Australia, and Japan.

Environmental activists were also active in deliberations on global environmental concerns. In 1992, Philippine NGO leaders distinguished themselves in citizen diplomacy through their energetic contributions to help steer the passage of NGO treaties on sustainable development during the Earth Summit in Rio de Janeiro. At the 1996 Asia-Pacific Economic Cooperation (APEC) Summit held in Manila, four parallel APEC conferences were simultaneously organized by Philippine NGO-PO formations in coordination with civil society representatives from other nations. At least two of these formations, the Manila People's Forum on APEC (MPFA) and the Sustainable Development: Asia-Pacific Initiative (SUSDEVAPI), vigorously emphasized the need to include sustainable development issues in trade deliberations in the Asia-Pacific region.

Impacts

The significance of the Philippine environmental movement as a political force can be realized by examining its impact on policy directions, governance processes, citizen empowerment, and corporate accountability. For a long time, collective challenges were waged by small communities defending local environments against encroachment by powerful outsiders. While most defensive actions eventually crumbled in the face of the mighty battering ram of big resource-mining and industrial interests, a few local successes created disturbing ripple effects on the status quo. Instructive in this regard was the tenacious resistance of the Kalinga and Bontoc tribal communities in the 1970s, which halted the construction of the Chico hydroelectric dam and forced the World Bank to withdraw from the project.

This protest action generated multi-level gains. At the community level, the indigenous people saved their villages from being flooded into extinction by the dam. On the other hand, the policy repercussion of the dam's rejection was felt both at the national level, where the government was pushed to adopt policy guidelines requiring the preparation of environmental impact statements (EISs) for large-scale development ventures, and at the global level, where the World Bank was compelled to incorporate environmental concerns in making investment choices (Aufderheide and Rich 1988). In addition, the opposition to the Chico Dam inspired similar movements in India and Thailand (Surendra 1987).

From the anti–Chico Dam effort in the 1970s, to the San Fernando logging blockade in the 1980s, and the Bolinao anti–cement plant movement in the 1990s, small communities exhibited various capacities in resisting large-scale development activities that threatened nature and livelihood systems. The success of specific local actions may be attributed to the capacity of communities to cooperate, organize, and forge alliances with sympathetic outside players. However, given the unevenness in organizational levels and cooperation within and between communities, the environmental movement adopted a bimodal strategy in sustaining ecological activism beyond the resolution of immediate local demands. This was characterized by the employment of these modes of action: (1) strategic engagement at the national and local levels aimed at affecting policy thrusts and governance structures, and (2) strategic empowerment at the community level by organizing local citizens and strengthening their rights to resources.

Following the success of local efforts that led to the declaration of timber-cutting prohibitions in provinces such as Palawan and Bukidnon, a campaign in the early 1990s pressured Congress to enact a nationwide logging ban law. The environmental movement, however, was no match for strong logging interests represented in the national legislature, as successive attempts to pass an anti-logging measure in the country were thwarted. A host of other proposed bills on environmental protection was placed in the freezer. This suggests the relative weakness of green activists in influencing environmental legislation. Getting better results from strategic engagement in the legislative process would require an upgrading of environmentalists' lobbying skills. At the same time, the environmental movement's capacity to mobilize voters to elect green legislators must be eventually tested. During the 1992 elections, the Green Forum took initial steps to inform the electorate about the environmental records of politicians running for office. Nevertheless, no major moves have been made since then by environmental groups in crafting a comprehensive electoral strategy aimed at capturing legislative seats.

Compared to the legislature, the environmental movement could create more strategic inroads toward affecting governance processes in the executive arm of the state. In 1992, the NGO community played a major role in the establishment of the Philippine Council for Sustainable Development (PCSD), together with the DENR and the Department of Foreign Affairs (DFA). Constituted by virtue of Executive Order No.15, the PCSD provides for NGO participation in the monitoring of the government's compliance with the official commitments made during the 1992 United Nations Conference on Environment and Development (UNCED) held in Rio de Janeiro, Brazil. It also has the authority to undertake policy research, perform advocacy work, and propose legislation on sustainable development issues. NGO representatives were involved in the technical working group that drafted the PCSD's operating guidelines. Under these guidelines, the NGO sector is given a counterpart role in the Council's decision-making process. It is composed of sixteen representatives from state agencies and seven representatives from the NGO sector. NGO members in the PCSD are selected through a process designed and implemented by the NGO community, rather than by the government. Despite having fewer Council members, the use of a consensus-seeking approach enables the NGO sector to raise vital environmental issues in PCSD deliberations.

Bureaucratic innovations influenced by the environmental movement were most pronounced in the expansion of the DENR's participatory and community-based resource management programs in the past ten years. The appointment of environmentalists from NGOs and academic institutions in high positions within the DENR hierarchy resulted in an increased emphasis on the role of local communities and NGOs in environmental protection activities. This departed from previous policy preferences exclusively focused on state distribution of public resource rights to large private enterprises. In community forestry programs, for instance, upland villagers were given the opportunity to negotiate land tenure agreements whereby the state gave them long-term management and production rights in public forest zones. Meanwhile, the ancestral land delineation program was established to demarcate and map the boundaries of forest areas claimed by indigenous communities as part of their ancestral domains. Traditional community management systems have ably protected the forests in the past prior to their displacement by expanding state and market forces.

Most environmental conflicts are contests over the distribution of rights to use and manage social goods such as water, air, land, and forest resources. For the environmental movement, the education and empowerment of local citizens are critical to the joint pursuit of livelihood and environmental protection strategies. In the context of strategic efforts to democratize access to resources, NGOs played a key role in organizing and mobilizing local people to secure legal tenure and control over resources. With the influx of environmental funds from the international donor community since the late 1980s, Philippine NGOs could access much-needed financial resources in assisting local communities in the preparation and implementation of sustainable development projects.

The dramatic expansion of donor funds for the environmental sector had negative effects as well. NGOs organized by private entrepreneurs and politicians proliferated (Meyer 1995). For instance, many opportunistic NGOs won government reforestation contracts in the late 1980s and early 1990s. The DENR estimated that as much as 15 percent of the funds spent on the reforestation program were wasted on corruption (Clarke 1995). Large-scale official funding was criticized for diverting the accountability of NGOs away from grassroots and internal constituencies, and such funding also overemphasizes quantitative outputs (Edwards and Hulme 1996). In addition, the competition for environmental funds also turned into turf battles even among legitimate

NGOs. Such rivalries potentially threaten cooperative actions among environmental NGOs in the future.

The environmental movement's capacity to affect business enterprises in exercising corporate accountability, on the other hand, is still fairly weak. Only in recent years have vigorous efforts been made to compel private firms to adopt full-cost accounting procedures involving the internalization of pollution and resource depletion expenses. The standard practice was to pass on the ecological damage resulting from investment and production activities to society at large. Amid growing environmental awareness and increasing pressure on governments to regulate ecologically destructive business operations, a nonprofit organization named the Philippine Business for the Environment, Inc. (PBE), was established in 1992 to assist the business community in addressing environmental concerns. PBE seeks to educate and convince business organizations to recognize environmental responsibility as a corporate priority. To this end, PBE advocates sound corporate environmental values and promotes the search for efficient and environmentally clean technology. In the short term, PBE expects to get 300 signatory companies to join its *Philippine Business Charter for Sustainable Development,* which encourages business firms to adopt a precautionary approach in the production of goods and services, an approach emphasizing investments in pollution prevention rather than in cleanup operations. The Charter also enjoins corporations to conduct regular environmental audits and provide appropriate information, not only to their shareholders, but to employees and the general public as well (Rubio 1997). It would be a remarkable feat, indeed, for environmentalists to actually compel business enterprises to adhere to sound environmental practices and ensure that corporate declarations of environmental concern are supported by concrete actions and not simply employed as a public relations strategy.

Conclusion

Environmental issues in the Philippines tend to be framed within the context of livelihood and equity concerns. In the past, the preferential distribution of resource rights to large resource-mining and industrial enterprises resulted in the displacement of small communities that sustainably managed resources using traditional knowledge and customary property systems. The promotion of community control over resources is therefore seen by the environmental movement as a vital component in making development both equitable and ecologically sensitive. This is undertaken through active efforts to help local people build strong organizations that will enable them to resist development aggression from powerful economic interests, as well as empower them to demand state recognition of community tenure and rights to resources.

Among the major streams of the environmental movement, nature conservation–related actions indicate the existence of once-rich natural resources whose rapid exhaustion exerts severe stress on the livelihood prospects of local people. The anti-nuclear stream, on the other hand, revolves around opposition to nuclear power plants and the former U.S. military bases. With the Philippine Senate's refusal to continue hosting the bases in the country, the campaign thrust shifted toward the demand for the American government to clean up the toxic wastes left behind in the baselands. On the other hand, revival of the nuclear power program is expected as the country attempts to catch up with its neighbors in the race for economic growth. Given the excessive energy demands arising from the industrialization drive, the pressure to build more power plants, including nuclear ones, will intensify conflicts between the state and the environmental movement. How the labor movement responds to these cleavages is critical in the development of alliance politics revolving around the use of nuclear power. The anti-pollution stream of the environmental movement is marked by launching protest activities against specific development projects. While particular victories were recorded in stopping the operation of certain projects, the efforts to address and offer programmatic alternatives to urban environmental management problems, such as air pollution, water supply deficiencies, sanitation and sewerage, solid waste collection, and toxic waste disposal, were generally weak. Meanwhile, the linkage between environmental degradation and deteriorating health conditions has not been fully explored, and its potential as a focal point for citizen mobilization remains untapped.

There is a growing, but still politically insignificant, green consumer sector expected to expand with the broadening of the middle class. The increase in environmental awareness and the rise of green markets will shore up the demand for goods produced under sustainable conditions. This trend will benefit the drive to place natural resource management authority in the hands of local people. Given the tremendous demands on NGO activists and academics to provide advocacy, research, technical, and capacity-building skills to citizens and communities so that they may meaningfully participate in ecological governance processes, the forging of better linkages between environmental groups and academic institutions at local, national, and global levels is not only desirable but extremely necessary.

In the foreseeable future, the environmental movement is expected to continue pursuing its sustainable development agenda through the twin strategies of citizen empowerment and policy engagement. It will remain as a critical voice and force in monitoring the enforcement of environmental regulations, aside from being a valuable partner in the joint implementation of environmental protection activities. To be a significant factor, however, in the passage of important environmental legislation, the environmental movement should mix mass street actions with systematic lobbying efforts in Congress. Sooner or later, environmental groups must also confront the challenge of designing an electoral strategy for voting environmentalists into positions of power. Already, the formation of electoral alliances at the local level is influenced by environmental concerns. In 1995, the leader of the main opposition group against the construction of a cement plant in Bolinao successfully won the mayoralty, based on an electoral promise to derail the cement project in the coastal town of Pangasinan. The growing importance of local alliances in determining environmental outcomes can also be attributed to the decentralization of government functions under the Local Government Code which, at the same time, provides for the participation of NGOs in local development and resource management councils at the municipal and provincial levels of government. With the transition of local governments into a major locus for decision-making processes affecting the environment, local coalition-building efforts now assume a critical space in the environmental movement's menu of strategic concerns. Indeed, a rapidly transforming societal climate presents formidable but exciting environmental challenges. How well the environmental movement responds to the new challenges depends much on its capacity to exercise strategic flexibility and innovativeness in the face of great political and ecological transitions.

References

Alario, Margarita. 1995. *Environmental Destruction, Risk Exposure and Social Asymmetry.* Lanham: University Press of America.

Anonuevo, Carlito. 1996. Personal communication. Berkeley, California.

Anzula, Alex. 1993. Personal communication. Haribon Foundation, San Juan, Metro-Manila.

Asian Development Bank. 1994. *Forestry Sector Study of the Philippines.* Manila: Agriculture Department, Asian Development Bank.

Aufderheide, Pat, and Bruce Rich. 1988. "Environmental Reform and the Multilateral Banks." *World Policy Journal* 5: 301–321.

Broad, Robin, with John Cavanagh. 1993. *Plundering Paradise: The Struggle for the Environment in the Philippines.* Berkeley and Los Angeles: University of California Press.

Buttel, Frederick. 1993. "Environmentalization and Greening: Origins, Processes and Implications." In *The Greening of Rural Policy: International Perspectives,* edited by Sarah Harper, pp. 12–26. London and New York: Belhaven Press.

Catholic Bishops Conference of the Philippines. 1991. "What Is Happening to Our Beautiful Land?" In *Responses to the Signs of the Times,* edited by Josol Abdon, pp. 306–320. Cebu: Redemptorist Publications.

Clarke, Gerard. 1995. "Non-Governmental Organizations and the Philippine State: 1986–1993." *Southeast Asia Research* 3: 67–91.

Edwards, Michael, and David Hulme. 1996. "Too Close for Comfort? The Impact of Official Aid on Nongovernmental Organizations." *World Development* 24: 961–973.

Factoran, Fulgencio, Jr. 1992. "Environment and Natural Resources." In *The Aquino Administration: Record and Legacy (1986–1992),* edited by Belinda Aquino, pp. 209–226. Quezon City: University of the Philippines Press.

Friedmann, John, and Haripriya Rangan. 1993. *In Defense of Livelihood: Comparative Studies on Environmental Action.* West Hartford: Kumarian Press.

Ganapin, Delfin, Jr. 1989. "Strategic Assessment of NGOs in Community Forestry and Environment." In *A Strategic Assessment of Non-Governmental Organizations in the Philippines,* edited by Antonio Quizon and Rhoda Reyes, pp. 85–124. Metro-Manila: ANGOC.

———. 1994. Personal communication. Honolulu, Hawaii.

Gonzales, Eugenio. 1995. "Autonomous Development Funds in the Philippines." *Development Dialogue* 2: 53–66.

Green Forum–Philippines. 1991. "Economic White Paper." Metro-Manila.

Hipolito, Malou. 1990. "Visions of Green." *Conjuncture* 3: 6.

Hsiao, Hsin-Huang Michael, Lester Milbrath, and Robert Weller. 1995. "Antecedents of an Environmental Movement in Taiwan." *Capitalism, Nature, Socialism* 6: 91–104.

Hutchcroft, Paul. 1994. "Booty Capitalism: Business-Government Relations in the Philippines." In *Business and Government in Industrializing Asia,* edited by Andrew MacIntyre, pp. 216–243. Ithaca: Cornell University Press.

Johnston, Barbara Rose. 1995. "Human Rights and the Environment." *Human Ecology* 23: 111–123.

Kalaw, Maximo, Jr. 1991a. "Political Organizing Promotes Sustainable Development in the Philippines." In *Earth Summit: Conversations with Architects of an Ecologically Sustainable Future,* edited by Steve Lerner, pp. 117–127. Bolinas, CA: Commonweal.

———. 1991b. "The Role and Involvement of Nongovernmental Organizations in the Sustainable Development of Coastal Resources." In *Managing ASEAN's Coastal Resources for Sustainable Development: Roles of Policymakers, Sci-*

entists, Donors, Media, and Communities, edited by T.E. Chua and L.F. Scura, pp. 103–106. Makati: ICLARM.

Kemmins, Daniel. 1990. *Community and the Politics of Place.* Norman: University of Oklahoma Press.

Kitschelt, Herbert. 1993. "Social Movements, Political Parties, and Democratic Theory." *The Annals of the American Academy of Political and Social Science* 528: 13–29.

Korten, Frances. 1993. "The High Costs of Environmental Loans." *Asia Pacific Issues,* No. 7. Honolulu: East–West Center.

Meyer, Carrie. 1995. "Opportunism and NGOs: Entrepreneurship and Green North–South Transfers." *World Development* 23: 1277–1289.

Montes, Manuel. 1988. "The Business Sector and Development Policy." In *National Development Policies and the Business Sector in the Philippines,* edited by Manuel Montes, pp. 23–77. Tokyo: Institute of Developing Economies.

Morales, Horacio. 1992. "Fighting Poverty Through Self-Help." *Third World Convergence* 20: 40–41.

Perez, Francis Ronald. 1993. Personal communication. Tambuyog Development Center, Quezon City.

Piccolomini, Michele. 1996. "Sustainable Development, Collective Action, and New Social Movements." In *Research in Social Movements, Conflicts and Change,* edited by Michael Dobkowski and I. Walimann, pp. 183–307. Greenwich: JAI Press.

Rio, Luz. 1993. Personal communication. People's Environmental Action Network, Quezon City.

Rubio, Rico. 1997. Personal communication. Philippine Business for the Environment, Pasig City.

Rucht, D. 1990. "The Strategies and Action Repertoires of New Movements." In *Challenging the Political Order,* edited by Russel Dalton and Manfred Kuechler, pp. 156–178. New York: Oxford University Press.

Rush, James. 1991. *The Last Tree.* New York: The Asia Society.

Sachs, Aaron. 1995. *Eco-Justice: Linking Human Rights and the Environment.* Washington, DC: Worldwatch Institute.

Sajise, Percy, Percy Sajise, Nicomedes Briones, Miguel Fortes, Edgardo Gomez, Rosario Jimenez, Enrique Pacardo, Nenita Tapay, Macrina Zafaralla, Prescillano Zamora, and Imelda Zosa-Feranil. 1992. *Saving the Present for the Future: The State of the Environment.* Quezon City: U.P. Center for Integrative and Development Studies.

Surendra, Lawrence. 1987. "Emerging Trends in Ecological and Environmental Movements in South and Southeast Asia." In *Protest Movements in South and South-East Asia,* edited by Rajeshwari Ghose. Hong Kong: University of Hong Kong.

Task Force Masinloc. 1991. "Position Paper: The Masinloc Coal-Fired Thermal Plant and Its Environmental Impact Statement." *Enviroscope* 7: 1–6.

Thomashow, Mitchell. 1995. *Ecological Identity: Becoming a Reflective Environmentalist.* Cambridge, MA: The MIT Press.

Walpole, Peter. 1994. Personal communication. Honolulu, Hawaii.

World Bank. 1989. *Philippines: Environment and Natural Resource Management Study.* Washington, DC: The World Bank.

Comparative Analyses

7

Grassroots Environmentalism in the United States: Implications for Asia's Environmental Movements

Andrew Szasz

Acronyms

ABC	American Broadcasting Company	NBC	National Broadcasting Company
CBS	Columbia Broadcasting Company	NIMBY	Not-In-My-Backyard
		NTC	National Toxics Campaign
CCHW	Citizens' Clearinghouse for Hazardous Waste	PAHLS	People Against Hazardous Landfill Sites
EPA	Environmental Protection Agency	RACHEL	Remote Access Chemical Hazards Electronic Library
GAO	General Accounting Office	RCRA	Resource Conservation and Recovery Act

Introduction

In one sense, "Asian societies versus the United States" seemed a good pairing for comparative analysis; the "dependent variable," the effect to be explained, seemed dramatically different, since in Asian societies environmentalism is a relatively new phenomenon. Judging from earlier chapters, these movements typically started in the 1970s. In contrast, American environmentalism usually dates its beginnings to the turn of the century; if one includes workers' health and/or urban sanitary movements, that beginning date can be pushed well back into the nineteenth century. Environmental movements in most Asian societies appear largely modest in size and influence. The movement in the United States is huge, composed of thousands of organizations, some with multi-million-dollar budgets and millions of members.

When I considered the other end, the "independent variables" or *causes,* rather than effects, the Asian societies/U.S. pairing seemed less promising for comparative purposes. Ideally, comparative/historical procedures work best when the things being compared differ only in one, or a small number of, ways but are alike in every other way. In the classic comparative study situation:

$$A \rightarrow X$$

$$B \rightarrow Y$$

A and B differ significantly in a few ways but are alike in many other ways, thereby "controlling" for those "variables" in a quasi-experimental fashion. Those few, discreet differences between A and B, then, must be somehow causally related to observed differences between X and Y. But these conditions for doing comparative analysis—few, and discreet, differences; or a high degree of similarity, otherwise—could not possibly be met. The Asian societies in this volume differ from the United States in many important respects: economic, political, cultural, demographic.

Thus, in this chapter, I first describe what I consider the most important strand of contemporary American environmentalism—the strand variously referred to as "the toxics movement," "grassroots environmentalism," or, most recently, "the movement for environmental justice." I will describe the following: the conditions that made this movement possible; its development, both organizational and ideological; and its impacts. After that, I will turn to the movements described in earlier chapters in this volume and identify ways that they are, and are not, similar to American grassroots environmentalism.

The Toxics Movement or Grassroots Environmentalism in the United States

The "environmental movement" in the United States today is such a diverse, multifaceted entity that it is not possible to either describe or theorize it as homogeneous. If one is to speak of today's U.S. environmental movement, one has either to describe this complex, fragmented multiplicity or pare down and choose one strand on which to focus.

In my work, I have chosen the latter course, focusing on what is labeled "the grassroots toxics movement" or, more recently, "the environmental justice movement." There are several good reasons for making this choice. First, this is a real movement, in all the senses that we think of when, as social scientists, we study "social movements." Here we see real organizing going on; people coming out of their homes, meeting, getting angry, planning actions, feeling that they *matter,* forging connections with others similarly mobilized in other communities. Second, this sector is also arguably the most interesting and dynamic sector of American environmentalism today. Starting with the ways that contamination of the environment affects public health, local land use, the quality of everyday social life, and focusing recently on the fact that the risks of industrial pollution disproportionately impact poor working people and disadvantaged minorities, the movement has begun to redefine the very term "environmentalism." The toxics movement is important, too, because it decisively rejects the "normalized" political tactics of earlier environmentalists—who preferred to educate the public and build constituencies for passing new laws through lobbyists and lawyers to pressure officials to fully implement such laws—in favor of more spontaneous, more immediate, more confrontational tactics. Finally, this facet of contemporary American environmentalism is important and interesting because it made a huge impact on both popular attitudes and public policy.

The case study that follows is based on research conducted by the author between 1989 and 1993. In that study, the author examined government documents (legislative histories, reports published by regulatory agencies), interviewed government officials, studied television news stories and print media, interviewed social movement leaders, gathered and analyzed social movement publications, and read the extensive secondary literature on toxic waste policy. The full case study is presented in the book, *EcoPopulism: Toxic Waste and the Movement for Environmental Justice* (Szasz 1994).

Favorable Preconditions

When we look back at the early or mid-1970s, clearly there was still no such thing as a grassroots toxics movement. Although later it would be determined that American industry generated hundreds of millions of tons of potentially hazardous wastes every year, at the time even federal regulators knew next to nothing about what toxics were being generated, where, in what quantities, or where or how those wastes were being disposed of. Average citizens could not possibly have known about any of this either. At most, people in a few, scattered communities may have been aware of some local contamination problems. Nevertheless, it is possible to point to certain preconditions that would, given the right spark, facilitate rapid social movement growth.

First, one might point out that the American economy had experienced a long period of trouble-free expansion characterized by steady growth and low rates of unemployment and inflation. True, that period had ended sometime during the 1970s, somewhat before the development of the movement. It is also true that by 1978, economic insecurity was on the rise, but the long boom had allowed citizens to care about non-economic interests, their health, and "quality of life" issues.

At the same time, there was significant quantitative growth in the amounts of waste by-products generated by industrial production, and those wastes were becoming more toxic. This was a result of the combined effects of a steadily expanding American economy (that is, the same factor that had made the first precondition, above, possible) and the chemicalization of production, a process that is an integral feature of capitalist development but which leaped forward in the second half of this century.

A third precondition was a fundamental shift in public perceptions of business, science, and technology. The traditional American attitude was one of trust and confidence. As President Calvin Coolidge said, back at the beginning of the century, "The business of America is business." Ever newer technology meant prosperity, more goods, a better life, an easier life. By 1980, this confidence was gone. Souring popular attitudes toward business and technology led to two factors important to the future of the toxics movement: popular fear of anything atomic and the rise of the modern environmental movement.

Some have persuasively argued that nuclear issues—fear of atomic war, dread of fallout, and, later, worries about the spread of nuclear power—played a key role in this fundamental change in the public's perception of modern technology. Fear of nuclear war was pervasive. Fallout, deadly but invisible, has been called the archetype of the contamination experience. One author has shown that Rachel Carson's descriptions of silent chemical poisoning evoked the image of atomic fallout, and that most of these descriptions' rhetorical power came from that association (Lutts 1985).

In addition, unlike in that earlier conservation moment, the environmentalism that arose in the 1960s instead emphasized that industrial activity pollutes the "ordinary" environment everywhere and, in the process, threatens people's quality of life, even their very health. Media coverage of dramatic pollution events such as that at Three Mile Island supported environmentalists' claims that unregulated industrial activity had ugly and disastrous consequences. Television news carried a steady stream of reports showing that many of the substances that people come into contact with, either as producers (chemicals, dusts, metals) or as consumers (notably, preservatives, pesticides, and other food residues), are toxic or carcinogenic. Viewers were reminded again and again that unregulated economic activity can produce catastrophes, and that neither industry nor government could be trusted to keep one safe. Technological innovation could no longer be equated with progress and material advancement.

The fourth specific precondition we might cite is the general rebirth of social activism in the United States in the 1960s, a rebirth that includes the civil rights movement, the women's movement, the antiwar movement— all the movements that, together, constitute the New Left. Modern environmentalism both contributed to this general rebirth of activism and was in turn affected by it. Earth Day was a "teach-in," an outreach and education model developed in the anti–Vietnam War movement. The surge of activism meant that environmental attitudes would be expressed not only through membership in traditional organizations, such as the Sierra Club, but also in direct, neighborhood-based confrontations.

Finally, the previous point should make us remember that the United States has a long history of social movements and protest. The nation's founding event was a revolt against colonial rule. American history is frequently depicted as a history of popular struggle against injustice. This history provides people with a sense that protest is legitimate; it also produces a political culture with a rich set of collective representations that provide a vocabulary for expressing grievances, legitimate protest, and provide people with an intuitive feel for the tactics of protest.

Thus, during the 1970s, despite the absence of a toxics movement, the following conditions existed: a healthy economy allowed citizens to value and wish to preserve non-economic interests; the objective level of risk was growing; at the same time, people had become suspicious of the very technology that had been such an integral factor in economic growth; and the activist bent of the period, in general, had made the rhetoric and tactics of protest legitimate again.

"Toxic Waste" on the TV

Between 1978 and 1980, "toxic waste" became a clearly formed issue in the popular imagination. Television coverage of Love Canal, and a handful of similar community contamination episodes, was largely the cause of this development.

The nation first heard about hazardous waste when CBS and ABC carried stories about events at Love Canal on August 2, 1978. Decades earlier, Hooker Chemical had dumped toxic chemical waste, "thousands of drums" (CBS 8/2/78) of it, into Love Canal, a partially completed and abandoned navigation channel. In 1952, the canal was covered up. A year later, Hooker sold the land to the Niagara Falls Board of Education. A school was built. Developers built homes and "unsuspecting families" (CBS 8/2/78) moved in. In the 1970s, after heavy rains, chemical wastes began to seep to the surface, both on the school grounds and into people's yards and basements. Federal and state officials confirmed the presence of eighty-eight chemicals, some in concentrations 250 to 5,000 times higher than acceptable safety levels. Eleven of these chemicals were suspected or known carcinogens; others were said to cause liver and kidney ailments (CBS 8/2/78; ABC 8/2/78; ABC 11/21/78).

Over the next two years, the networks' nightly news programs alone carried about 190 minutes of news about hazardous waste. Whether people watched television in the morning ("CBS Morning News," "The Today Show," "Good Morning, America"), during the day ("Donahue"), at the dinner hour ("McNeil-Lehrer," the networks' nightly news shows, "60 Minutes"), or late night ("Nightline"), they saw stories about Love Canal (Levine 1982). The networks' reporters, the elite of the newscorps, and premier opinion-makers, made it clear that Love Canal was an unmitigated disaster for the residents: a "calamity"; chemical poison "that has been steadily and silently building up for a long time" (ABC 8/2/78) is now "seeping . . . coming out of the ground" (CBS 8/2/78) into people's lives. Officials recommended that the people most affected should evacuate the area—first 37 families with pregnant women and children under two, then 97 families, eventually 239. Television showed families packing up all their belongings, moving to temporary shelter, leaving behind a street full of boarded-up homes. Love Canal stories then appeared in almost every type of popular magazine such as the newsweeklies (*Time, Newsweek, U.S. News and World Report*).

These early stories also began to suggest that what had happened to the people at Love Canal could well happen in many other communities, that the horror of chemicals coming out of the ground into your home and making your children ill could happen to *you*. EPA officials said that waste "has been disposed in unsafe ways" and that dumps sites are "like ticking time bombs" (CBS 8/9/78). The EPA was said to have found at least 400 other cases, according to some news reports (CBS 8/9/78), or 638 cases according to others (ABC 11/21/78). It was also said that there might, in fact, be as many as thousands of cases (ABC 11/12/78). U.S. industry was said to be generating 30 to 40 million tons of waste that "could have a severe adverse effect on human and animal life" (CBS 8/9/78).

Opinion polls confirmed that mass media coverage and EPA findings had a big impact on people's perceptions. An ABC News/Harris poll fielded in June 1980, shortly after coverage of the Love Canal chromosome damage study (May 17), the taking hostage of two EPA officials (May 19), and the president's declaration of a federal emergency at Love Canal (May 21), found that 93 percent of the public favored making federal disposal standards "much more strict"; 86 percent favored making "toxic chemical dumps and spills a very high priority for federal action"; 88 percent favored "providing funds to allow people who live in such areas and whose health may have been impaired to move out as soon as possible" (Mazur 1984; Szasz 1982: 350).

Local Actions Grew More Numerous, Networking Began

The shift in public perception was reflected almost immediately in a surge of local activism. People who had suspected that their communities might be contaminated but had been uncertain and hesitant to do anything about their concerns suddenly felt entitled to speak out. In other locales, people became convinced that they had to organize to oppose any attempt to site a new waste facility in the community. Only a few years before, back in 1976, less than half of toxic waste facility operators had said that public opposition was a problem for them. By 1979, a GAO survey of government and industry officials found that "*Virtually all* of the disposal industry officials interviewed indicated that public opposition was a major problem. . . . *Most* State officials we interviewed cited [public opposition] as the major barrier and expected public opposition to increase in the future" (U.S. General Accounting Office 1978: 11, emphasis added).

Publicity also seems to have encouraged networking. Before 1978, instances of siting opposition were, with almost no exception, conducted without any contact with or help from others. After 1978, more than half the cases reported in the literature had begun to network, bring in speakers from communities fighting the same company, share experiences, and learn from others' tactics. Will Collette told us that "one hundred and fifty-some-odd citizen groups contacted Lois [Gibbs] while she was still at Love Canal."

Two Kinds of Local Action

As local actions proliferated, it was possible to see that they could be categorized as either a "contamination protest" or a "siting opposition." In the first type, people organized because they became convinced that they had already become toxic victims; in the second, they organized because they feared they *would become* victims if they did not act *now* to prevent a proposed siting plan.

Contamination Protests

Contamination episodes are the stuff of nightmares (see Edelstein 1988; Levine 1982; Kroll-Smith and Couch 1991). Typically, the hazard is not directly visible to the victims. It is never clearly *known* to be there; it is *suspected,* but its extent, its intensity, and the actual level of threat it presents cannot be gauged. Worse, even if contamination episodes have a clear, identifiable starting point, like an explosion or a spill, they persist for long periods and typically do not have a definite endpoint after which the threat is over, people can relax, and normal life can resume.

That threat is omnipresent, but invisible; pervasive uncertainty; no end in sight. These conditions produce extreme emotional reactions:

"intense fear . . . chronic anxiety . . . demoralization . . . feelings of helplessness" (Kroll-Smith and Couch 1991: 6, 7, 8). Unable to bear the pervasive sense of uncertainty, people tend to develop firm, subjectively certain beliefs about the "true" situation. They have no doubts that their bodies and their loved ones' bodies have been violated, polluted, poisoned. People who find themselves the innocent victims of toxic contamination feel that, in addition to the material violation of their bodies, their moral-economic sense of fairness or justice has been grievously violated. That feeling is only intensified as the victims find that officials are unable or unwilling to remedy their plight (Kroll-Smith and Couch 1991: 9).

The very invisibility of such hazards once made it difficult for people to construe themselves as contamination victims, but media coverage of others' protests in other contaminated communities changes that. As our interviews with activists show, media coverage emboldened other people to say that they, too, had been contaminated and victimized.

Siting Opposition

People had not always opposed the siting of hazardous waste facilities in their communities. The 1973 EPA survey, cited earlier, shows that, at that time, people had not yet learned to fear such facilities. By 1979–80, all the evidence suggests that attitudes had changed and siting opposition had become widespread (U.S. Environmental Protection Agency 1979, 1980; U.S. General Accounting Office 1978; U.S. Council on Environmental Quality 1980).

The EPA (1979) study of siting opposition documented the extraordinarily wide spectrum of interests that people felt would be at risk if a hazardous waste facility were constructed in their community. Concerns for health and safety were raised most insistently. Concerns included fear of catastrophic events such as fires, explosions, toxic spills; fear of insidious/chronic pollution, especially groundwater contamination; and fear of what Centaur Associates called "political wastes," substances that had been extensively publicized, such as PCBs and dioxin. A second cluster of interests, mentioned less often but still important, involved nuisance and undesirable life-style impacts. Nuisance issues included concern about dust, noise, odors, traffic, and rodents. Life-style issues included both general interference with local life-styles and more specific concerns with visual impact. Fear of economic impacts constituted a third cluster of concerns. These ranged from fear of adverse impacts on individual property values to more general threats to the community's dominant economic activities, such as tourism and agriculture. Proposed TSD (transportation, storage, or disposal) facilities might, it was feared, interfere with more desirable community goals and land uses, such as planned industrial development, housing, or hoped-for development of recreational space.

Perceived violations of moral economy are also important in siting opposition. In the Centaur case studies, moral-economic threats appear in several guises. Residents felt it was wrong for their community to have to take other communities' wastes. In some communities, residents were upset to discover that the nature of the proposed facility had been misrepresented to them. Citizens often felt that regulators, who, after all, ought to be serving them and assuring their safety, seemed unresponsive to their concerns. Citizens also felt that their nominal right to "participate" was phony, that powerful economic and political actors elsewhere would ultimately do whatever they had planned to do anyway, regardless of local sentiment.

Stigma—the threatened loss of social status, the symbolic soiling of the community and its image—was another issue that came up often. People felt it was stigmatizing, shameful, to be dumped on, to be forced to live with others' waste products. Only folks considered to be at the bottom of society's class and status hierarchies would be subjected to such treatment.

Participants, Goals, Tactics

Until the toxics movement, the environmental movement in the United States had been criticized for its demographic narrowness, for being too white and middle-class. Grassroots environmentalism is quite different from that depiction.

Industrial areas are typically associated with poor and working people's neighborhoods. In the United States, where class and race are very highly correlated, this also means that people of color, especially African Americans and Latinos, are also more likely to be found near industrial areas. Contamination is associated with industrial activity; inevitably, the demographics of contamination protest groups reflect the social processes that concentrate poor and working people, both white and minority, near industrial sites. In addition, since it is family health, home life, and community that are threatened by contamination, women are disproportionately represented in both the leadership and membership in contamination protest groups.

The criterion for siting new toxic waste facilities is similar, in many ways, to traditional industrial siting criteria. The waste company seeks a site where land is cheap, that is well served by transportation infrastructures—rail, major highways, navigable water routes—and that is zoned for non-residential land use. Thus, again, the same segments of the population are likely to be most affected and therefore can be expected to be active in siting opposition. A number of studies suggest that, in the case of siting opposition, a larger area surrounding the proposed facility is often roused to opposition. Such a larger area tends to be demographically more diverse. Siting opposition groups, then, tend to be a microcosm of the potentially affected region: "almost the entire community . . . turns out to be environmentalists—the Kiwanis, the Rotary, the League of Women Voters, sometimes even the banks and the Chamber of Commerce. The environmental position is taken by almost everyone" (Robbins 1982: 505).

The *goal* of each type of mobilization is pretty straightforward. In cases where citizens suspect contamination, they want to have their suspicions officially confirmed and want to be compensated, to be made whole. That can include removal of the contamination; health monitoring and medical care; government purchase of contaminated homes, money for relocating, or monetary compensation for lost wages. In cases of siting opposition, the goal is simpler still: stopping the proposed project, preventing the siting.

Finally, *tactics* vary widely, but one can safety generalize that the overall "tenor" or "ethos" of the movement is confrontational. Contamination protests may start out innocently enough, with neighbors talking to neighbors, gathering information in a process Brown (1987) labeled "popular epidemiology." But such organizing often turns oppositional as the victims struggle to get reluctant officials to first take them seriously and then agree to spend millions of dollars to deal with the problem. Siting opponents have used many different tactics. Here, too, action commonly begins with citizens expressing their views and wants using routine and non-militant means: getting people to sign petitions, testifying at public hearings, filing court cases. But if these early non-militant actions do not bring the siting effort to a halt, things get militant quite quickly, moving to demonstrations, militant blockades of roads, or anonymous threats of violence. The fundamentally militant, confrontational spirit of siting opposition infuses even the most routine of tactics; for example, public hearings can turn into menacing mass rallies that take on near-riot overtones.

Movement Dynamics in the 1980s

After the 1978–80 watershed, the movement entered a qualitatively new phase. Local actions became very widespread. Formal movement infrastructural organizations developed. The movement's boundaries expanded and came to encompass an increasingly diversified set of local pollution issues. The movement experienced rapid ideological evolution.

Quantitative Growth

The Citizens' Clearinghouse for Hazardous Waste (CCHW) publishes an annual count of the grassroots groups it has served in some way: over 600 groups by the end of 1984, over 1,000 by the end of 1985, 1,700 by 1986, 2,739 by 1987, and 4,687 by 1988 (Citizens' Clearinghouse 1984; 1985; 1986a; 1987; 1988). In 1988 alone, CCHW claims to have sent organizers to work with citizen groups in 162 cities in 30 states and the District of Columbia. CCHW regional organizers told us that, at any one time, they are in phone contact with dozens of groups in their region. The two other national-level infrastructural organizations, the National Toxics Campaign and Greenpeace, say they have worked with about 2,000 and 1,000 local groups, respectively (interviews with Gary Cohen, National Toxics Campaign; Margie Kelley, Greenpeace).

Building a Formal Organizational Infrastructure

Informal networking was only a first step toward creation of a formal movement infrastructure. The first and still most important of these formations, the Citizens' Clearinghouse for Hazardous Waste (CCHW), came out of the Love Canal experience. As calls for help from other communities kept coming, Lois Gibbs, the leader of the Love Canal Homeowners' Association, decided to set up an organization that could "give other people the kind of help she wished she had gotten when she first started at Love Canal" (CCHW 1986b: 15–16).

State and regional groupings were organized. State-level coalitions appeared in every region of the United States—the Deep South, New England, the industrial Great Lakes region, the Mid-Atlantic, the rural Midwest, North Central, and the Far West.

New national-level organizations, such as the National Toxics Campaign (NTC), developed. Although now defunct, NTC worked with about 2,000 local organizations, offering these groups CCHW-style organizing help, technical assistance, and laboratory testing. Greenpeace, an environmental organization that predates the surge of neighborhood-based toxics organizing, transformed itself in response to the movement and became an important element in the movement's infrastructure.

The movement generated its own information services. The Environmental Research Foundation in Princeton, N.J., for example, provided the movement with accessible summaries of relevant scientific research on aspects of the toxics problem. It offered a computerized database, the Remote Access Chemical Hazards Electronic Library, or RACHEL. Weekly summaries of new and important developments were distributed by newsletter, "RACHEL's Hazardous Waste News." The movement was served by a number of other computer networks, such as Greenpeace's bulletin board, "Environet," and by numerous newsletters.

By the end of the 1980s, then, the "hazardous waste movement" consisted of a vast, somewhat loosely articulated network of many local, often short-lived, groups, statewide and regional coalitions, and national-level organizations providing sophisticated information services and organizing assistance. Such movement infrastructure gives a movement stability and continuity. This is especially important to a movement that is as localized and decentralized as the toxics movement. Had it *not* generated a permanent organizational infrastructure, the toxics movement would have stayed at the level of an objective but not yet subjective force; in Sartre's terms, an entity *in itself* but not *for itself.* Local actions would have occurred, but they would have been more like a continuously boiling pot of water—lots of heat and steam but no forward motion, no development. With an infrastructure, the movement had collective memory, an ability to learn from previous experience, a capacity to organize its resources, improve its tactical skills, develop a more sophisticated movement ideology, and, finally, convey these hard-earned lessons to new communities just beginning to mobilize.

Issue Expansion

The toxic by-products of industrial production are hardly the sole source of localized environmental degradation. A community can face threats from a host of other sources: the smokestack emissions of a local factory, unsafe disposal of infectious hospital wastes, toxics stored at a nearby military base. Over the decade, local groups sprang up around many such issues. They, too, contacted the organizations of the hazardous waste movement and asked for their help. Core movement organizations may have begun with a single issue, often just a single facility, but, over time, as they responded to these requests for help, they expanded their focus to other types of problems.

Initially, CCHW dealt almost exclusively with Love Canal–like cases of community contamination. By 1986, CCHW was helping communities fight facility siting, both hazardous and solid waste sites, landfills, incinerators, and waste-to-energy facilities. It was helping other communities deal with deep well injection, military toxics, pesticides, industrial plant emissions, and transportation of wastes. By 1988, CCHW literature was talking about global issues such as the greenhouse effect and ozone depletion; the Five-Year Plan of Action adopted in 1989 resolves to "broaden [the] movement [to] include *all* environmental hazards" (CCHW 1988; CCHW 1989: 57–58). In this way, the "hazardous waste" movement gradually became a much more broadly defined "toxics" movement, then an even more broadly defined movement.

Movement newsletters clearly show the progression. The PAHLS newsletter eventually carried stories about a wide set of environmental issues, pesticides, radioactive waste, PCBs, military nerve gas, food irradiation, ozone depletion, electronic pollution, acid rain, global warming, oil spills, and Agent Orange. In an article on movement strategy, RACHEL's editor Peter Montague wrote

> it would be beneficial to broaden the . . . concerns of our Movement . . . [to] pollution of the workplace; gross industrial air pollution of whole cities and regions; pesticide pollution and industrial pollution of our food; automobile pollution; indoor air pollution; . . . And in the next few years, grass-roots activists will need to pay serious attention to what look like bunny-hugger issues but aren't: habitat destruction, loss of wildlife species, and loss of wetlands. (Montague 1989: 104)

*Ideological Development: From NIMBYism
Toward a Radical Environmental Populism*

The hazardous waste and toxics movement is often characterized by its critics in industry and government as a "NIMBY," or "Not-In-My-Backyard," phenomenon. But that is no longer true today. I have described how the movement expanded from "hazardous waste" to a host of other toxics issues. That expansion was accompanied by an increasingly comprehensive, totalizing critique of modern economic production and forms of political power.

When the problem was conceived of as "our contaminated community," the cause was "that landfill" or "that careless chemical firm." When the problem was conceived of as hazardous industrial waste generally, the cause of the problem was Waste Management, Inc., Browning-Ferris, the disposal industry, polluting firms, and do-nothing state and federal officials. As the movement grew and addressed an ever larger set of problems, the cause came to be defined very broadly, in terms of a whole system of technology and chemical production, driven by profit, unchecked by a government that serves private wealth rather than public interest:

> We are endangered because the polluters, in their quest for profit, have exhibited a callous disregard for the lives and health of people. The corporate polluters have used their enormous power to . . . weaken regulation, and to avoid paying damages for injuries they have caused. . . . Government has failed to protect the American people. The regulatory program is ineffectual. (National Toxics Campaign, no date: 1)

The movement has not settled on a single, clear political ideology. Rather, one finds a certain eclecticism, a coexistence of multiple political symbol systems that have little in common but that can be mobilized to legitimate a position of radical critique and activism. Beyond specific referents to the American Revolution and the Bible, the clearest and most consistent ideology of the movement is a rather traditional radicalism that depicts American history as, most centrally, a struggle of the small people against big government and big business. American *populism* viewed that history as always shaped by the conflict between "the people" and the privileged, powerful elites who wish to dominate and exploit them. Thus, environmental damage today is depicted as the latest in the long list of injustices that have been caused by "greedy corporate polluters and their friends in government" (Citizens' Clearinghouse for Hazardous Wastes 1986b: 4). Comprising this list are the following:

> corporate polluters . . . their quest for profit [and] callous disregard for the lives and health of people. . . . Government [that] has failed to protect the American people. . . . *Who pays and who profits?* . . . the polluters profit while the rest of us pay! (National Toxics Campaign, no date: 1, 4) government bureaucrats who have lost their connection to the people they serve; . . . corporate decision-makers who have lost their connection to the people affected by their decisions. (Montague 1989: 104)

It seems most apt, then, to describe the movement's ideological position as a *radical environmental populism*. This phrase *situates* the movement in a larger history of American radicalism while it *distinguishes* the movement both from earlier forms of populism and from other tendencies in contemporary environmentalism.

Totalizing concepts of root causes imply radical cures. The movement is not explicitly socialist or anti-capitalist, but the reforms it advocates would, if adopted, amount to a fundamental restructuring of the current relationship between economy and society. The movement's leading groups envision a radical democratization of politics. CCHW (1989: 57–60) says that social governance of production, if it ever happens, should not mean governance by officials and bureaucrats, but "direct citizen representation in *all* decision-making." NTC (no date: 5–6) calls for "measures at every level of government to empower citizens and communities in their efforts to protect public health and community well-being." Barry Commoner (1989: 12), the most famous environmentalist now associated with the movement, speaks of "social governance of the means of production."

Ideological Development II: From EcoPopulism
Toward Environmental and Social Justice

While mainstream environmentalists continue to restrict themselves to their one cause, at least officially and publicly, and tend to avoid becoming involved with other social causes, the toxics movement has continued to broaden its vision of the connection between environmental action and more traditional social justice issues.

Its leading organizations explicitly identify the movement with what they depict as a long and proud history of social struggles in America, with the Labor Movement, the civil rights movement, the anti-war, and New Left movements of the 1960s, and the women's movement (Citizens' Clearinghouse for Hazardous Waste 1986b, 1989; Zeff, Love, and Stults 1989: 1). The movement's core organizations reach out to and seek common ground with a variety of causes, ranging from the elderly, labor, race, and women, to more recent ones, such as homelessness and AIDS.

Why or how this evolution from environmental populism to a broader social change agenda happened is not difficult to discern. The key moment was the refusal of the tactical and ideological alternative—mainstream, reform environmentalism—and the articulation of the perspective I earlier labeled radical environmental populism. Having made that "choice," the toxics movement found itself squarely within a broader left/opposition culture consisting of numerous other social movements that had similar views about the root causes of various oppressions and also similar tactics. In addition, and more specifically, the movement found itself necessarily dealing with issues of class, racism, and sexism.

Race had to be addressed because toxics production and disposal take place to a disproportionate degree in or near communities of the working poor and people of color. Core movement organizations that wished to reach out and help organize minority communities or poor, multiracial communities had to deal with racial tensions, not just toxics. Thus, in contrast to earlier environmentalist toxics movements, where there was little attempt to link that problem's cause to the civil rights movement and other movements against racial inequality, the intersection of racial discrimination and exposure to toxic hazards is one of the core themes of the hazardous waste and toxics movement. Conceptually, this intersection of heretofore separate causes has given birth to a new emphasis on "environmental racism" that enriches and deepens both sets of social issues. In the decade of the 1990s, *environmental justice* has become the movement's number one issue and its most powerful slogan.

The movement had to deal with sexism, or patriarchy, because the foci of toxics organizing are the home, community, integrity of the family, and health—all traditionally women's concerns—and because, as a consequence, women make up the majority, probably the vast majority, of both the membership and the leadership of movement organizations. In this way, the hazardous waste and toxics movement provided its own answer to eco-feminists' call for an integration of women's liberation and environmentalism.

The results, in recent years—both the general place in the political spectrum that the movement found itself in and the specific organizing challenges it has had to deal with—have affirmed that environmentalism is a social justice issue that must necessarily forge solidarity with all the other great social causes of the day.

> We can reach out to others who, in their own ways, are struggling to recapture lost values of individual rights, fairness, justice and equality of opportunity: activists for civil rights (Asian, African-American, Hispanic, and Native Peoples), organized labor, women, gay men and lesbians, housing and tenants' rights, farmers, welfare rights, affordable health care, animal rights, consumer rights, and safe energy, among others. (Montague 1989: 104)

In summary, the toxics movement can no longer be characterized as narrow, selfish, or short-sighted. Quite the opposite. Even if, tactically, the movement still largely takes the form of local actions against single local targets, those local actions are informed more and more by explicit, long-term goals of radical social change and by visions of a just society. It is true that people who are just becoming active today still tend to start from a narrow, NIMBY position. But when they contact the movement's infrastructure to ask for help, they not only get help, they get a full dose of the movement's radical analysis. And they are exhorted to stay involved, become part of the movement, help others. Charges of NIMBYism may have been justified a decade ago; they are no longer fair or accurate today.

Two Reactions to the Movement

The political system has had two very different reactions to the movement. On the one hand, the officials who were charged with administering hazardous waste statutes wanted to insulate themselves from the effects of the movement. They searched for strategies that would neutralize what they saw as disruptive intrusions from below. At the same time, though, lawmakers felt compelled to respond to citizens' profound fear of toxic waste, and their desire to be protected from it.

First of all, as the toxics movement grew more powerful and successful—in the case of siting opposition, *spectacularly* successful—officials began to discuss ways to neutralize this unwelcome exercise of local popular power. Examining the literature on siting, I found five distinct "strategies of disempowerment" described.

1. *Siting in Out-of-the-Way Places.* Perhaps the simplest idea was to site undesirable waste facilities in areas that are already heavily industrial, in underpopulated rural areas, or areas that are otherwise far removed from communities. As the EPA's consultants pointed out, "When the public is unaware of a siting attempt, they are unlikely to oppose it" (U.S. Environmental Protection Agency 1979: 18).

2. *Selecting Communities That Are Powerless or Most Likely to Be Compliant.* One could select locales where people are politically conservative, pro-business, and still have a high degree of trust in experts and in technology, or select communities where people are socially and materially disadvantaged, powerless, or ill-informed—communities that lack the resources, skills, confidence, and sense of entitlement necessary to successfully organize resistance (Cerrell Associates and Powell 1984).

3. *Preemption.* Siting proponents worried that local governments would listen to outpourings of fear and anger, then use their authority over local land use to block siting attempts. "Preemption" of local control by either state or federal governments would neutralize local resistance by taking authority from the political institutions most responsive to it.

4. *Compensation.* People are rational economic actors. Why wouldn't they refuse to bear costs that exceed potential benefits? If so, the remedy is obviously some form of compensation. Developers could offer direct money payments or non-monetary forms of compensation, such as to improve roads, buy the community a new fire engine, provide the community with a new park.

5. *Expanded Participation.* Policy analysts argued that the only way to restore trust and secure public acceptance was to fundamentally rethink and redesign the process of citizen participation. If officials wished to have a community's consent, they had to approach it with respect, not with the patronizing and dismissive notion that they were dealing with irrational "NIMBYs." Officials had to be willing to make the community a real partner in facility planning. Citizens had to be brought into the process from the very beginning and had to be given a voice at every stage of project development.

Actual siting policy often involves a combination of the above strategies. Popular dread of "toxic waste" is so intense, though, that in fact none of these have been at all successful. At the level of the community, the toxics movement has been incredibly successful and has exercised a virtually unchallengeable veto over the construction of new toxic waste facilities.

There was a second kind of official reaction to the movement, fundamentally different from the first. While one part of officialdom was intent on finding a way to neutralize the movement at the local level, elected officials, especially U.S. senators and congressmen, believed that the movement represented real mass sentiment—dread of "toxic waste"—and that they had to pay attention to this if they were not to be punished by the electorate when they next ran for office.

To get a sense of the strength of this latter reaction, one has to recall the larger political climate of the early 1980s. "Deregulation" was one of the battle cries of the newly elected Reagan administration. The environmental and health and safety laws that were already in place came under heavy assault. New initiatives were avoided. Congress did not even dare debate the various statutes—the Clean Air and Clean Water Acts, for example—that came up for routine reauthorization during this time. Hazardous waste regulations proved to be the only exception. The Reagan administration's blunt attempts to cripple implementation of the two toxic waste laws, the Resource Conservation and Recovery Act (RCRA) and, especially, the Superfund law that was passed after Love Canal to clean up toxic dumps that were threatening public health, spawned a public outcry and became a full-blown political scandal in 1983. After that, Congress went on to defy the deregulatory ethos of the times and significantly strengthened both laws when they came up for reauthorization in 1984 and 1986, respectively.

Evaluating Movement Impacts

A recent survey of the social movements literature says that social scientists have not paid sufficient attention to movements' impacts. In my study of the toxics movement, I attempted to assess that movement's various impacts, and do so in the broadest possible terms. I have concluded the following.

If achievements are considered narrowly—that is, in terms of the percentage of all wastes safely disposed of or the number of old, leaking Superfund sites cleaned up—the movement has not been a success. Yes, the movement pushed elected officials to strengthen regulatory laws, but, as is so often the case with regulatory law, there is a vast gap between what Congress intended and what has actually been accomplished. Thus, the impact on society's actual disposal practices has been much less than would appear from simply examining the law. Government auditors find that even the best, newly built, and fully licensed landfills are likely to leak, that incinerators often malfunction, and so forth. These auditors find, too, that the Environmental Protection Agency does not have the budget or staffing to ensure that all the companies that handle, store, transport, and dispose of toxic wastes are in compliance with the law. Other studies show that only a tiny fraction of Superfund sites have been successfully cleaned up.

Still, I found that the movement-driven strengthening of toxic waste laws has had a number of important, if indirect, benefits. Regulatory laws not only police, set standards, and enforce those standards, they also stimulate the production of new data. Even if the RCRA and Superfund law have not been as successful as one would hope in actually cleaning up toxics, they have encouraged the creation of a large amount of new information concerning the generation and distribution of toxics, the effects of chemicals on the human body and on other species, and so on. The new information is the result of the regulation-driven building of a whole new *research infrastructure* of laboratories and scientists trained and funded to study toxics. All of that is critical if society is *ever* to be able to develop meaningful controls over the generation and disposal of the toxic by-products of economic activity.

Important as it is, the development of treatment and disposal infrastructure only improves how toxics are dealt with once they have been created. I found that the toxics movement forced a policy change that is potentially far more important—a turn from policies that emphasize better *control* of waste disposal toward those that encourage pollution *prevention,* or, as it is also known, source reduction. By the end of the 1980s, both government and industry officials were praising source reduction as the most desirable, possibly the only workable, solution to the nation's waste problems.

I wish to argue that the toxics movement caused this shift. It did not do so intentionally. Rather, this impact resulted from the simultaneous, combined impact of two factors: at the local level, the failure of policymakers' various disempowerment tactics; and at the national level, legislators' desire to placate the movement—which they perceived as having behind it a huge mass of voters/supporters—with stronger hazardous waste laws. Stronger regulation increased the cost of legal waste disposal and strengthened legal liability so that companies would pay dearly if caught disposing of wastes illegally. The price increase might have been more modest if supply could have kept up with demand; that is, if the disposal industry could have responded by rapidly building new disposal facilities. But this would not be. Almost every proposal to site landfills, incinerators, and so on, met with vehement opposition. Because efforts to neutralize local opposition did not work, new waste facilities were not built. Thus, while regulations forced demand, the movement vetoed increasing the supply, and the price for legitimate disposal rose very fast. Land disposal, for example, used to cost about $15 per ton. By 1986, the cost of land disposal was up to $250 per ton and the cost of incinerating waste $500 to $1,500 a ton (RACHEL #5, December 29, 1996; Ottinger 1985: 20–21).

My argument, then, is that the hazardous waste movement was responsible for the progress toward waste reduction. Not in the simple and direct sense that it demanded pollution prevention (though its most advanced leaders did that, too); rather, the movement was responsible by creating a "scissor" effect: at the centers of formal political action, the movement caused regulations to be strengthened. Locally, the movement threw a wrench into the siting process, making it nearly impossible to build new disposal and treatment capacity. The *combined* impact, the movement's contradictory and simultaneous presence at these two levels, is the single most important factor that caused industry, which not long ago wanted nothing to do with waste reduction, now to "voluntarily" embrace it.

Finally, the movement may potentially have an impact on progressive politics in the United States more generally. I argued earlier that the toxics movement both began to define its own mission in broader terms and moved to forge coalitional bonds with other movements. If things continue to develop in this direction, the movement might prove to have a more general impact on democratic politics.

With labor in decline, it has not been clear which, if any, of the "new social movements" would make the move, would go beyond its particularistic cause and take upon itself the vacated position of the leading/unifying element of the various movements that challenge the existing organization of society. The hazardous waste movement has made explicit gestures in this direction. It has redefined its environmental mission in terms of a larger critique of society; it has made common causes with other movements and has said that, ultimately, they are all joined in the same struggle. Some of its most visionary leaders have imagined a future in which grassroots environmentalism spearheads the resurgence of a mass-based progressive movement in the United States.

Comparisons with Asian Environmental Movements

How does the American case differ from the Asian environmental movements described in other chapters? Reading the case studies of South Korea, Taiwan, Hong Kong, and the Philippines, I find that the Asian cases certainly differ from the United States case in significant ways, but I am struck more by the similarities, both at the level of environmental destruction and the movements that arise.

The Presence of Grassroots Environmentalism

All four case studies confirm the emergence not only of environmentalism, but of a specifically *grassroots* form of environmentalism—local, at times militant—immediately recognizable as very much like the grassroots toxics movement in the United States. Typically, this particular type of environmentalism is not the only one, is not the first, and is not necessarily the prototyped or dominant form. Grassroots movements are preceded by NGOs that have a small, highly educated, elite membership; they begin at a later point, and they do so largely independently of the existing NGOs.

Unfettered Economic Growth

More than fifty years ago, the economic anthropologist Karl Polanyi, in his justly famous work *The Great Transformation,* argued that the very processes that unleash modern, market-centered economic development—deregulation; the removal of traditional socio-cultural constraints on land and labor; their transformation into commodities pure and simple; the substitution of the motive of endless, abstract pursuit of economic gain for older economic motivations that emphasized, instead, security and maintenance of a traditional standard of living—

would necessarily produce massive, adverse social and environmental impacts: "Nature would be reduced to its elements, neighborhoods and landscapes defiled, rivers polluted . . . no society could stand the effects of such a system . . . the ravages of this satanic mill" (Polanyi 1944: 72–73).

An Environmentalism Driven by Very Immediate Human Interests

In Asia, as in the United States, grassroots environmentalism is a response to the linked social/ecological changes that come with unfettered economic growth, along with rapid industrialization and intensive resource extraction activities that are the hallmarks of "development." In the United States, as the name "toxics movement" suggests, grassroots environmentalism mainly targets *downstream* impacts; that is, the polluting discharge of the waste by-products of production. The Asian cases differ somewhat in that grassroots environmental groups address both downstream impacts and *upstream* ones, as well. Certainly, much grassroots organizing deals with pollution, but groups also arise to protest when resource extraction activities withdraw too many resources too quickly (deforestation, overfishing), or when they degrade the local environment in ways that threaten traditional livelihoods of farmers, fishers, and indigenous people.

In every Asian case study country (territory), resistance to the building of nuclear power plants is an important, high-profile facet of environmental protest (see Chapter 10). In the United States, too, fear of nukes, weapons testing, radioactive fallout, and nuclear power plant safety had a special place in the development of contemporary environmentalism. Nuclear power is such an extraordinary threat, which inspires such dread, that it undermines whatever enthusiasm (or perhaps just acquiescence in the face of the juggernaut of modernization) people may have felt toward new technology and endless economic modernization. But what needs to be emphasized, I think, is the role played by more mundane threats—*pollution* and *threat to traditional means of livelihood*—as the kinds of threats critical in unleashing local, grassroots environmental protest. This is true in both the U.S. and Asian cases, although threat to livelihood has been less prominent in the United States and has taken a somewhat different form (threat to value of one's home; concern that communities with waste sites would be less attractive for types of economic development or for tourism).

In the United States, the more recent, people-oriented, "victim" environmentalism of the grassroots toxics movement seems a significant departure from the immediately preceding period, when environmentalism was strongly identified with nature preservation, establishing parks shielded from development, protecting endangered species, and so on. The Asian studies depict an environmentalism that, like the American grassroots movement, is almost never about just nature (one component of the movement in Taiwan is an exception) but always about how the transformation of nature threatens human interests, be they material (health, means of subsistence, traditional livelihoods) or moral (sense of unfairness, being victimized by the powerful).

Movement Composition, Movement Tactics

Grassroots environmentalism everywhere is a movement of victims, and/or of people convinced that unless they act they are certain to *become* victims; it is not a movement of educated elites with a greater vision of ecosystem preservation. Thus, the composition of the movement in any locale, region, or nation is determined by the specific pattern of economic development that has occurred or is being planned; it can be urban residents protesting a local industry's emissions, or rural people protesting development that threatens their livelihood. Contamination protest and siting opposition are, thus, important "tributaries" that feed into and constitute the movement in every society.

Although several studies emphasize that important sectors of the environmental movement in Asian societies shun militant, confrontational tactics—notably the more formal environmental organizations and NGOs—the more grassroots-type groups organized in the face of specific local threats seem everywhere to gravitate toward more militant approaches. This, too, is similar to the U.S. case, where the older, more established environmental NGOs prefer public education, lobbying the legislators, and using the legal system, while grassroots groups protest, disrupt meetings, throw themselves in front of bulldozers and dumptrucks, and sometimes threaten violence.

In my summary, I cited as a general precondition the fact that popular understanding of U.S. history legitimates protest as a way to express grievances. After all, at least in fondly repeated myth, a revolutionary act was the founding moment of the nation. In none of the Asian cases, I believe, is there anything like this identification of national history with a history of legitimate social protest. They all have a much weaker democratic tradition. Confrontation and protest as ways to express grievances are a much more recent phenomenon; the goal has been to fight for democratic rights, not (as in the U.S.) to fully exercise them. Although this is somewhat speculative, I would venture that in such societies, there are powerful tendencies toward more non-confrontational social movement tactics, but when movements are militant or confrontational, they may quickly take on anti-statist or revolutionary overtones. In contrast, in the United States, since confrontation is so much a part of popular political culture, conflict—even militant, violent conflict—does not necessarily or automatically take on anti-systemic connotations. This, in turn, has implications for the connection between environmentalism and democratization, a point to which I return below.

Movement Trajectories, Environmental Impacts

Having identified the logic of unfettered economic growth as the culprit in both the United States and Asia, it is perhaps not surprising that people's responses, their sense of victimization, and the militancy of their gut responses, would be quite similar. But similar motivations and actions do not necessarily generate similar movement trajectories and impacts. Here, the differences between the case study societies assert themselves.

The U.S. case is one of a decade of rapid quantitative growth with respect to movement self-organization and ideological maturation. The movement accomplishes a lot: local struggles often succeed; laws get strengthened, an improvement even if those laws are not fully implemented; the whole discourse on waste turns from silence and neglect toward systematic efforts at source reduction and cradle-to-grave waste management.

Grassroots environmentalism seems generally to be on the rise in all the Asian cases, but there are significant differences in the pattern of development. In Taiwan, local actions have proliferated, but as I read Professor Hsiao's chapter, there was not much weaving together of the many local struggles, the building of a unifying movement infrastructure. Popular attitudes are changing and local protests are often victorious, but it is not clear that such victories have been translated into an overall shift in the nation's economic and environmental policies. And that seems to also describe South Korea.

Hong Kong's movement seems to have been different from those of both Taiwan and South Korea. Hong Kong's local actions have been modest in number. There is little communication between local protest groups and the territorywide NGOs that could have, had they wished, helped those locals begin to coalesce. Resistance from local elites in rural struggles, for example, is strong and has been largely successful. If grassroots groups are beaten back when activism is at an early stage of development, when actions are sporadic and few in number, the movement fails to develop real momentum. Professors Chiu, Hung, and Lai also describe how the political energies that might have continued to infuse the grassroots movement were diverted into electoral politics. Although the movement seems to have an impact mostly at the level of the individual green consumer, Hong Kong's environment nevertheless has improved because of the massive migration of manufacturing and other polluting industries across the border to mainland China.

In contrast, Professor Magno's chapter on the Philippines depicts a movement that has developed from reactive protest to proactive participation in the development of more sustainable economic practices. In the 1990s, the movement pursues its agenda through the twin strategies of citizen empowerment and policy engagement. The movement will continue to be a critical voice and force in monitoring the enforcement of environmental regulations, aside from being a valuable partner in the joint implementation of environmental protection activities.

Ideological Evolution; Broader Political Impacts

Turning, finally, to the question of movements' ideological trajectories, I first point out that the ideological development that happened with the American toxics movement during the 1980s is meaningful only in an American context characterized by mass political naiveté and the tendency to compartmentalize social issues. It is that context that develops toxic NIMBYism into a radical environmental populism and ultimately links environmental action with other social justice issues so noteworthy.

That said, I did see something like this in the South Korean, Taiwanese, and Philippine cases, but the ideological evolution is not so dramatic, probably because the nondemocratic form of the state shortens the distance to be traveled between the experience of environmental victimization and the conviction that the solution lies in a broader democratization of society and in popular empowerment.

Similarities continue when we look at actual political impacts. In the United States, the grassroots movement and the environmental justice movement began to see themselves not only as fighting for environmental goals but also as a force that could revitalize progressive politics in the U.S., more generally. Although the topic of the connection between environmentalism and democratization in Asian societies is given fuller treatment elsewhere in this book, I wish to remark on the fact that there is an intimate link between the two in every case study. The specifics of the relationship vary, certainly. In Taiwan, anti-pollution struggles preceded and contributed to the buildup of a more general agitation for democratization; in South Korea, democratization unleashed both mass media coverage of environmental issues and protest activity. In the Philippines, environmental goals are pursued within a larger shift toward local, participatory planning processes. Interestingly, if sadly, the relationship is not always a positive one. In Hong Kong, activists' involvement in democratic processes, electoral politics, and their greater consultation in policymaking, paradoxically drained resources and manpower from environmental struggles.

This relationship between environmentalism and social justice emerges inevitably from another point of similarity I have emphasized—the *fusion* of many different motives when people oppose industrial toxics. The fact that people cannot separate the material threats to health and livelihood from the moral insults *at the moment they are moved to enter the movement* inevitably means that the movement cannot rest at taking on environmental degradation or public health issues alone, but must inevitably address larger political questions, as well.

Discussion

Let us recall the diagram I presented at the beginning of this chapter:

$$A \rightarrow X$$

$$B \rightarrow Y$$

To repeat: the usual logic of the comparative method is to select A and B carefully so that there are a few discreet differences. Then one can reasonably argue that differences found in the phenomenon of interest, X and Y, may in large part be explained by those differences between A and B.

As I mentioned at the beginning, I had some concern that A and B were in this instance so profoundly different, that the Asian societies studied by my colleagues in the Workshop differed from the United States in so many important respects—economic, political, cultural, demographic—that the logic of the comparative method would break down.

It seems to me now that I need not have been so concerned. First, although these societies do differ in dramatic ways, meaningful comparisons and causal explorations are possible. For example, the different histories, political cultures, forms of the state—hence different political opportunity structures—straightforwardly account for the differences in movement trajectories and impacts. Second, and to me much more intriguing, I found a surprising situation in which A and B were drastically different, but such profound differences seemingly produced rather similar outcomes, not so much X and Y, as X' and X".

$$A \rightarrow X'$$

$$B \rightarrow X''$$

Given the immense differences between the United States and the various Asian societies described in other chapters, big differences in various nations' environmentalism (X, Y) are to be expected. When we expect differences but find, instead, similarities or convergences, we have a *puzzle* or an *anomaly* that begs to be *analyzed* and *explained*. Looking once more at the discussion just completed, for me three similarities stand out above all else: (1) unfettered economic development simultaneously puts at risk a host of interests, none of which are (in real life, as opposed to in our concepts) strictly separable from each other; (2) "environmental movement" is somewhat of a misnomer because people become active not just to save the "environment"; environmental degradation and contamination are only one symptom of a larger, more complex threat, and people react to that whole indivisible complex, not to any single component of it; (3) inevitably, because of (1) and (2), "environmental" movements are closely tied to larger movements for social change.

References

American Broadcasting Company (ABC). "Nightly News." August 2, 1978; August 4, 1978; August 7, 1978; August 11, 1978; November 11, 1978; November 12, 1998; November 21, 1978.

Brown, Phil. 1987. "Popular Epidemiology: Community Response to Toxic Waste-Induced Disease." *Science, Technology and Human Values* 12(3–4): 78–85.

Cerrell Associates, and J. Stephen Powell. 1984. "Political Difficulties Facing Waste-to-Energy Conversion Plant Siting." Sacramento: California Waste Management Board.

Citizens' Clearinghouse for Hazardous Wastes (CCHW). 1984. *Annual Report, 1984.* Arlington, VA: CCHW.

———. 1985. *Annual Report, 1985.* Arlington, VA: CCHW.

———. 1986a. *Annual Report, 1986.* Arlington, VA: CCHW.

———. 1986b. *Five Years of Progress, 1981–6.* Arlington, VA: CCHW.

———. 1987. *Annual Report, 1987.* Arlington, VA: CCHW.

———. 1988. *Annual Report, 1988.* Arlington, VA: CCHW.

———. 1989. "Grassroots Convention '89 Songbook." Arlington, VA: CCHW.

Columbia Broadcasting System (CBS). "Nightly News." August 2, 1978; August 7, 1978; August 9, 1978.

Commoner, Barry. 1989. "Why We Have Failed." *Greenpeace* 14 (September/Ocober): 12–13.

Edelstein, Michael R. 1988. *Contaminated Communities.* Boulder: Westview Press.

Kroll-Smith, Steve, and Stephen R. Couch. 1991. "Social Impacts of Toxic Contamination." Carson City: Nevada Agency for Nuclear Projects, Yucca Mountain Socioeconomic Project.

Levine, Adeline G. 1982. *Love Canal: Science, Politics, and People.* Lexington: Lexington Books.

Lutts, Ralph H. 1985. "Chemical Fallout: Rachel Carson's *Silent Spring,* Radioactive Fallout, and the Environmental Movement." *Environmental Review* 9(3): 211–225.

Mazur, Allan. 1984. "The Journalists and Technology: Reporting About Love Canal and Three Mile Island." *Minerva* 21(1): 45–66.

Montague, Peter. 1989. "What We Must Do—A Grass-roots Offensive Against Toxics in the 90s." *The Workbook* 14(3): 90–113.

National Broadcasting Company (NBC). "Nightly News." September 24, 1978.

National Toxics Campaign (NTC). No date. "Toxics Prevention: A Citizens' Platform." Boston, MA: National Toxic Campaign.

Ottinger, Richard. 1985. "Strengthening of the Resource Conservation and Recovery Act in 1984: The Original Loopholes, the Amendments, and the Political Factors Behind Their Passage." *Pace Environmental Law Review* 3(1): 1–28.

Polanyi, Karl. 1944. *The Great Transformation: The Political and Economic Origins of Our Time.* Boston: Beacon Press.

RACHEL's Hazardous Waste News. Various issues. Princeton: Environmental Research Foundation.

Robbins, Richard L. 1982. "Methods to Gain Community Support for a Hazardous Waste Facility or a Superfund Cleanup." In *Hazardous Waste Manage-*

ment for the 80s, edited by T.L. Sweeney, H.G. Bhatt, R.M. Sykes, and O.J. Sproul, pp. 503–518. Ann Arbor: Ann Arbor Science Publishers.

Szasz, Andrew. 1982. "The Dynamics of Social Regulation: A Study of the Formation and Evolution of the Occupational Safety and Health Administration." Ph.D. dissertation, Department of Sociology, University of Wisconsin, Madison.

————. 1994. *EcoPopulism: Toxic Waste and the Movement for Environmental Justice.* Minneapolis: University of Minnesota Press.

U.S. Council on Environmental Quality. 1980. "Public Opinion on Environmental Issues: Results of a National Public Opinion Survey." Washington, DC: Government Printing Office.

U.S. Environmental Protection Agency (EPA). 1979. "Siting of Hazardous Waste Management Facilities and Public Opposition." Washington, DC: Government Printing Office.

————. 1980. "Hazardous Waste Facility Siting: A Critical Problem." Washington, DC: Government Printing Office.

U.S. General Accounting Office. 1978. "How to Dispose of Hazardous Waste." Washington, DC: Government Printing Office.

Zeff, Robbin L., Marsha Love, and Karen Stults. 1989. "Empowering Ourselves: Women and Toxics Organizing." Arlington, VA: Citizens' Clearinghouse for Hazardous Wastes.

8

Culture and Asian Styles of Environmental Movements

Hsin-Huang Michael Hsiao, On-Kwok Lai,
Hwa-Jen Liu, Francisco A. Magno, Laura Edles,
and Alvin Y. So

Acronyms

BCCs	Basic Christian Communities	NGOs	Non-Governmental
BECs	Basic Ecclesial Communities		Organizations
CBCP	Catholic Bishops Conference of	NIEs	Newly Industrializing Economies
	the Philippines	POs	People's Organizations
KMT	Kuomintang	PSK	Pagbugtaw sa Kamatuoran
	(Nationalist Party)		(To be awakened to the truth)

Introduction

According to Pye (1985), the paternalistic nature of Asian political culture creates obstacles for political critics, labor agitators, student rebels, environmental activists, and other challengers to the status quo. This is because Asian distaste for open criticism of authority, the fear of upsetting the unity of the community, and the knowledge that any violation of the community's rules of propriety will lead to ostracism all combine to limit the appeal of Western democracy and social movements. Due to the Confucian emphasis on harmony and the demand for consensus, adversarial relationships are muted, and critics are taught the benefits of conformity. Deyo (1989) also points out that labor peace in the Asian NIEs is generally attributed to the political

culture, which stresses "hierarchy, cooperation, a preference for mediation over confrontation, industriousness, deference to elders, and most
important, the subordination of individual to family, group, and state."

Despite these cultural barriers, however, a robust environmental
movement is developing rapidly in East Asia and Southeast Asia in the
late twentieth century. This raises intriguing "macro" and "micro" questions, such as: (1) What specific cultural "tools" (i.e., values, strategies
for action, rituals, and symbols) rooted in what specific cultural traditions (e.g., Taoism, Buddhism, Christianity, and folk religions) do environmental movements use to challenge the norms/values of orthodox
Confucian paternalism? (2) How exactly have cultural systems played a
role in the micro-mobilization of environmental movements? Specifically, what particular "frames," symbols, and rituals provide a legitimate
base from which to challenge the status quo? How are identity and
solidarity within the environmental movement attained and sustained?

In order to answer the above questions, we would like to briefly
introduce the concepts and methods of cultural analysis before study-
ing Asian environmental movements.

Cultural Analysis

Since the 1980s, we have seen a renewed interest in culture in the
substantive area of social movements. This new cultural emphasis is a
direct response to the fact that the "resource mobilization" and "political process" perspectives dominant in the United States in the 1970s
"privileged the political, organizational and network/structural aspects
of social movements while giving the more cultural or ideational dimensions of collective action short shrift" (McAdam 1994: 36). Of
course, the materialist bent of the 1970s was itself a reaction against
the earlier "collective behavior" tradition, which seemed to highlight
the *irrational* and even pathological nature of collective action. Thus,
in this new culturalist period, social movement theorists resurrect cultural issues of identity, solidarity, and so forth, while emphasizing that
people are active, skilled users of culture, and that they have the capacity to resist and redefine the message of the state and other dominant
institutions. In emphasizing agency and contingency, recent cultural
analysts create a more multidimensional rendering of culture.

Methodologically, recent cultural analysts have turned away from
the exploration of absolute values and beliefs as revealed in survey

data (as did earlier modernization theorists such as Pye), and toward discourse or textual analysis, and the study of symbolization. Analysts such as Snow et al. (1986) explore the frame alignment processes by which organizers seek to join the cognitive orientations of individuals with those of social movement organizations.

"Frames" are symbolic or moral codes that actors use to make sense of the world. These symbolic frames of reference are found in the official *texts* of the movement (declarations, speeches, pamphlets, etc.) and in the everyday *talk* of the organizations (revealed through conversation analysis and participant observation). More important, "frames" operate at both a (rational) conscious and a (non-rational) unconscious level. Thus while environmental activists and opposition elites wittingly frame issues so that they might be read in a particular way, elites necessarily create this frame using the relatively unexplored, pre-existing systems of meaning. In terms of reception or interpretation, symbols are multivocal rather than univocal. Thus movement and opposition elites may intend to frame an issue in a particular way, but this frame calls up different, unanticipated symbols and values that may even contradict the goals of the organization.

What symbolic anthropology helps reveal is that frames often revolve around the construction and identification of the *sacred* and the *profane*. The "sacred" is the emotionally charged symbol of the good; the "profane" is its symbolic opposite, the emotionally charged symbol of the bad, which in the religious realm is denoted by evil. These emotionally charged symbols contrast with routine signs that lack this heightened effect. Interestingly, environmental movements all share a specific core dichotomy: the environment/nature (whether it is a particular river, endangered animal, etc.) is itself "sacred" and the profane are the specific practices (e.g., the construction of a nuclear power plant, chemical fertilization, logging, etc.) that represent the defilement, rape, or extermination of the sacred, often literally *pollution*. In the Asian context, cultural analysis would identify the symbols and values through which movement participants activate salient frames of the sacred and profane, and how and why these frames are successfully or unsuccessfully resisted by the state or anti-environmentalists.

Of course, symbols and frames do not exist in a world by themselves; they are intimately entwined with action. Thus, it is imperative to explore not only "discourse" but "ritual acts" as well as the everyday life of the environmental organization itself. This provides a more well-rounded understanding of the environmental movement, and it reveals the fit between movement discourse and movement action. Cultural analysis of ritualization reveals the meaning behind and within, for example, sites of protest (e.g., outside a Buddhist temple), the costumes of actors (e.g., wearing a green T-shirt or button), the staging of protests (e.g., using banners, folk songs, etc.), and the dramatic acts themselves (e.g., the burning of a toy petrochemical company).

In sum, cultural analysis helps explain why certain ritual acts are successful in mobilizing the environmental movement while others are not. In addition, cultural analysis reveals how discourse and ritualization impact the solidarity, identity, and consciousness of movement participants, which also helps explain why a movement is successful.

In the following sections, cultural analysis will be applied to the study of environmental movements in Taiwan, the Philippines, and Hong Kong. The discussion will focus upon discourse and rituals. It will be argued that although environmentalism in these territories had Western origins and borrowed heavily from Western Green thinking, there also has been an indigenization process of environmentalism over the past two decades. Domestic religious discourse (folk religion, the Catholic Church, Buddhism), cultural values (familism, Feng Shui, and indigenous traditions), and rituals (religious parades, funerals, and the Catholic mass) have played a significant role in "framing," enhancing the solidarity, and empowering the environmental movements—leading to the emergence of Asian styles of environmental movements in the 1990s.

Taiwan: Folk Religion, Familism, and Multiculturalism

Taiwan's environmental movement successfully raised its people's concerns over environmental issues by inventing a "collective action frame" that combined Western environmentalism, Taiwanese folk religion, and Chinese traditional familism. Moreover, the rise of this movement also shows the potentiality of multiculturalism by including alternative viewpoints and voices from indigenous people and women in the environmental discourse.

Western Environmentalism

In Taiwan, the controversy over "development vs. ecosystem" in the early 1980s was largely inspired by Western Green thinking (Weller and Hsiao 1998). This was introduced and promoted by a pool of concerned Taiwanese intellectuals who disproportionately held American graduate degrees; they tend to be the younger, better-educated members of the new middle classes who are either working in the "non-productive," personal service sectors, or students and groups only marginally integrated in the labor market. The membership structure of Taiwan's several major national environmental organizations mainly consists of university professors, journalists, lawyers, engineers, and college students.

By bringing up neglected environmental issues in the 1970s and the early 1980s, Taiwan's environmental movements significantly aroused people's awareness of the environmental crises around them. For example, today more than 80 percent of the Taiwanese people regard the environment's quality as serious or very serious. Environmental movements also receive social support from more than 50 percent of the population in various opinion surveys (Hsiao 1998).

In Taiwan, national environmental organizations see themselves as reiterating Western developments in environmental consciousness and organization. They mainly focus on global issues such as deforestation, nuclear power, the ozone layer, and the greenhouse effect, avoiding local culture and community completely. Strongly influenced by Western environmentalism, Taiwanese national environmental organizations somehow reject the localism inherent in the use of Asian culture.

In contrast, incorporating the suffering and grievances of victimized people in their communities, local environmental activists and advocates have transformed and reinterpreted the academic debate into simple statements and slogans compatible with extant cultural schemas (folk religions and familism) and are able to reach a wider audience.

Temples, Religious Parades, and Ghost Festivals

In Taiwan, pollution disputes between polluting enterprises and local residents often draw upon preexisting social networks and folk religions in the negotiation process. Local temples serve as fund-raising agents for protests, a public space for information exchange and mass gatherings, and, most important, a well-established network to mobilize people (Hsiao 1988: 133). Rituals of folk religion are transformed into vehicles for mobilization and enhancing the legitimacy of environmental protests.

For example, protests against Taiwan's fifth naphtha cracker made very effective use of folk religion. Since many leaders of local protests were folk religion specialists, they brought in Shen Nong—the God of agriculture—to support their protests. They used the simplest method of divination, throwing two curved pieces of bamboo root (*poe*), which can come up "yes," "no," or "laughing." Defying the odds, local religious leaders said the *poe* came up "yes" nine times in a row. They said when the dominant Kuomintang (KMT, the Nationalist Party) tried the same device, the *poe* always showed up "no." Consequently, when activists told local residents that the planned protest was approved and blessed by deities as shown through the *poe,* this religious sanction effectively increased the number of participants in various large-scale demonstrations. As Weller and Hsiao (1998) point out, "as protectors of community welfare, and often as symbols of community as opposed to national or other interests, deities provide easy cultural opportunities for these [anti-pollution] movements."

In the blockade of China Petrochemical Plant, a thousand riot police were called out in force to prevent a renewal of the blockade. In response, local activists utilized the ritual of religious parades to reestablish the blockade. Activists mobilized the temple's traditional martial arts performing groups to support them while they set up a spirit altar at the gate. These performing groups involved dozens of young martial arts enthusiasts, armed with spears and swords, who performed traditional routines at important local festivals. They wore operatic costumes and make-up, and their steps were ritualized. Nevertheless, their weapons were real; the performers could fight, and the elements of real physical threat and religious backing were obvious to everyone. As a result, the police had to back down.

Local activists also used traditional ghost festivals to present their claims. The ghost festival, which included a parade of hells and costumed ghosts, was updated by local activists to include punishments for modern environmental sins. Local activists had schoolchildren paint the traditional water lanterns (sent down the river to announce the ceremony to drowned ghosts) with environmental themes. Activists talked about the river itself as an ancestor or the mother of civilization who was killed by her bad offspring. This theme captured the ideas of filial debt that allowed protesters to characterize pollution as an unfilial attack (*beixian wenhua*).

Familism, Funerals, and Gender

Thus, familism was frequently invoked in local environmental protests. The Taiwanese environmental movement even finds a niche in the familial argument that "parents leave the best for their children." It is well known that Taiwanese parents work hard in order to save resources for descendants or attempt to maximize an estate to be handed down. The way that environmentalism comes into play is that "resources" and "estates" are presented as not only material ones (house, land, cash, stock, etc.) but also include "the environment." In other words, the environment is interpreted as part of an estate that must be passed along to descendants (Weller and Hsiao 1998). Parents have the responsibility to hand down a cleaner and less polluted environment to their children, and environmental protection becomes a means to protect children. It is common to see banners like "Protect [the somewhere] Shore for Our Children and Grandchildren" and "Leave a Clean Planet for Our Children" in many locally based environmental protests and demonstrations. A fisherman's protest in Hualian, for example, read in part: "Dear people of Hualian County, teachers, mothers: Let us unite for the sake of our beloved sons and daughters, and absolutely oppose the China Paper factory, which continues to poison Hualian's seas and air."

It is also common for these demonstrations and protests to become family events: many parents brought their kids to go along. In a society strongly emphasizing the bond between parents and children, the deteriorating environment provoked the consciousness of "parenting" to act or fight in order to protect children. This is quite different from Western environmentalism embedded in individualistic tradition.

In addition, funeral rituals are some natural carriers for local environmental protests. In most cases, funerals place the local land, river, or sea as a dead parent. Such funerals fight for the moral high ground. By implication, holding such a funeral accuses the state or polluting companies of murdering the environment. In the three-year fight against the fifth naphtha cracker, the high point was the so-called "battle of the coffins." The protesters carried four coffins, intending to set up a spirit altar at the west gate of the factory compound, and thus reestablish their blockade. These coffins suggested the idea of mourning for a slain environment, just as they conjured up images of the discarded Confucian responsibility to the welfare of future generations.

The protest also added an element of threat, because the group carried traditional funeral wreaths, but wrote the names of factory managers on them.

Key players in Taiwan's environmental movement have been women. Considering the overall indifference of Taiwanese women to public issues, the environmental movement has an unusually high proportion of female participation and female-dominated movement organizations. The Homemakers' Union, an environmental movement organization made up of middle-class housewives, distinguishes itself from other male-dominated organizations by rooting its concerns in "softer" and "less academic" issues like recycling and energy conservation. Through cartoons and slogans, it also creates an image of "nurturing women" with regard to the relationship between human beings and nature. One example is a brochure in which a woman was pushing the bandaged earth in a wheelchair, with the slogan "Women take care of the wounded earth" (Lu 1991; Weller and Hsiao 1998). Through environmental issues, Taiwanese women step into a public sphere and make their voices heard.

Nevertheless, women participants tend to pay more attention to environmental issues relating to household and motherhood than other environmental matters. Household issues might be a fruitful strategy to extend the coverage of Taiwan's environmentalism and to draw mass participation from a less mobilized female pool. On the other hand, invoking household issues may reinforce the sexist stereotypes in the Taiwanese mass media and strengthen gender inequalities in the Taiwanese family—two obstacles that the Taiwanese women's movement long strived to overcome.

Protests by Indigenous People

Backed by the government's industrial policies, big conglomerates built polluting factories near or on the homeland of indigenous people. Also, "over the past 12 years, the government established six National Parks, of which, three are located at the historical homeland and hunting grounds of the indigenous Taiwanese" (Chi et al. 1996: 13). Once again these decisions were made without the native people's consent.

As a result, the indigenous people first got involved in the environmental movements in the mid-1980s by protesting the state's decision to remove their sacred ancestors' graves in road construction, opposing the expansion of a nuclear waste storage site and the development of a national park, and rejecting the construction of large-scale dams. Some of the slogans used by the indigenous people were: "to save our ancestors' homeland," "to safeguard our peaceful life," "do not pollute our children and their children."

In order to emphasize that they were the original inhabitants of the land to be destroyed, they wore traditional clothes, followed traditional customs in staging the protest, and spoke in their native languages. In doing so, the indigenous people tried to tell the state and the Han Chinese that the aborigines are the true masters of the homeland, and that no one has the right to ruin their land. The Yami tribe even applied the native concept of evil spirits (*yawned*) to condemn the nuclear waste from afar.

From the above cases, we detect a mixture of indigenous people's traditions (concepts, rituals, language) and contemporary environmentalism (protecting the environment and human life-styles) in Taiwan's environmental movements. There are also instances in which the younger, educated indigenous people played important initiating roles to persuade their elders to join the protests. It is this combination of the traditional and the modern, youth and the elderly, and even insiders (within the tribe) and outsiders (environmental activists, journalists, and intellectuals) that made the environmental movement of the indigenous people "culturally rich" and appealing.

The Philippines: The Church and Indigenous Tradition

The Catholic Church

The Philippines is a predominantly Roman Catholic society and the Church is a major social institution influencing beliefs and values. The Church in the Philippines historically evolved as a major bastion of political conservatism. In the 1960s, however, through the social teachings of Vatican II enunciating the Church's preferential option for the poor as well as the emergence of liberation theology urging Christians to actively fight for the oppressed, a section of the Church in the Philippines became socially and politically active.

While local priests and nuns immersed in poor communities were more likely to take an activist stance on social issues than their superiors, a small group (around 20 percent) of bishops was classified as activists or "progressives" who spoke out against state failures and social inequities much more boldly, particularly during the authoritarian period. The progressives were described as supportive of the "community of liberation" model of the Church; they were often assigned to administer dioceses in frontier areas of the country (Youngblood 1990).

In the 1970s, Basic Christian Communities (BCCs) were established in the parishes as an organizational infrastructure, weaving together the practice of faith with the livelihood, human rights, and social justice concerns of local villagers. A collection of parishes falls under the jurisdiction of a "diocese" headed by a bishop. In certain instances, bishops could also be active in environmental campaigns, as in the case of Bishop Gaudencio Rosales of Bukidnon, who supported the logging barricades in the parish of San Fernando.

On many occasions, villagers expressed concern about the environment and asked the local priest to help them understand their problems. The local priest would normally report on what was happening in his parish in meetings within the diocese. In an interview on how the anti-logging campaign was launched in Bukidnon, Bishop Rosales said:

> We went about it as a Church, as a diocese, through the BEC's [basic ecclesial communities] that are very strong in the parishes. It started in the BEC in the parish of San Fernando, which was in fact cited in the CBCP [Catholic Bishops Conference of the Philippines] pastoral letter. But that was way back in 1987. Once we had decided to take the issue, we began a massive information drive. It was all we talked about in our homilies in all the Masses throughout the diocese—from the Cathedral to the kapilyas [chapels] in the small sitios and barrios. The sisters and the lay leaders would conduct seminars among the people. The people saw the connection between the loss of their livelihood and the denudation of the forests and they decided, "Stop it!" Personally, it really amazed me. Not only by listening to them, but by praying with them, feeling their helplessness. I had to do a lot of reading about the whole thing—ecology, environment, etc. I went there (as bishop in 1982) completely ignorant about trees. And I found it was a blessing to be assigned in Mindanao, because the experience opened me to a lot of things, broadened my horizons, helped to really understand, what I now call the dialogues between man and nature. (Rosales 1992)

The parishes that were active in organizing BCCs and in pursuing social action programs at the height of martial law during the 1970s turned into ecologically oriented campaigns as resource mining and polluting activities of powerful economic corporations threatened the livelihood prospects of poor communities in the post-Marcos era. In the late 1980s, local church people were actively involved in helping people organize livelihood projects and campaign for environmental protection. When a broad environmental coalition called Green Forum was created in 1989, church-based groups were intrinsic components. In fact, Green Forum is also known as the NGO-PO-Church Forum on Social Equity, Sustainable Development, and Environment. In anti-logging campaigns in the towns of San Fernando (Bukidnon Province), Gabaldon (Nueva Ecija), and Midsalip (Zamboanga del Sur), local priests and church people supported the local villagers in their fight against big loggers who denude the mountains and cause droughts and floods affecting the farms in the lowland areas.

An interesting case was the series of actions launched by poor peasants in San Fernando, Bukidnon (Northern Mindanao), against logging activities. The rice and corn farms in the area depended on rainwater, since there was no irrigation system. With forest loss due to excessive logging, water became scarce due to the deterioration of the watersheds and fertile topsoil diminished due to soil erosion. In 1987, the local people requested the Redemptorists, a Catholic religious order based in the town during that period, to conduct ecology workshops in the community, to help them find the linkage between their deteriorating agricultural produce and environmental change. Many residents who participated in the workshops belonged to a local church-based environmental group named Pagbugtaw sa Kamatuoran (PSK), which literally translates into "to be awakened to the truth." Established in the early 1980s, the PSK provided organized opposition to the government's plan to build a dam in the Pulangi River, which would have flooded a large area of San Fernando. With the cancellation of the dam project, the PSK became inactive until the logging issue erupted.

The Stewardship of Nature

Environmental activists within the church are guided by the Christian belief in the responsibility of human beings as the stewards or guardians of nature, which is God's "creation" (the very idea of Genesis itself). The environmental movement's demand for the shift toward community management of natural resources is framed within the

Christian context in terms of community "stewardship" over resources.

In the Bishops' Plenary Assembly in 1988, a draft of a paper written by ecological advocates within the Church was circulated and approved by the bishops for circulation in all the churches in the Philippines as a pastoral letter entitled "What Is Happening to Our Beautiful Land?" This pastoral letter was later released to the media and read in Sunday Mass in churches. "As we reflect on what is happening in the light of the Gospel," this pastoral letter lamented, "we are convinced that this assault on creation is sinful and contrary to the teachings of our faith." Citing the biblical notion of Genesis or creation, the bishops emphasized that "God created this world; that He loves His world and is pleased with it; and that He created man and woman in His image and charged them to be stewards of His creation. God, who created our world, loves life and wishes to share this life with every creature."

Furthermore, the pastoral letter linked religious commitment with ecological responsibility in these terms: "As we look at what is happening before our eyes, and think of the horrendous consequences for the land and the people we would do well to remember that God, who created this beautiful land, will hold us responsible for plundering it and leaving it desolate. So will future generations of Filipinos."

In a call to action, it was indicated that "the task of preserving and healing is a daunting one given human greed and the relentless drive of our plunder economy. But we must not lose hope. God has gifted us with creativity and ingenuity. He has planted in our hearts a love for our land, which bursts forth in our songs and poetry. We can harness our creativity in the service of life and shun anything that leads to death" (Catholic Bishops Conference of the Philippines 1990). The bishops, at the same time, lauded the efforts of the local people of Bukidnon and Zamboanga del Sur who "defended what remains of their forest with their own bodies." In the face of the rampant assault on the environment, the pastoral letter urged the people "to avoid a fatalistic attitude" and to instead "organize around local ecological issues."

Catholic Mass

In July 1987, after a Catholic mass in the morning (a religious ritual ostensibly performed to strengthen the group's solidarity and resolve in their fight for justice), the local villagers proceeded to form a human blockade to prevent the logging trucks coming from the forest from leaving the town. According to Father Pat Kelly, a Canadian mission-ary providing support to the protesters, on the twelfth day of the log-ging blockade, a military detachment appeared. The villagers held a mass. There were 35–40 soldiers and 80–90 people. The people were crying, but wouldn't move (Broad with Cavanagh 1993).

Scheduling the Mass to begin the day of the protest activities, as in the above case of the logging barricade in San Fernando, Bukidnon, could be interpreted as a preparation for the painful struggle that lay ahead. By professing their faith and commitment to endure suffering just like Christ, and oneness with their community (the Christian com-munity), which was also village-centered in this case, local environ-mental activists were declaring in ritualistic fashion their readiness to persevere, as all good Christian soldiers–ecological warriors do, in the fight for nature and justice. To show their solidarity as part of a single community, in singing their praises to God (e.g., the "Our Father" prayer) during Mass, the people usually hold and raise each other's hands. The San Fernando logging barricade became a prelude to the practice of linking arms and using bodies to block the logging trucks leaving the forest with their haul of freshly cut timber.

Indigenous Tradition

Aside from the values of social justice and stewardship of nature pro-moted by Church-based ecological activists, the environmental move-ment also draws important values from the nature-based belief systems of indigenous people, which are highly protective of the environment. In a document entitled "Kabuuan: Spirituality and Development, Envi-ronment and the Integrity of Creation" prepared by Philippine NGOs led by the Green Forum for the 1992 Parallel NGO Forum on Environ-ment and Development held in Rio de Janeiro, Brazil, such indigenous systems as communal forest protection, shared water rights, and rever-ence for the soil were identified as key practices in conserving nature.

For example, the T'bolis of South Cotobato have a reverent attitude toward the land, which they consider the body of one of the sons of D'wata (the highest God); on this body, a variety of trees and plants grows profusely, covering it. In addition, among indigenous communi-ties in the Cordillera region in the northern Philippines, dead ancestors are traditionally believed to be owners of property and are expected to intervene in village affairs, especially in matters affecting the management of natural resources. Ancestors are known to be displeased by the alienation of land handed down through generations. These "ancestral lands" include the irrigated rice fields, which are considered non-alienable to non-kinsmen with the exception of emergency situations where non-kinsmen can produce the ritual requirements (e.g., animals to be sacrificed). These beliefs restrict access to land, thus protecting it from excessive use (Prill-Brett 1995).

Indigenous people also believe that there are spirits inhabiting the forest, streams, springs, cliffs, rivers, and caves, and that these spirits have prior rights to these areas. Any violation of the sacred abode of these spirits, especially at certain times of the day, would invite misfortune, accidents, illness, and calamities in the village. Mountain springs important to the continued production of irrigated rice paddies would dry up the moment the spirit of the spring abandons the area. A ritual called *apey* is usually performed, involving the building of a fire at the source of the spring; a chicken sacrifice offered to "warm up" the spring is thought to increase the flow of water. Soap and other pollution-causing substances brought to the spring are said to offend the water spirit, leading to its transfer to another village. On the other hand, the cutting of the sacred trees called the *papatayan* in Bontoc is *inayan* (taboo), and is supposed to bring misfortune to the offending party and the community as a whole. The practice of *lapat* between the Isneg and Tigguians requires the imposition of a taboo within a designated area, over a certain period of time, which disallows the exploitation of natural resources (Prill-Brett 1995).

Hong Kong: Buddhism, Taoism, and Feng Shui

Soft Environmentalism

Unlike their counterparts in Taiwan and the Philippines, the leaders of Hong Kong territorywide environmental organizations tend to adopt a non-confrontational strategy of mobilization, through which they seek to work within existing parameters of the colonial government and capitalist consumer society. Instead of criticizing and challenging the colonial government and polluting corporations, the Hong Kong environmental leaders seek sponsorship and funding from big corporations, including Shell, Esso Green Fund, and China Light & Power. The focus of Hong Kong's environmental movements is raising environmental consciousness through such educational programs as exhibitions, festivals, fairs, and competitions, and corporate funding provides the major financial support to run these educational activities. The goal is to achieve greener consumption, consciousness, and life-style through policies such as paper saving and recycling, bringing your own bag to shop (using fewer plastic bags), organic farming in the New Territories, eco-tours to tropical rain forests, and vegetarianism.

For Chau (1995: 100), raising "green" consciousness in Hong Kong is a more important task than engaging in so-called "confrontational" environmental movements. This is because the transformation of a green consciousness and life-style will produce the following results: "(1) the supporters for the 'green' movements will rapidly increase, and (2) the most serious societal problems such as the 1997 transition, the pressure of living, illness, and the meaning of existence will be resolved, so will be the ecological crisis."

The "Greening" of Buddhism and Taoism

In Hong Kong, Buddhism and Taoism were invoked to promote "green" values. Buddhism is said to attach great importance to the conservation and protection of the environment. Chau (1989: 209) cites a Buddhist story in which monks are forbidden to cut down trees. Once, when a monk cut a tree's branch, the spirit of that tree complained to the Buddha that by cutting down the branch, the monk cut off his child's arms.

In addition, Buddhism regards survival as an undeniable right of all species; as co-inhabitants of this planet, other species have the same right to survival that human beings enjoy. There is another Buddhist story in which three princes see a tigress, surrounded by five cubs of seven days old. Hunger and thirst have exhausted the tigress, and her body is quite weak. On seeing her, a prince calls out, "the poor animal suffers from having given birth to the five cubs only a week ago! If she finds nothing to eat, she will either eat her own young, or die of hunger!" When the prince sacrifices himself to feed the hungry tigress and save her cubs, this act propels him to full enlightenment and Buddhahood (Wall 1994).

Taoism, too, is perceived as capable of providing a metaphysical foundation for environmental ethics. The sayings of Lao Tzu, the founder of Taoism, are frequently reinterpreted to justify the claims of environmentalism. For example, Lao Tzu's saying "a tower of nine storeys begins with a heap of earth. The journey of one thousand li [miles] starts from where one stands," is read as "things simply work in accordance with the laws of nature. Anyone who tries to do things in violation of the laws of nature is doomed to failure." The sayings in Taoism that "he who takes an action fails" and "the sage takes no action and therefore does not fail" are interpreted as "he who takes action in violation of the laws of nature fails" and "the sage acts in accordance with the laws of nature and therefore does not fail" (Ip 1986: 101).

In addition, Buddhist leaders and organizations are frequently mobilized to promote environmental movements. Fok Tou-Hui, the leader of Fa Ju Xue Wu (Academy for Buddhist Teaching), is a close friend of Simon Chau, the symbolic leader of Hong Kong's environmental movements. Po Lin Che (the largest Buddhist temple, with its giant Buddha statue on Lantau Island) is highly receptive to the Green Power's calling for a vegetarian life-style.

Green Life-style and Consciousness in Hong Kong

Besides the "greening" of Buddhism and Taoist teaching, the Buddhist life-style is articulated as an integral part of the environmental movement in Hong Kong. For example, the Buddhist life-style is used to endorse Green Power's vegetarianism. Meals should be based mostly on cereals, and there should be decreased or non-consumption of sharks' fins, swallows' nests, snakes, and other kinds of exotic food, because Buddhism believes that it is wrong to kill animals.

In addition, Buddhism is said to endorse the use of renewable materials over non-renewable ones. From a Buddhist point of view, non-renewable goods must be used only if they are indispensable, and then only with the greatest care and the most meticulous concern for conservation. To use non-renewable goods heedlessly or extravagantly is an act of violence against nature (Wall 1994).

Furthermore, Chinese traditional medicine and medical practices are also endorsed by Hong Kong environmental leaders. Natural health therapy (a preventive medicine that involves the flushing of intestinal organs periodically), herbal medicine, acupuncture, breathing exercises (*chikung*), foot reflexive massage, meditation, and yoga are all promoted by green activists (Chau 1995: 100).

Promoting the indigenization of Western environmentalism, environmental leaders were very successful in raising green consciousness in Hong Kong in the early 1990s. There were green programs on most radio and TV channels—like "Green Studio" produced by Radio Television Hong Kong, "Green Time" broadcasted by the Asia Television, as well as green columns in major newspapers. Subsequently, the five leaders of Green Power all became occupied in key cultural industries as radio program director, mass media consultant, press editor cum producer, public relations consultant, and columnist–writer.

Feng Shui (Cosmology)

It may be mentioned in passing that the new town development in Hong Kong highlighted the irony of and controversies around Feng Shui, the Taoist Cosmology of Wind and Water (Freedman 1979). The interpretations of Feng Shui are in the hands of self-proclaimed experts who work with sets of prior assumptions about specific spatial localities without much validity, reliability, and verification. It is not unusual that the Feng Shui experts' opinions strongly influence development programs in the New Territories. In many cases, Feng Shui experts are employed by powerful local leaders to defend their property rights.

Coupled with the colonial governance in the New Territories, which endorsed a system of division of authority at the level of local governance in the New Territories with the Rural Committees (centrally coordinated by the Heung Yee Kuk, with rather strong power, vis-à-vis the colonial government, to interpret the extent of local traditionalism and heritage), the Feng Shui cosmology has been used by local leaders to justify their "compensatory" claims for the violation of the natural environment in the New Territories when constructing housing, roads, railway lines, and harbors. In other words, environmental struggles around the Feng Shui cosmology often evolve around monetary compensation. This is because the Hong Kong colonial government was willing to pay considerable sums of money as compensation to local power holders in order to gain the latter's agreement in the New Territories' development projects (Bruun 1995). As a result, instead of promoting the goal of sustainable development, the power-driven and profit-led Feng Shui discourse is actually helping transform the New Territories into a polluted locality.

Conclusion: Asian Styles of Environmental Movements

In many Asian countries, environmental movements are an imported product from the West. Environmental movement leaders are Western educated and strongly influenced by the Western green discourse. Nevertheless, in the mobilization of community residents to protest, local activists began a process of indigenization through which Asian religions, cultural values, and rituals are incorporated into the environmental moments.

Common to all three cases discussed in this chapter, local activists invoke religious sanctions to legitimize protest activities. In the 1980s, when many Asian states were under authoritarian rule, local activists needed religious forces to unite community residents and consolidate support against political repression and violence. In Taiwan, local temples are important sites of environmental protests. Local deities, religious parades, and ghost festivals are key components of environmental protests against the polluting companies. In the Philippines, the Catholic Church, as a central institution, is a focal point for citizen mobilization in environmental struggles at the local level. Its religious Mass is often used to bless environmental movements. In Hong Kong, Buddhism and Taoism are invoked to endorse green lifestyles stressed by the leaders of territorywide environmental organizations.

Besides religion, there is a reinterpretation of dominant Confucian values for environmental purposes. In addition, familism is invoked to condemn polluting companies, because the latter threaten the local people's *zisun* (descendants). Funerals are used to mourn the murder of the environment. And motherhood is invoked to enlist the support of women to protect the wounded earth.

Finally, environmental movements frequently invoke indigenous traditions in order to protect their communities and life-styles. Taiwan's environmental movements lend support to the aborigines' fight for their unique way of life and land ownership. In the Philippines, indigenous communities use the spirits of ancestors who reside in the mountains, trees, and lakes in their efforts to protect the natural environment from poaching by developers. However, in Hong Kong, the cosmology of Feng Shui is invoked by powerful landowners in the New Territories for monetary gain and political power.

The above analysis questions Pye's conception of the paternalistic nature of Asian political culture, which endorses the status quo. Instead of stressing harmony, consensus, and conformity, Asian religions, cultural values, and rituals provide fertile ground to promote radical environmental discourses and movements.

In fact, this indigenization of Western environmentalism through the incorporation of radical Asian religions, cultural values, and rituals empowers local environmental protests, enabling them to challenge dominant authoritarian states in the 1980s. Furthermore, the fusion of local religion and native cultural values into environmental movements also created distinctive styles of Asian environmentalism, in contrast to its Western green counterpart.

It would be very interesting to see whether the cultural analysis in this chapter can be applied to other Asian countries with a different cultural configuration. For example, how do the Buddhist-dominated Thai culture and the Muslim-dominated Indonesian culture affect the development of environmental movements? As a pioneer study, this chapter has contributed by bringing culture back into the analysis of environmental movements in Asia.

References

Broad, Robin, with John Cavanagh. 1993. *Plundering Paradise: The Struggle for the Environment in the Philippines.* Berkeley: University of California Press.

Bruun, Ole. 1995. "Fengshui and the Chinese Perception of Nature." In *Asian Perceptions of Nature: A Critical Approach,* edited by Ole Bruun and A. Kalland. Surrey: Curzon Press.

Catholic Bishops Conference of the Philippines. 1990. *Catholic Bishops Conference of the Philippines: Letters and Statements, 1984–1990.* Manila: CBCP.

Chau, Simon. 1989. *Green Thinking.* (In Chinese). Hong Kong: Ming Chang Publisher.

———. 1995. *The Magic of Life.* (In Chinese). Hong Kong: Ching Wen Publisher.

Chi, Chun-Chieh, H.H. Michael Hsiao, and Juju Chin-Shou Wang. 1996. "Evolution and Conflict of Environmental Discourse in Taiwan." Paper presented at the Annual Meeting of the Association for Asian Studies, Honolulu, Hawaii.

Deyo, Frederic. 1989. *Beneath the Miracle: Labor Subordination in the New Asian Industrialism.* Berkeley: University of California Press.

Freedman, Maurice. 1979. "Geomancy." In *The Study of Chinese Society,* edited by William Skinner. Stanford: Stanford University Press.

Hsiao, Hsin-Huang Michael. 1988. *Anti-Pollution Protest Movement in Taiwan in the 1980s.* (In Chinese). Taipei: Environmental Protection Administration.

———. 1994. "The Character and Changes of Taiwan's Local Environmental

Protest Movements, 1980–1991." (In Chinese). In *Environmental Protection and Industrial Policies,* edited by Taiwan Research Fund, pp. 550–573. Taipei: Vanguard Publications.

———. 1998. "Normative Conflicts in Contemporary Taiwan." In *The Limit of Social Cohesion,* edited by Peter Berger, pp. 320–351. Boulder: Westview Press.

Ip, Po-Keung. 1986. "Taoism and Environmental Ethics." In *Religion and Environmental Crisis,* edited by E.C. Hargrove. Athens: University of Georgia Press.

Lu, Hwei-Syin. 1991. "Women's Self-Growth Groups and Empowerment of the 'Uterine Family' in Taiwan." *Bulletin of the Institute of Ethnology* 71: 29–62.

McAdam, Doug. 1994. "Culture and Social Movements." In *New Social Movements,* edited by Enrique Laraña, Hank Johnston, and Joseph Gusfield. Philadelphia: Temple University Press.

Prill-Brett, June. 1995. "Indigenous Knowledge System on Natural Resource Conflict Management." *Diliman Review* 43: 57–64.

Pye, Lucian. 1985. *Asian Power and Politics: The Cultural Dimensions of Authority.* Cambridge: Harvard University Press.

Rosales, Gaudencio. 1992. "Interview: People Can Prevail over Forest Raiders." *Manila Chronicle* (February 26).

Snow, David, E. Burke Rochford, Jr., Steven K. Worden, and Robert D. Benford. 1986. "Frame Alignment Processes, Micromobilization, and Movement Participation." *American Sociological Review* 51: 464–481.

Wall, D. 1994. *Green History.* London: Routledge.

Weller, Robert, and Hsin-Huang Michael Hsiao. 1998. "Culture, Gender, and Community in Taiwan's Environmental Movement." In *Environmental Movements in Asia,* edited by Arne Kalland and Gerald Persoon. Copenhagen: Nordic Institute for Asian Studies.

Youngblood, Robert. 1990. *Marcos Against the Church: Economic Development and Political Repression in the Philippines.* Ithaca: Cornell University Press.

9

The Impact of Democratization on Environmental Movements

Su-Hoon Lee, Hsin-Huang Michael Hsiao, Hwa-Jen Liu,
On-Kwok Lai, Francisco A. Magno, and Alvin Y. So

Acronyms

CPAR	Congress for People's Agrarian Reform	KMT	Kuomintang (Nationalist Party)
CSMs	Civil Society Movements	NGOs	Non-Governmental
DPP	Democratic Progressive Party		Organizations
EIS	Environmental Impact Statements	POs	People's Organizations
		PRRM	Philippine Rural Reconstruc-
EPA	Environmental Protection Agency		tion Movement
		SRDDP	Sustainable Rural District
KAPMA	Korea Anti-Pollution Movement Association		Development Program
		USAID	United States Agency for
KFEM	Korean Federation of Environmental Movements		International Development
		WWF	World Wildlife Fund

Introduction

The 1980s were heralded as a decade of democratization throughout the world. The demise of military regimes in Latin America in the late 1970s was followed by another wave of democratization in Asia in the 1980s. The Philippines ended its long-lasting dictatorial rule in 1986 when Marcos was removed from power in a popular upheaval. In the mid-1980s, burgeoning movements pressing for democratization emerged in South Korea and Taiwan. In the late 1980s, democratic transitions took place in many former socialist states in Eastern Europe, including Poland and Czechoslovakia. By the 1990s, electoral politics, with the presence of opposition parties and challenging bids for presidency by multiple candidates, were basically institutionalized in many Asian states, with pressures growing in many others.

Civil society, once suppressed, began to emerge in these former authoritarian states. In the 1990s, environmental movements (encompassing anti-pollution, environmental protection, anti-nuclear, and peace movements), economic justice movements, feminist movements, and consumer protection movements became highly active. These so-called "civil society movements" (CSMs) were not classical class struggles, because their interests transcended class lines and did not necessarily intend to destroy capitalism. Instead, civil society movements aimed to serve societal interests through reforming the existing capitalist system. In this respect, civil society movements tended toward a social democracy model with an emphasis on the welfare state.

Observing the simultaneous unfolding of democratization and environmental movements in Asia, researchers want to examine the intricate relationship between these two phenomena. The aim of this chapter is to examine the impact of democratization on environmental movements in Asia. Thus, the central research question of this chapter is: What role has democratization played in the emergence and transformation of environmental movements in Asia?*

To start with, democratization is conceived as a process that goes through the following three phases: (1) *liberalization,* with the relaxation of authoritarian rule; (2) *democratic transition,* characterized by the emergence of competitive elections at the national level and the insertion of civil rights clauses into the constitution; and (3) *democratic consolidation,* which refers to the institutionalization of electoral rules in the civil society. Democratic consolidation is indicated by the

---

*This chapter will focus on the impact of democratization on the contour of environmental movements in Asia. Of course, it would be important to study the impact of environmental movements on the contour of democratization in Asia too. Although the issues concerning environmental impact on democratization will be touched upon here and there, this subject is too complicated to be dealt with in this chapter.

fact that the ruling party is willing to step down and concede power to an opposition party after experiencing electoral defeat.

To what extent, then, are the contours of environmental movements shaped by the three phases of democratization? In other words, in what ways have democratic transitions and consolidation led to the emergence and transformation of environmental movements? And in what ways has incomplete democratization (the inability to attain democratic consolidation) modified the path of environmental movements?

To answer the above questions, this chapter will examine three cases (South Korea, Taiwan, and the Philippines) in which democratic consolidation has occurred and one other case (Hong Kong) in which there is incomplete democratization. It will be argued that while these four countries' democracy movements and environmental movements share a similar pattern of partnership during the phase of liberalization, a variety of patterns emerge in environmental movements during the phases of democratic transition and consolidation. Where democratization has been achieved—in the cases of Taiwan, South Korea, and the Philippines—environmental movements acted either as *partners* or *guardians* to the democratic forces. On the other hand, where democratic consolidation is elusive or incomplete, as in the case of Hong Kong, environmental movements were detoured to *bystanders* from democracy movements.

South Korea: Partnership All the Way

Environmental activists trace the roots of South Korea's environmental movements to the democratization of the 1970s and the early 1980s. In South Korea, environmental and democratic movements were partners throughout the three phases of liberalization (1983–87), democratic transition (1987–92), and democratic consolidation (1992 to the present).

The Period of Liberalization (1983–1987)

Asian industrialization in the post–World War II era was a product of authoritarian states. State repression kept labor docile and cheap; state and business monopolies channeled resources to export-oriented industrialization; and state censorship ensured that high-speed, export-oriented industrialization strategy prevailed over other social values or political goals.

Under such authoritarian rule in South Korea, Chun Doo Hwan came to power through a military coup in 1980. Chun used extraordinary measures to squash opposition and pacify civil society in his first three years. Chun's rule was no less harsh than Park Chung Hee's rule during his last years in power, buttressed as it was by the sheer exercise of coercive force. But the regime could not stand on continuous repression alone. After three years of fierce efforts, Chun succeeded in stabilizing his regime as the South Korean economy began to grow in double-digit figures. Chun's regime was also allowed to host the 1988 Summer Olympic Games in Seoul, thus boosting Chun's prestige in the international arena.

In late 1983, Chun decided to boost his political legitimacy through a series of liberalization measures (Seong 1993: 110). The government released dozens of political prisoners, allowed activist students and professors to return to their schools, and granted more freedom of activity for civic organizations. This liberalization, though limited in scope, greatly intensified anti-regime struggles among students, opposition parties, and all other dissident groups (Hsiao and Koo 1997).

In this period of liberalization, South Korean environmental and democratic movements became partners to promote each other's cause. There was a fusion of goals between these two movements. The South Korean environmental movements raised questions about the harmful consequences of the state's high-speed industrialization; they thereby were highly critical of the authoritarian state. For example, since pollution was a product of business monopoly and military repression, the end to this authoritarian regime through democratization was thus seen by South Korean environmental activists as the most appropriate path to stop ever-increasing, life-threatening pollution.

On the other hand, the South Korean democracy movements often disguised themselves as environmental movements in order to avoid political suppression. Up to the 1980s, anti-pollution was one of the few arenas in which the Korean military regime allowed public demonstrations. Environmental movements, which involved ordinary community residents and carried moral authority, were much harder to suppress than democracy movements.

The South Korean environmental and democracy movements also utilized a common confrontation strategy to accomplish their goals. Strongly influenced by the protest strategy of the democracy movement against the military regime, the anti-pollution movement in the early 1980s was radicalized, resistant, and confrontational.

Democratic Transition (1987–1992)

In early 1987, the revelation that a college student was tortured to death by the police played a catalytic role in mobilizing a huge number of protests. Student street demonstrations occurred daily, joined by many workers and urban residents. In June 1987, street demonstrations had grown too big and too widely spread to be controlled by the police alone. Subsequently, Roh Tae Woo, the chairperson of the ruling Democratic Justice Party and a military academy classmate of Chun Doo Hwan, accepted all the demands made by the opposition party and agreed to hold a direct presidential election at the end of 1987. This was seen as the beginning of the democratic transition in South Korea (Hsiao and Koo 1997).

During this period of democratic transition, there was a loosening of the coercive state and the activation of civil society (Lee 1993). As a result, Korean environmental movements greatly expanded their organizations and scope of activities. The Korean Anti-Pollution Movement Association (KAPMA) was formed in 1988, and the Korean Anti-Nuclear and Anti-Pollution Peace Movement Research Institute as well as the National Headquarters for the Nuclear Power Eradication Movement were formed in 1989. Moreover, these Seoul-based organizations were empowered by local anti-pollution struggles in Ulsan, Pusan, Yeocheon, Mokpo, and Youngkwang.

There was also a shift in movement strategy from militant confrontation to peaceful protest. During the democratic transition, the South Korean environmental movements' strategy changed to non-violence and peaceful action, in contrast to the previous militant and confrontational strategy of the democracy movement against the repressive military regime. In this new era, the Korean environmental movements put a priority on creating a mass base, acquiring expertise (on the issues that they took up), and sought mass media attention and public sympathy on their side.

Democratic Consolidation (1992 to the Present)

With the election of Kim Young Sam to the presidency in the December 1992 election, South Korea achieved democratic consolidation. A new civilian government replaced the past military regimes, signaling democratic consolidation from authoritarian rule. In 1993, Kim Young

Sam prosecuted many of the past military elite members, investigated past political corruption, carried out a radical shakeup of the military establishment, and jailed two former military presidents (Hsiao and Koo 1997).

In this period of democratic consolidation, environmental movements were still partners with democratic forces. For one thing, many former leaders of democracy movements transformed themselves into leaders of environmental movements and other social movements. Consider the Korean Federation of Environmental Movements (KFEM), the largest and most active environmental organization in South Korea. Choi Yul, KFEM's secretary-general, is a former democratization movement activist. Under the Park regime, Choi was involved in the famous 1975 "Myongdong Cathedral incident" and arrested on charges of violation of Emergency Decree No. 9—General Park's notorious weapon to repress political dissidents. Choi was later sentenced to prison for six years. In fact, at least four of the eight members of the Executive Committee of the Korea Anti-Pollution Movement Association (as it was known before transforming itself into the KFEM) were activists in democracy movements.

In addition, environmental leaders actively participated in electoral politics. In the 1995 local elections, KFEM solicited "environmental candidates" to run for multilayered positions in the government. KFEM supported a total of 46 candidates, of which 32 won the election and 2 won mayoral positions.

On the other hand, observing the growing influence of the environmental movements in electoral politics, Korean political leaders have shown serious interest in environmental issues. Many political leaders selected environmental movement leaders as their policy advisers or full-time aides, sponsored conferences on environmental issues, and some political leaders even maintained close personal ties with environmental activists. During elections, the environment becomes a popular issue and virtually every candidate claims to be pro-environment. In this respect, democratic consolidation has empowered the environmental movements in South Korea.

Taiwan: From Partners to Guardians

Similar to the South Korean case, Taiwanese environmental movements and democracy movements were partners during the phase of liberalization (1980–87). However, in contrast to the South Korean case, Taiwanese environmental leaders were highly skeptical of the democratic forces during the phases of democratic transition and consolidation (1987–present).

Liberalization (1980–1987)

In the early 1980s, the ruling Kuomintang (KMT—the Nationalist Party) softened its attitudes toward the opposition forces. Instead of using repressive measures to arrest the growth of opposition forces, President Chiang Ching-kuo opted for a mediated dialogue with opposition leaders. It was under this liberalization policy that opposition forces formed a quasi-party under the name of the Public Policy Research Association, which later evolved into the opposition Democratic Progressive Party (DPP) in September 1986.

As in Korea, liberalization led to the emergence of many new social movements in Taiwanese civil society. In Taiwan, democracy movements and environmental movements became the two strongest movements challenging the authoritarian rule of the KMT. Although other social movements—including those of consumers, women, students, and aborigines—emerged and grew in the early 1980s, only democracy and environmental movements had the potential to transform the authoritarian state into a democratic one. In Taiwan, the importance of the environmental movement rested on its ubiquitous nature and direct impact on local politics. The Taiwanese anti-pollution protests of the environmental movement were never limited to certain locations (such as an urban/rural dichotomy), but occurred nationwide, in almost every city and county. According to a calculation of the number of protests launched by seven social movements from 1983 to 1988, the protests of the environmental movement occurred 582 times and made up about one-fifth of all protests (Wu 1990: 57–59). As Hsiao (1994: 553) states: "among all social movements, the environmental movement is the one that has extended most widely and [is] most localized."

Also similar to the South Korean case, Taiwanese environmental movements were partners with democracy movements in challenging the authoritarian KMT rule. For example, most Taiwanese pollution disputes never ended in movement victory. Shutdowns of polluting factories or prevention of certain industries from invading neighborhoods might be the ultimate goals of protests, but the achievement of these was very rare. Thus, the pervasive and multiplied grievances of anti-pollution residents were soon transformed into hostility toward the authoritarian rule of the KMT, which had been unable to either control the polluting industries or alleviate the victims' pain. These grievances also metamorphosed into support toward democratic leaders who strongly challenged the KMT's rule. Though political scientists seldom study party affiliation and preference among movement constituents in general, it is safe to say that angry anti-pollution residents contributed to voting gains for anti-KMT candidates, and that the protests served as a tool to shake and break down the cohesiveness of the KMT's local control.

In turn, the legitimization of Taiwanese environmental movements created a set of collective action repertoires and a "public sphere" that political dissidents and social activists could utilize to facilitate the reorganization of the political structure. Subsequently, democratic forces frequently participated in the anti-pollution movement to discredit the authoritarian state, facilitating the rise of opposition forces, the institutionalization of opposition parties, and the transformation of authoritarian one-party rule to a fledgling, functioning multiple-party system.

Democratic Transition and Consolidation (1987 to the Present)

In 1987, Chiang Ching-kuo not only tolerated the establishment of the opposition DPP, but also lifted martial law, which led to another wave of organized protest and new social movements, signaling the democratic transition in Taiwan. In the early 1990s, the Temporary Provision to suppress domestic rebellion was repealed, the Period of Mobilization and Combating Rebellion was put to an end, and a constitutional amendment was approved. All these policies represented a political break from undemocratic, extra-constitutional structures and the restoration of a constitution for the government of Taiwan. The mid-1990s saw the first popular and direct elections of mayors in two major cities, the Taiwan provincial governor, and the president of Taiwan. Most important, the capturing of some of these important posts by opposition DPP members indicated, to a certain extent, that Taiwan has achieved democratic consolidation, because the ruling KMT was willing to relinquish its power over these important posts after electoral defeats.

At first glance, Taiwan's environmental movement also seems to have been a beneficiary of democratization. Induced by green thinking and frequent environmental protests, several legislative and institutional reforms took place in Taiwan. Tougher measures of pollution control were adopted, and two important environmental laws (Pollution Disputes Resolution Law and Environmental Impacts Assessment Act) were passed and enacted. In addition, the Environmental Protection Administration (EPA) was promoted to a cabinet-level agency in 1987.

But it is hardly the case that these reforms have effectively improved Taiwan's deteriorating environment. Or, to put it differently, besides these legislative and institutional reforms, the environmental movement itself has not substantially benefited from Taiwan's democratization. The environmental movement may find legislators of opposition parties to voice its demands, but so can the pro-growth business/industrial sector. As Tarrow (1994: 170) states: "The structure of politics through which movement demands are processed forces them into a common crucible from which modest reforms are the most likely outcome of the struggle." Taiwan's new environmental regulations have indeed been the products of bargains and compromises between pro-environment and pro-growth legislators. Also, due to pressure from pro-growth legislators, party cadres, and government bureaucrats, the extent to which these "soft" regulations have been fully implemented by the EPA was also critically questioned by environmental groups.

In addition to undermining and compromising environmental regulation and policies, in the past decade the KMT party has developed close alliances with the business/industrial sector and launched various ambitious economic development projects, including the building of a nuclear power plant, the taking over of coastal wetlands for industrial facilities, and even facilitating construction of petrochemical industrial parks. Through its control of the electoral majority and agenda-setting processes, in most cases, the KMT defeated the environmental movement and its law-making allies in the Legislative Yuan, and many pro-growth policies were adopted and ironically legitimized by procedural democracy.

Even worse, there is some indication that the Democratic Progressive Party (DPP), the biggest opposition party and once the most solid political advocate of the environmental movement, has not proven firm on environmental causes. Its stands on environmental issues are tenuous. The stronger the DPP becomes, the more difficult it is to figure out its priorities on the environment–growth policy controversy. For example, though the DPP took a position against the construction of a fourth nuclear power plant, several DPP magistrates eagerly invited highly polluting industries to move to their counties at the expense of coastal wetlands. Though environmentalism is one of the most important policy platforms that DPP candidates adopted to gain votes during past elections, environmental groups now criticize the DPP for accepting unacceptable compromises in "under-the-table" negotiations with the ruling KMT regarding environmental issues. The founding of the Green Party in 1995, consisting of more than twenty environmental and welfare groups, was the clearest sign that environmental activists were disappointed at the DPP's shifting environmental stands as it approaches the center of power in Taiwan's politics.

Finally, as democratization proceeded, many substantial political donations flowed into major political parties instead of social movement organizations, the centralization of financial contributions causing many environmental groups to suffer from increased financial pressures. The environmental movement is now tightly guarding its former movement allies, the opposition political parties.

What, then, explains the dissolution of the partnership between environmental movements and the DPP, representative of democratic forces during Taiwan's democratic consolidation? This may be due to the de-radicalization of the DPP after the institutionalization of competitive elections. The DPP, as a minority opposition party, wants to win over the ruling KMT and control the government through winning the elections. The DPP thus needs support, particularly financial support, from anti- or non-environmental constituencies (such as businesspeople, labor unions, and moderate politicians). If the DPP calculates that it wins more votes through a scaled-down environmental agenda, it will adopt such a platform in order to turn itself into a ruling party.

On the other hand, in South Korea, after the military regime was replaced by a civilian government, there was no dominant party system like the KMT in Taiwan. As civil society is highly critical of big business conglomerates, and as the public is highly receptive to notions of economic justice and environmentalism, Korean political parties compete with one another to win voter approval with their environmental platforms.

The Philippines: From Subsidiary to Partnership

Like South Korea and Taiwan, the Philippines also reveals the crucial impact of democratic consolidation on environmental movements. In the Philippines, the environmental movement developed as a subsidiary of the broad democracy movement in the late 1970s. Given the temper of the times, the democratic agenda took center stage. In strategic terms, collective action in various conflict areas, including environment-related ones, was geared toward heightening the struggle against authoritarian rule. However, with the collapse of the Marcos regime in 1986, the environmental movement was freed from the restrictive demands of the anti-regime struggle. It became an equal partner with other democratic players in the social arena in the continuing effort to expand and deepen citizen participation in decision-making processes both at the state and local levels through the pursuit of a sustainable development agenda to empower local communities in gaining rights of tenure and control over public goods such as forest, mineral, and coastal resources.

Liberalization (1978–1985)

After the imposition of martial law in 1972, coercive measures were habitually employed by the Marcos regime and its business allies to silence opposition to their development policies. Subsequently in the period of liberalization from 1978 to 1985, environmental demands were often subsumed under the broad demands of democratic movements. Environmental coalitions were established in the late 1970s in opposition to giant infrastructure and development projects launched by the state and its business allies. Examples of these include protests against the negative environmental impact of the Chico River Dam in the Cordilleras and the Bataan Nuclear Power Plant in Morong. Opposition to these business activities was aimed not only at preventing ecological degradation, but also at discrediting the Marcos regime's economic agenda favoring its big business allies. Nested in the strategic context of democratic struggles, it became standard procedure to voice environmental demands (e.g., stop the Chico Dam construction) together with democratic calls to remove the Marcos regime from power. Thus, the face of Macli-ing Dulag (the anti–Chico Dam leader) often appeared together with those of slain opposition figures, like Benigno Aquino, Jr., in large paintings paraded in Manila's streets during the huge anti-Marcos rallies of the 1980s.

Due to the subordination of the environmental movements to democracy movements, the type of environmental activism that spilled over into the 1980s was influenced by the values and agendas of the democratic movement. It highlighted the negative relationship between environmental protection and authoritarianism. Indeed, environmental movements were formed in opposition to the ecological abuses that arose from the exclusion of public participation in development planning, the concentration of resources in a few hands, and the intolerance of alternative development strategies fostered under undemocratic political and economic structures.

The case of the Haribon Foundation is a good illustration of how a traditional conservation group, caught in the swirling tide of the democratization process, turned into a politically active and socially oriented environmental organization in the mid-1980s. Founded as a birdwatching society in 1972 by personnel from the Asian Development Bank and the U.S. embassy in Manila, Haribon began to shift its exclusive focus on birds to active advocacy of native biological diversity, natural resources, and indigenous culture under the leadership of Celso Roque. According to Roque, "poverty and the distorted distributional aspects of the political economy have grave ecological consequences" (Rush 1991). In 1986, Haribon launched a national campaign to save Palawan Province (where rich tropical forest ecosystems could still be found) from big logging companies. Haribon's brochure entitled "Save Our Only Planet Earth" asserted the "need for management of natural resources to be community-based, socially equitable, and scientifically sound." The demand for community-based resource management was linked to the effort to democratize access to natural resources, which under martial law was concentrated in the hands of big business allies of the Marcos regime.

Democratic Transition and Democratic Consolidation (1986 to the Present)

The democratic transition in the Philippines was marked by the downfall of the Marcos government in the face of a combined popular uprising and military insurrection. Political prisoners were freed and civil rights were restored under the Aquino government. A new constitution was fashioned in 1987 setting term limits for elected positions. However, a spate of military coup attempts rocked the government and successfully prevented initiatives from a certain section of the civilian leadership from prosecuting military officials guilty of human rights violations under the previous government. Due to the Aquino administration's lack of political will, many politicians and business allies of the Marcos regime escaped prosecution for corruption. In this sense, South Korea was more successful than the Philippines in redressing the severe injustice and abuse of power committed under dictatorial rule by punishing its worst perpetrators.

In formal political terms, democratic consolidation, defined on the basis of the institutionalization of competitive electoral processes, was achieved with the removal of the last coup threat in 1989, the holding of general elections in 1992, and a general sense of respect for the procedural requirements of circulating power through the ballot system. However, the restoration of electoral competition allowed the traditional politicians, including previous supporters of Marcos, to recycle themselves in the political scene. To a large extent, success in Philippine electoral politics was measured in terms of the capacity of candidates to activate access to financial resources necessary to oil campaign machineries during election time. The failure to institutionalize a party-list system also contributed to the maintenance of weak party structures, which facilitated the liberal switching of politicians from one party to another.

Nevertheless, under an elite-based democracy as opposed to authoritarianism, basic political freedoms and civil liberties received greater protection. Political opportunities for citizen mobilization and organized dissent widened. Government officials have also been subjected to intense public scrutiny by a vigorous mass media. Whereas national security was held sacred and in fact used as the "reason of state" in suppressing citizen rights during the dictatorship, with democratic consolidation environmentalists are instead advocating a notion of "natural security," which gives utmost priority to environmental protection and the life-based support systems of people. Thus, environmental groups pushed for the reduction of the defense budget and the redirection of funding priorities toward environmental protection and livelihood concerns.

In the post-Marcos era, a wide array of non-governmental organizations (NGOs) and people's organizations (POs) flourished. POs continued in the activist tradition of organizing citizens along sectoral and mass lines. NGOs, on the other hand, were established to provide research, training, technical, and organizational assistance to POs and unorganized local communities. Umbrella coalitions and networks of POs and NGOs, such as the Congress for a People's Agrarian Reform (CPAR), challenged state positions on land reform, fisheries reform, and foreign debt management. In 1989, more than 200 NGOs, POs, and church groups joined to form the Green Forum, the nation's biggest environmental coalition.

The civil society/NGO-PO formations in the country developed out of a long period of organizing and mobilizing people at the grassroots level to fight the dictatorship. With democratic consolidation, empowerment strategies were cultivated not only to enable people to participate in political processes, but to provide them as well with the capacity to defend their communities and local environments from development aggression against rich and influential outsiders. Thus, environmental campaigns were also struggles for the democratization of rights to resources. There has been a convergence of the radical democratic pursuit of citizen empowerment and the environmentalist demand for sustainable development. A good illustration of the simultaneous pursuit of empowerment strategies and local development initiatives can be seen in the experience of the Philippine Rural Reconstruction Movement (PRRM). Under the leadership of Horacio Morales, Jr., and Isagani Serrano, the PRRM's approach of education to combat ignorance, livelihood to fight poverty, health to fight disease, and self-government to fight civic inertia was expanded to a new framework called the Sustainable Rural District Development Program (SRDDP) on the scale of a district or a small province.

There are two main institutional developments that affected the dynamics of the Philippine NGOs. First, the 1987 Constitution emphasized that the state shall encourage NGOs and community-based organizations that promote local welfare. With the passage of the 1991 Local Government Code, NGOs are further provided the opportunity to participate in local development councils and resource management councils in municipalities and provinces all over the country. In addition, transnational funding agencies encouraged the growth of NGO activities at the community level. In the 1980s, many transnational funding agencies channeled food and relief aid to development NGOs and Church-based groups for distribution to poor communities in the rural areas. In the 1990s, the "debt-for-nature" swaps of the World Wildlife Fund (WWF) and the United States Agency for International Development (USAID) pumped in millions of dollars to the NGOs to participate in the implementation of environmental management projects in rural communities.

With the decentralization of state functions to local governments, partnerships between democratic and environmental activists were forged in order to effectively influence policymaking processes at the local level. In recent years, local electoral alliances successfully supported the mayoralty bids of environment-friendly candidates such as Sofronio Blando, who opposed illegal logging and advocated community-based forest management in the mountain town of Nagtipunan. Environmental groups have also been active in challenging big infrastructure and development projects sponsored by the state and its business allies. For instance, environmental protests delayed the construction of a coal-fired power plant in Calaca, Batangas, for three years. The joint use of strategic engagement and pressure politics by the environmental movement also yielded positive results. In 1990, the government adopted the Philippine Strategy for Sustainable Development, which compelled the incorporation of environmental concerns in development projects. Consequently, Environmental Impact Statements (EISs) are now required before large business investment activities are allowed to operate in the country.

In general, the return of competitive elections opened up greater opportunities for the environmental movement to elevate ecological issues into public concerns. In late 1991, the Green Forum launched its Earthvote Project aimed at developing a green electorate at the national level. With media support, it released a green guide for voters on how to choose candidates on the basis of ecological criteria. During the 1992 electoral campaign, the major presidential candidates, especially Fidel Ramos and Jovito Salonga, addressed environmental issues in their campaign speeches. Ramos, who eventually won the presidential elections, signed an executive order creating the Presidential Council for Sustainable Development, mandated with the task of proposing environmental policies and monitoring the government's compliance with environmental standards set during the Earth Summit in Brazil.

In the post-Marcos period, many democratic activists ended up occupying important government positions, and they have allied themselves with environmentalists in the advocacy of important environmental policies. During the debates in the early 1990s over a proposed law calling for a nationwide logging ban, legislators, especially in the Senate, who were active in the anti-Marcos opposition, supported the environmentalist position, while the more traditional oligarchy in the House of Representatives firmly resisted timber-cutting restrictions. While the logging ban initiative was eventually defeated, the character of alliance-making during the crucial policy struggles on the issue indicates how democrats and environmentalists could be important partners in the pursuit of sustainable development issues. Previous defeats in legislative battles such as the logging issue also show why environmental groups should develop a more comprehensive electoral strategy that builds on the Green Forum's Earthvote experience.

Hong Kong: From Partners to Bystanders

In Hong Kong, environmental movements started as partners to democracy movements in the early phase of democratic transition. But as Hong Kong's democratization ran into difficulties, environmental movements quickly dissociated themselves from democracy movements and adopted a "soft" strategy toward environmentalism.

Liberalization (Pre-1985) and Democratic Transition (Mid-1980s)

The Hong Kong case is quite different from other Asian cases because the former had a uniquely liberal colonial state. Unlike the authoritarian regimes in South Korea and the Philippines in the early 1980s, the colonial government in Hong Kong was liberal, with freedom of speech, freedom of political organization and public protest, and the absence of censorship. However, unlike the democratic regimes in South Korea and the Philippines in the 1990s, the colonial government of Hong Kong was highly undemocratic. The governor of Hong Kong was appointed by the British Parliament, with no input from Hong Kong citizens. Up to 1985, members of the Legislative Council of Hong Kong were appointed by the governor of Hong Kong, and elections to the top government posts and the Legislative Council were non-existent.

After the London government agreed to return the sovereignty of Hong Kong to China in 1984, economic integration between Hong Kong and mainland China intensified. Hong Kong capitalists began to relocate their factories across the border in China for cheaper production costs, leading to an estimated loss of 5 million jobs in the manufacturing sector. In addition, London, over Chinese opposition, initiated a modest reform to introduce a small number of indirectly elected seats through functional (occupational) constituencies to the legislature. In response, a robust democracy movement arose in Hong Kong since the mid-1980s, pushing for more directly elected seats in the legislature, a more accountable government and legislature, and human rights and civil liberties.

What was the relationship between the nascent democratization movement and environmental movements in colonial Hong Kong? At its inception through the Daya Bay Anti-Nuclear Movement in 1986, it seemed
that Hong Kong's environmental movement would, similar to its counterparts in South Korea and the Philippines, follow the path of partnership
with the democracy movement. In the Daya Bay incident, environmentalists joined forces with democratic activists to criticize the Hong Kong
government for its lack of representation; they adopted a public confrontation strategy; and there was a sharing of leadership and members between environmental movements and democracy movements.

Furthermore, at the community level, electoral politics and the new
consultative governance structure since the 1980s—like the District
Boards and the Regional and Urban Councils—provided fertile ground
for democratic activists to mobilize communities around environmental issues. On the other hand, community groups with concerns for
environmental and livelihood issues also cooperated with pro-democracy agencies, as in the Tsing Yi and Kwai Chung protests against
environmental hazards.

Incomplete Democratization (Late 1980s to the Present)

The growing power of the democratic forces in the mid-1980s threatened the Beijing government and Hong Kong business interests. The
latter feared that rapid democratization would bring political instability, more taxes, more rules and regulations, and a welfare society to
Hong Kong. Subsequently, an "unholy" alliance was formed between
the Beijing government and Hong Kong's big business community to
slow the process of democratization in Hong Kong. In drafting the
Basic Law (the mini-constitution of Hong Kong after 1997) in the late
1980s, the unholy alliance imposed a restricted democracy for the
post-1997 Hong Kong government. Only a third of the legislature seats
would be directly elected, and the chief executive of the Hong Kong
Special Administrative Region would be selected by a Selection Committee of 700 rather than elected through popular votes.

In light of democratic frustrations in Hong Kong in the late 1980s,
environmental movements quickly changed paths, adopting a "soft"
approach, and becoming bystanders to the democracy movements.
First, a high degree of differentiation of leadership and membership
existed between the two movements. Although coming from the same

middle-class professional background, Hong Kong's democracy activists seldom joined the territorywide environmental organizations, and Hong Kong's territorywide environmental organizations and activists (with the exception of the Reverend Fung Chi-Wood) seldom joined and participated in democratic protests. In this respect, cooperation and interpenetration between democracy movements and environmental movements were rather limited.

Second, the goals and world views of Hong Kong's pro-democracy organizations and territorywide environmental organizations differed. Hong Kong's democracy activists wanted a more representative government, a more accountable legislature, more autonomy from Beijing, more guarantees for human rights and civil liberties, more welfare, and a better working environment for the grassroots population. In contrast, the leaders of Hong Kong's territorywide environmental organizations tended to take a philosophical perspective on "protecting the environment by changing individual life-style." "Green Life-style" then became the focus of educational programs, exhibitions, and publications of environmental organizations. Thus, while the democracy movement's goal was to achieve structural, institutional transformations, territorywide environmental organizations stressed more individual, psychological, and life-style changes.

Third, the movement strategies of Hong Kong's pro-democracy organizations and territorywide environmental organizations were different. Perhaps due to their apolitical life-style and historical non-involvement in public protests, none of the territorywide environmental groups was ready to engage in political confrontation via public demonstrations. This "soft approach" toward environmentalism may be a result of the pro-establishment attitude of these environmental organizations, which want to work with the colonial government and business groups and seek the latter's funding support for their educational and promotional programs. On the other hand, pro-democracy groups, because of their experience in mobilizing grassroots populations in social protests since the 1970s, are highly militant and possess a much higher inclination for collective action than environmental groups. The pro-democracy groups are highly critical of the colonial government, big business, and Beijing; they see mass rallies as the best way to achieve their goals.

Finally, Hong Kong's environmental and democracy movements are competing for media coverage and scarce movement resources. For instance, the media coverage on the Daya Bay Anti-Nuclear Movement started to fade in 1987 when the journalists turned their attention to cover the democratic battles over direct elections for the 1988 Legislative Council. In addition, although other movement organizations such as the Professional Teachers' Union, Social Workers' General Union, and the Christian Industrial Committee strongly supported the Daya Bay protest in 1986, the energy of these movement organizations quickly shifted from the environment to direct elections and the drafting of the Basic Law when these democratic issues arose in 1988.

In the 1990s, pro-democracy groups began to incorporate environmental issues into their party platforms and agendas. Pro-democracy groups now have spokespersons on environmental affairs, and democracy activists often argue for environmental issues in the legislature and at various levels of the consultative governmental structure. However, environmental groups still rarely participate in democracy movements or endorse their mass mobilization strategies. It seems that Hong Kong's environmental movements are fated to be merely bystanders to the democracy movements.

Conclusion

It is interesting to note the temporal coincidence of democratic transitions and environmental movements in Asia. South Korea, Taiwan, the Philippines, and Hong Kong all achieved democratic breakthroughs at more or less the same time in the mid-1980s. Moreover, the environmental movements of these four countries/territories quickly blossomed in the initial stages of democratic transition. Observing this simultaneous unfolding of democracy and environmental movements, this chapter examined how democratic transitions and democratic consolidation shaped the contours of the environmental movements in the four Asian countries, and vice versa.

During the critical transition from liberalization to democratic breakthroughs in the four Asian countries, environmental movements and democracy movements were generally partners, cross-fertilizing and empowering each other. Being the two strongest social movements in society, democracy and environmental movements shared the same goals of overthrowing authoritarian regimes and creating a better environment. Very often, democracy movements disguised themselves as environmental movements to avoid political suppression, and environmental activists felt the need to institute a democratic state before the environment could be improved. There was a fusion of leadership and members between the two movements, and they adopted a common confrontation strategy to challenge the authoritarian regime and the polluters.

However, although the environmental movements and democracy movements in the four Asian countries were partners during the democratic breakthrough, these movements exhibited a variety of relationships in the course of democratic transition and democratic consolidation.

In South Korea, where democratic consolidation was achieved, as indicated by the civilian replacement of the military regime, environmental movements continued their partnership with democratic forces. Environmental leaders are active in promoting environmental candidates to run for elections, and political leaders have adopted a pro-environmental platform to appeal to environmental organizations and the general public.

Like South Korea, Taiwan has, to a certain extent, achieved democratic consolidation, as the opposition DPP was able to capture some important government posts in recent elections. However, many DPP members, absorbed in intense electoral politics in order to defeat the ruling KMT, wavered on critical environmental issues. Distrustful of the DPP, Taiwanese environmental groups formed a Green Party so as to keep a close watch on DPP environmental policies.

In the Philippines, too, the environmental movement developed as a subsidiary to the broad democracy movement in the late 1970s. Given the temper of the times, the democratic agenda took center stage as the Filipino social movements focused on the struggle against authoritarian rule. However, with the collapse of the Marcos regime in 1986, the environmental movement was freed from the restrictive demands of the anti-regime struggle. Due to the 1987 constitutional reforms and the transnational findings, the Filipino environmental movements— through NGOs and POs—have become an equal partner with other democratic players in the political arena. The NGOs articulated a sustainable development agenda to empower local communities in gaining control over natural coastal resources and to influence the state to address environmental issues.

Whereas environmental movements are either partners or guardians of the democratic forces in South Korea, Taiwan, and the Philippines, environmental movements in Hong Kong have become dissociated from the democracy movements. Despite the brief unity of the two during the initial phase of the democratic transition in 1986, they soon went their separate ways in Hong Kong. Leaders and members of the territorywide environmental organizations seldom join or participate in pro-democracy groups. While environmental leaders focus on transforming life-styles, democratic organizations want to promote institutional change. While environmental leaders prefer a "soft" approach to work with governmental officials and businesspeople, democracy activists do not hesitate to use confrontational strategies to challenge the establishment. And while the democrats are trying to articulate some environmental issues in their party platforms, the environmental leaders remain bystanders in the democracy movement.

From the above analysis, the different phases of democratization and degrees to which democratic consolidation has been achieved are decisive factors in shaping the relationship between environmental movements and democracy movements in Asian states. The transition from authoritarianism to democratic breakthroughs tends to provoke a strong partnership between environmental movements and democracy movements. In the states in which democratic consolidation has occurred, intense electoral competition may tempt some democratic leaders and organizations to waver in their stands on environmental issues in order to win elections. On the other hand, in states in which democratic consolidation has yet to be achieved, environmental movements tend to become dissociated from democratic movements or even become bystanders to the democracy movements.

Since this chapter draws mostly from the four case studies of South Korea, the Philippines, Taiwan, and Hong Kong, it would be interesting to investigate whether the above analysis can extend to other Asian states. Will environmental movements develop a strong partnership with democracy movements during the phases of liberalization and democratic transition in Thailand? To what extent is the Thai case similar to the Philippine case? Will democratic consolidation in Thailand empower or restrain environmental movements? Only when there are enough studies along these lines can we accumulate sufficient knowledge about the complexity of the relationship between democratization and environmental movements, and only then, it is hoped, can we build theories of environmental transformation in Asian states.

References

Hsiao, Hsin-Huang Michael. 1994. "The Character and Changes of Taiwan's Local Environmental Protest Movement: 1980–1991." (In Chinese.) In *Environmental Protection and Industrial Policies,* edited by Taiwan Research Fund, pp. 550–573. Taipei: Vanguard Publication Co.

Hsiao, Hsin-Huang Michael, and Hagen Koo. 1997. "The Middle Class and Democratization in East Asia: Taiwan and South Korea Compared." In *Consolidating the Third Wave Democracies,* edited by Larry Diamond, Marc F. Plattner, Yun-han Chu, and Hung-Mao Tien, pp. 312–333. Baltimore: Johns Hopkins University Press.

Lee, Su-Hoon. 1993. "Transitional Politics of Korea, 1987–1992: Activation of Civil Society." *Pacific Affairs* 66: 351–367.

Rush, James. 1991. *The Last Tree.* New York: The Asia Society.

Seong, Kyoung-Ryung. 1993. "Social Origins of Korea's Political Democratization: A Social Movement Approach." (In Korean.) In *New Currents in Korean Politics and Society,* edited by Institute of Far Eastern Studies, Kyungnam University, pp. 85–132. Seoul: Nanam Publishing House.

Tarrow, Sidney. 1994. *Power in Movement: Social Movements, Collective Action and Politics.* Cambridge: Cambridge University Press.

Wu, Je-Ming. 1990. *Social Protests During the Period of Transformation of Taiwan's Political Regime.* (In Chinese.) Unpublished master's thesis. Graduate Institute of Political Science, National Taiwan University.

10

The Making of Anti-Nuclear Movements in East Asia: State–Movements Relationships and Policy Outcomes

Hsin-Huang Michael Hsiao, Hwa-Jen Liu,
Su-Hoon Lee, On-Kwok Lai, and Yok-shiu F. Lee

Acronyms

IAEA	International Atomic Energy Association	KMT	Kuomintang (Nationalist Party)
KEPCO	Korea Electric Power Company	NGOs	Non-Governmental Organizations
		NIMBY	Not-In-My-Backyard

Introduction

In the newly industrialized economies of Taiwan, South Korea, and Hong Kong in the second half of the 1980s, a near-simultaneous emergence of anti-nuclear movements took place. There are strong reasons to believe that the "Chernobyl effect" played a significant role in spurring activism and conferring a certain degree of legitimacy to the anti-nuclear movements in the region. Negative education campaigns by domestic anti-nuclear groups also enhanced the public's awareness and perception of the nuclear risk and added momentum to anti-nuclear movements. The public was rightfully concerned with the nuclear issue because nuclear power projects are very expensive and pose potentially high health risks to a large region or an entire country's population.

In Taiwan, starting in the early 1980s, people's environmental concerns raised by pollution disputes started to include nuclear energy issues. Similar to the experience in the United States, "many [environmental] activists as well as members of the public interpreted energy issues, especially that of nuclear energy, to be environmental in nature, so that many members of the environmental movement moved easily into anti-nuclear activities" (Jasper 1990: 110). When the proposal to construct a fourth nuclear power plant in northern Taiwan was made public in 1985, Taiwan's anti-nuclear movement—consisting of local residents, scholars, opposition political party members, and environmental NGOs—became a noticeable force in the media and established for itself a formal identity in the environmental discourse. Taiwan's government is now confronted with an almost intractable problem of locating suitable and socially acceptable dumping sites in the crowded island state for the disposing of increasing amounts of nuclear waste, another serious concern fueling the agenda and activities of the anti-nuclear movement.

In 1987, two years after the advent of Taiwan's anti-nuclear movements, the anti-nuclear movement in South Korea was launched when local fishermen in Youngkwang county started a campaign calling for compensation for the loss of their income and livelihood due to nearby nuclear power plants. Today, anti-nuclear proponents say that South Korea is suffering from a deep nuclear crisis. Eleven commercial nuclear power plants are currently in operation; reports of various types of nuclear accidents are frequently filed. According to a 1988 assessment conducted by the National Assembly, operations in seven plants have been halted by 193 accidents since the first nuclear power plant went into operation in 1978 (Bello and Rosenfeld 1990: 108–109). Like the result of the state's "rush to develop" its nuclear power generation program, the country's nuclear power plants were, according to one nuclear expert, prone to accidents (Bello and Rosenfeld 1990: 109). All proposed construction sites for new plants are now met with vehement resistance by local residents. Like Taiwan, South Korea is also plagued by a nuclear waste storage crisis as all the on-site, temporary, spent-fuel repositories are reaching the limits of their capacity.

The anti-nuclear campaign in Hong Kong was started by its organizers in the second half of the 1980s, at about the same time that anti-nuclear activists first gained prominence in Taiwan and South Korea. In the colony, the anti-nuclear groups were organized to oppose the siting and construction of a small-scale nuclear power plant in the Daya Bay area in southern China. Located about fifty kilometers northeast of Hong Kong and proposed after the 1986 Chernobyl accident, the Daya Bay nuclear facility stirred up one of the most controversial debates in the territory in the 1980s. At that time, opponents of the project were highly skeptical about China's technical and managerial capability to safely operate the facility. Yet, despite being one of the few cases in the history of Hong Kong's protest movement where a coalition with a strong grassroots element successfully mobilized for an environmental cause, the Anti–Daya Bay campaign wound down rapidly. After the Guangdong Nuclear Power Plant Joint Venture Company, which sponsored the Daya Bay project, concluded and signed contracts with key suppliers, many leaders of the protest campaign conceded defeat and switched their attention to other battlefields. In contrast to the anti-nuclear movements in Taiwan and South Korea, which still constitute a major current in the environmental movements in both societies, anti-nuclear protest in Hong Kong has ceased to exist except as a part of the colony's environmental movement history.

In this chapter, we attempt to investigate and compare the "making" of anti-nuclear movements in Taiwan, South Korea, and Hong Kong by tracing the evolution of the political opportunity structures in which the movements were embedded in these three societies. We propose that the policy outcomes regarding nuclear power production in both Taiwan and South Korea are contingent upon the nature of the state, on one hand, and the strength of the anti-nuclear movement, on the other. The peculiarity of the anti-nuclear movement in Hong Kong, with its spontaneity and short life-span, is examined in detail in comparison with those in Taiwan and South Korea, to illustrate the key factors contributing to the common and divergent patterns of political change and anti-nuclear activism.

Geopolitics and the Nuclear Power Choice

Nuclear power is a peculiar issue; the state as an entity has very strong vested interests in developing and nurturing the nuclear power industry, an industry that projects a national symbol and is closely linked to the issue of sovereignty. Strategic considerations have thus played a prominent role in the nuclear decisions of certain states, particularly during the Cold War, when some form of nuclear and/or energy security was considered a paramount concern by regimes in the East Asian region. In Taiwan, the oil crisis of the 1970s lent initial impetus to the Nationalist government's pro-nuclear decision to use nuclear reactors to resolve the energy crisis. In South Korea, geopolitical considerations played a significant part in the state's decision to adopt a nuclear power program. There were strong reasons to believe that then-president Park Chung Hee wanted to develop some kind of nuclear weapon in a nuclear power program to strengthen the country's self-defense capability.

As the organizer of the political environment within which social movements operate, the provider of opportunities for action, and the ruler imposing restrictions on movement activities, the state occupies a central position throughout our analysis of anti-nuclear movements. In the past, most East Asian social movement literature focused on a formal conception of political opportunities, that is, formal protection of civil and political rights (Jenkins and Klandermans 1995). We attempt to go beyond this conventional approach by examining the extent to which (1) the institutional structure of the state, especially its centralization and policymaking capacities, and (2) the structure of political power, such as the extent of division among elites, influence the configuration of political opportunities. Moreover, with regard to anti-nuclear movements specifically, we examine the impact of state ownership of both electricity companies and the nuclear power industry on state–movement relationships and policy outcomes.

In Taiwan and South Korea, the initial choice to turn to nuclear energy was made under highly centralized or authoritarian regimes by a small circle of bureaucrats and managers embracing technological enthusiasm. In Taiwan, a highly centralized policymaking system set up in the early 1970s charted the course for importing nuclear technology and developing nuclear power. The small voice from academia critical of nuclear energy and questioning its safety neither drew public attention nor successfully challenged the ideology of "advanced technology" until the mid-1980s.

In South Korea, under the authoritarian regime headed by President Park Chung Hee in the 1970s, the government chose the nuclear path to sustain its high-speed, export-oriented industrial development strategy. The first commercial nuclear power plant began operations in 1978, in a town called Kori located in the southeastern coastal region near Pusan. By 1990, there were eleven commercial nuclear power plants in operation in the country, five in various stages of construction, and fifty-five more planned to be built by the year 2031 (Cho 1990: 184). With high-speed economic growth identified as the most important national goal, no one dared question the government's nuclear-power generation scheme, which was projected as crucial for the success of the national development strategy (Lee 1997).

In the case of Hong Kong, the nuclear power plant in question was set up a short distance from the territory's border by the Chinese state. The target of the anti-nuclear movement thus laid outside the territory's border in southern China. National leaders considered the nuclear energy program in southern China not only one of the major strategies to deal with the country's power shortage, but also regarded it as a symbol of prestige and prowess to demonstrate China's high-technology take-off in her modernization programs (Yee and Wong 1987).

Moreover, the decision to opt for nuclear power was reinforced by state ownership of electricity companies (in Taiwan and South Korea) and a government-franchised, quasi-monopolistic arrangement in electricity supply (in Hong Kong). In Taiwan, electricity is a monopoly run by the state-owned Taiwan Power Company. Close links between the state and the electricity industry sped up the pace of deployment of nuclear reactors in Taiwan and deepened its dependence on nuclear energy. By 1985, before the advent of the anti-nuclear movement, three nuclear power plants and six reactors had been built, altogether generating up to 52 percent of Taiwan's electricity supply (*Chinese World Almanac* 1995). Although the share of nuclear energy in total electricity production declined to around 30 percent by 1994, the state and the Taiwan Power Company have remained aggressive in their joint pursuit of additional nuclear facilities.

In South Korea, at the height of the nuclear power program, more than 50 percent of that country's electricity supply also came from nuclear sources (Bello and Rosenfeld 1990: 103; Hart-Landsberg 1988: 268). And similar to the experience of Taiwan, the proportion of nuclear-generated electricity declined to around one-third of the total power supply by the mid-1990s. Nevertheless, the production and distribution of electricity is still dominated by a state monopoly, the Korea Electric Power Company, which is committed to further expansion of nuclear facilities (Lee 1997).

Although Hong Kong differs from both Taiwan and South Korea in that the electricity industry is not monopolized by the state, there are strong government-sanctioned incentives for public utilities to pursue expansion of their investments, including nuclear power plants. Most public utilities in Hong Kong are franchised by the colonial government through a "scheme of control" that allows them to enjoy a quasi-monopolistic position in the market, usually with a "guaranteed" yearly rate of return of around 15 percent in accordance with their respective total assets (Lam 1996). Since the asset base is used to determine overall realizable profit, the "scheme of control" provides a very strong incentive for public utility companies in Hong Kong to expand their asset bases and, hence, their investment portfolios.

In the case of the Daya Bay Nuclear Power Plant, the Hong Kong government provided further impetus for the project by guaranteeing to purchase the electricity generated by the plant both to secure global financing for the investment and to qualify the project as a local activity that fell under the "scheme of control." Thus, given that the Daya Bay Nuclear Power Plant was simply a profit-making venture as far as the China Light & Power Co., Ltd. was concerned, the latter's decision was heavily buttressed by both the "scheme of control" and the Hong Kong government's guarantee to purchase the electricity generated by that plant (Guangdong NPJV 1988; Yee and Wong 1987).

Furthermore, in all three cases, the deliberation on the nuclear option was heavily swayed by the structural interests of international nuclear industries, technocratic government elites, and local businesses which converged to promote the local nuclear power industry. In Taiwan, all six nuclear reactors were imports manufactured by U.S. vendors such as General Electric and Westinghouse (Thomas 1988: 71). The U.S. nuclear power industry, which faces a declining domestic market, also dominates the nuclear energy market in South Korea (Lee 1997). In southern China, the Daya Bay Nuclear Power Plant was a joint venture supported by the tripartite interests of British, French, and Chinese companies.

Political Liberalization and the Beginning of Anti-Nuclear Protests

The 1980s recorded the opening of the political process in Taiwan, South Korea, and Hong Kong. This process of political liberalization had significant implications for the environmental movements in general and for the anti-nuclear movements specifically in all three countries/territories, as exemplified by a decentralizing state and a changing pattern of political opportunities in each society.

In Taiwan, civil society was repressed under martial law, which stifled any large-scale, organized social response to environmental ills. The lifting of martial law in 1987 was thus a watershed in the history of environmental activism in Taiwan. Within months after martial law was lifted, for instance, the Taiwan Environmental Protection Union was formed (Hsiao et al. 1995). Before martial law was lifted, all confrontations regarding nuclear energy had occurred mainly outside the realm of higher policymaking bodies. "Unlawful" protests, demonstrations, seminars, and public hearings were organized by political dissidents, concerned intellectuals, and the residents of the proposed site of the fourth nuclear power plant in northern Taiwan. They united under one "anti-nuclear" banner and fought against the "pro-nuclear" coalition made up of the ruling Kuomintang Party, Taiwan Power Company, and the private industrial sector.

After the lifting of martial law, in addition to continuing their "street fight" strategies, the anti-nuclear activists launched a yearly large-scale demonstration, which would draw up to thirty thousand participants (Association for the Referendum on the Fourth Nuclear Power Plant 1995). Moreover, the anti-nuclear groups called the general public's attention to the anger and grievances of those who claimed to be victims of nuclear waste dumping and the radiation effects of nuclear power plants (Chi et al. 1996). For instance, the aborigines from Lan-yu (Orchid Island) protested against the government's "environmental racism" by refusing to accept any more nuclear waste shipped to their homeland. All these activities apparently helped raise public awareness of the nuclear issue, so much so that in a 1994 "unofficial" referendum of the residents of a proposed site for a nuclear power plant, 96 percent of the residents rejected the project.

In South Korea, open discussion of the nuclear issue was considered taboo under the authoritarian regimes in the 1970s and up to the mid-1980s. After the state started to liberalize in the late 1980s, debates questioning the efficiency and safety of nuclear power plants found their way into the public arena. In fact, the beginning of the history of South Korea's anti-nuclear movement has been traced to 1987, when residents of Youngkwang County, the site of two operating nuclear power plants and two proposed plants, launched a campaign calling for compensation for the decline of local fishery output. Similar to their counterparts in Taiwan, anti-nuclear movement leaders in South Korea took advantage of a liberalizing state and organized mass rallies and signature collection campaigns to oppose the construction of the two proposed nuclear power plants (Lee 1997).

Nuclear weapons per se, however, are not found on the agenda of the anti-nuclear movement in South Korea nowadays. It has been a "public secret" that a sizable number of nuclear warheads have been placed in South Korea, and North Korea has consistently voiced its objections to this to Seoul and Washington. Up until the late 1980s, nuclear weapons were one object of a public debate over nuclear issues. However, due in part to the anti-nuclear movement and in larger part to the progress made between the two Koreas, South Korea proper was made a "non-nuclearized" area in December 1991 when the historical "Non-nuclearization Declaration" was officially announced by Seoul and Pyongyang, committing both sides to stop storing, processing, and producing nuclear weapons (Cotton 1993: 291–292). Although Pyongyang shocked Seoul and the international community in April 1992 by announcing the withdrawal of its membership from the International Atomic Energy Association (IAEA), nuclear warheads that were known to be scattered around South Korea have been retrieved. Hence, even though South Koreans are still concerned with the issue of global proliferation of nuclear weaponry, nuclear weapons are no longer a dominant domestic issue on the agenda of the anti-nuclear groups in South Korea.

In Hong Kong, the colonial governance structure has always been instrumental in limiting citizens' participation in the decision-making process. Then, in the mid-1980s, preparing for its withdrawal from the territory in 1997, the colonial government deliberately instituted a decolonized governance structure with added consultative elements. The introduction of an elected District Board system in 1982 and of elected Urban and Regional Councils in 1985–86 coincided with an upsurge in public concern with environmental issues. The emergence of a predominantly elected Legislative Council in 1991 added further momentum in the transformation of the political context for environmental policymaking in the territory (Hung 1993).

The immediate effect of the introduction of electoral politics was liberalization in the political arena, with more than two hundred elected officials given the mandate to probe social, economic, and environmental agendas in the colony. In response to the NIMBY mentality of the general public, around one-quarter of the elected officials were involved in the anti–Daya Bay project movement. Moreover, the

Joint Conference for Shelving the Daya Bay Nuclear Power Plant, a coalition of 107 organizations, undertook popular protest activities similar to those in Taiwan and South Korea, such as mass demonstrations and a territorywide signature campaign (Lai forthcoming).

In short, the opening of the centralized political regimes in the 1980s in all three societies led to a changing pattern of political opportunities that were highly conducive to the emergence of the anti-nuclear movements.

Strength of the Anti-Nuclear Movements and Policy Outcomes

While changing political opportunity structures allow for the emergence of anti-nuclear voices, the extent to which policy outcomes are altered is contingent upon the strength of the anti-nuclear movements themselves. This strength comes from combining several attributes of each anti-nuclear movement: the extent of the movement's political alliance with political parties such as the opposition parties and/or the "green party," the degree of its capacity for micro-mobilization, and the scope of its ability to shape or reshape public opinion (Burstein et al. 1995; Gamson and Modigliani 1989).

In both Taiwan and South Korea, anti-nuclear movements have been able to gain strength over a relatively short period of time, but they have only exerted limited influence over the course of nuclear policy agendas in both societies. The movements in both regimes have appeared to be successful in penetrating and weakening, but not totally refuting, the discourse of "the inevitability of nuclear energy" proposed by the state and supported by business interests. Nevertheless, in Taiwan, it was the movement's establishment of close alliances with political opposition parties that provided the major impetus behind its limited success in delaying and scaling down the government's nuclear program. And in South Korea, it was the campaign's capacity for micro-mobilization of local residents at the street level for organized and violent actions that served as the driving force in pushing the state to make concessions in its nuclear ambitions.

In Taiwan, the debate over nuclear choice was first waged by academics who refuted the "Taiwan's nuclear power plant is 100 percent safe" proposition promoted by the Taiwan Power Company and then challenged the "domestic energy shortage" and the "inevitability of nuclear energy" arguments put forth by technical and economic bureaucrats at the Nuclear Energy Committee and the Economic Ministry. This debate was later joined by political dissidents who formed opposition parties and won elections to become members of legislative bodies. Starting in 1987, three highly visible opposition parties (the Democratic Progressive Party, the New Party, and the Green Party), in spite of their differing agendas and conflicting political ideologies, adopted the same anti-nuclear stance. They questioned the government's long-established nuclear energy policy, proposed new energy alternatives, and boycotted the budget for the proposed new nuclear power plant. Local residents, mobilized by the Taiwan Environmental Protection Union into organizing regional chapters, also proved to be very important partners in local anti-nuclear protests.

In addition to the mass-based anti-nuclear demonstrations, sharp cleavages that developed among the elites (e.g., KMT members versus opposition party politicians, technological bureaucrats versus environmentally inclined academics) over nuclear policy became hindrances to the state's nuclear energy development. For instance, due to widespread opposition coming from both popular and elite groups, the proposal of the new nuclear power plant was deferred three times, and the Legislative Yuan twice froze the government budget for the new plant.

However, Taiwan's anti-nuclear movement was not able to fully engage the state in the discourse of the nuclear power controversy for the following reasons. First of all, the government neither participated in any public debate with anti-nuclear groups nor approved a nationwide referendum on the construction of the new power plant. Second, taking advantage of the public's ignorance of the nuclear issue, the government instilled a belief in "the inevitability of building the fourth nuclear power plant" by creating the illusion of an energy shortage. For example, whenever the anti-nuclear movement appeared to be soaring and socially influential, the Taiwan Power Company conveniently limited and rationed the electricity supply for residential areas to generate public fear of power shortages. Third, under the pro-growth ideology upheld by the state and the business sector, aggressive publicity campaigns to promote "nuclear energy safety" and "nuclear industry as a leading industry and a necessary infrastructure" effectively neutralized anti-nuclear claims and consequently minimized public suspicion of nuclear power. As a result, Taiwan's anti-nuclear movement was not able to shake the determination of the pro-nuclear executive branch of the government.

Unlike Taiwan, at least into the 1980s, South Korea's political elites were able to move ahead with their nuclear program despite reservations expressed by some opposition party members. In 1988, some opposition party members at the National Assembly took issue with the government over the pending construction of two nuclear power plants in Youngkwang. In the following year, outside the confines of the National Assembly, elite-based organizations (e.g., pharmacists, medical doctors) joined popular community-based organizations to form the National Headquarters for the Nuclear Power Eradication Movement (Cho 1990: 190). Originally set up on an ad-hoc basis to coordinate and to help bring organization and efficiency to the activities of the resident-level anti-nuclear groups throughout the country, the National Headquarters has been credited with raising public awareness about the nuclear issue to a significant extent.

However, opposition party members found it difficult to challenge the nuclear power program because it is considered a nationalist project. Hence, there is no effective opposition to the nuclear program in the National Assembly. Thus, in spite of the campaign activities promoted by the National Headquarters, the government eventually proceeded and completed two new nuclear power plants. The failure to hold back and scale down the nuclear program through formal political processes helps explain the increasing tendency to turn to street-level, mass-based, and violent protests. Beginning in 1989, resident-level movements enlarged the scope of residents' attention from nuclear energy to issues such as nuclear weapons, nuclear arms reductions, and, particularly, illegal nuclear waste disposal. In fact, since the early 1990s, the struggle against the government's plan to build a permanent and centralized nuclear waste repository site has become a new major element of the anti-nuclear movement in South Korea. Such a struggle has evolved into a nationwide issue, with anti-nuclear activists and local resident groups invariably engaging in organized and violent protest actions against the state.

For example, in 1990, after anti-nuclear activists learned that the government had secretly identified Anmyondo, a remote island off the west coast of the peninsula in Chungnam Province, as a site for a permanent nuclear waste repository, they organized the islanders to launch protests against the yet unannounced project. The islanders were especially enraged by the government's deceptive announcement that the island was selected for a research complex site and not a nuclear waste disposal site. After local residents found out the truth, the entire island exploded in riots. Even children joined the riots. Police stations and public buildings were attacked and some were set on fire. Shops were looted, people were injured, and parents refused to send their children to school. When the uprising showed no signs of subsiding, the Minister of Science and Technology, Dr. Chung Kun Mo, appeared on the TV evening news to announce his resignation. The government was forced to withdraw its plan and look for another site.

In 1994, a similar event took place when the South Korean government announced that the town of Uljin had been identified as a new alternative site for nuclear waste storage. Violent protests and demonstrations were organized, roads blockaded, tires burned, and fire bombs thrown. A sizable police force was called in to quell the violence but again the Ministry of Science and Technology was forced to withdraw its plan.

Immediately after this episode, the government hurriedly announced its proposal to designate Kulopdo, a tiny island about fifty miles from the port city of Inchon on the west coast, as an alternative storage site. The island had only ten residents who, according to the government, agreed to accept compensation for their land. Environmentalists, however, objected to the government's selection. They raised questions on the island's suitability, based on the claim that the island was vulnerable to geological dynamics, and they organized the islanders and the people of the neighboring Dukjok island. Local residents then quickly turned their backs on the government and claimed that they would never move from their homes for any monetary reward.

Altogether these stories clearly indicate that the state in South Korea, unlike in the past, can no longer impose and implement its nuclear policy without consent and cooperation from the population directly affected by its nuclear program. They also reveal a widening gap of credibility on the part of the state in relating to the larger society on nuclear issues. In a major way, these victories of the anti-nuclear movement in South Korea, like those in Taiwan, are testimony to its gathering strength in successfully re-shaping public opinion in its favor and in mobilizing the masses for its cause.

In Hong Kong, the anti-nuclear movement has been branded as perhaps the only case in the history of Hong Kong's protest movement in which a coalition of societal forces with a strong grassroots element was successfully mobilized for an environmental cause. Local environmental groups such as Friends of the Earth and the Conservancy Association were instrumental in shaping the anti-nuclear debate at the early stage of the movement (Paterson 1984), yet their role was mostly overshadowed, if not totally replaced, by the Joint Conference for Shelving the Daya Bay Nuclear Power Plant. The formation of this anti-nuclear movement agency was dominated by an extension and consolidation of different sectoral coalitions, or an amalgamation of mostly community groups, of the protest movements of the 1970s. The Joint Conference was formed by 107 organizations, most of which were historically rooted in community protests and the electoral politics of the 1980s. Conversely, environmental groups, though well respected, were less influential in the decision-making process in the Joint Conference. In the end, the Joint Conference opted for confrontational mass actions, including demonstrations, petitions, and signature campaigns, tactics that had not been fully articulated by the environmental groups. At the height of the movement, over one million signatures were collected in a signature campaign against the Daya Bay project, and the anti-nuclear protest was credited with forging a strong sense of identity among the Hong Kong people vis-à-vis the British colonial government and the authoritarian Chinese state.

The apparent success of the Joint Conference in mobilizing massive popular support for its cause (e.g., through the signature campaign), however, also reveals the fundamental weaknesses of Hong Kong's anti-nuclear movement with regard to its influence over the policy outcome and the construction of the nuclear power plant in question. The decision to opt for collective mobilization and confrontational strategies to challenge the nuclear power plant project reflected the fact that the civic forces in Hong Kong were totally kept out of the decision-making structure of the Daya Bay project, which involved only multinational business interests (French and British) and three governmental representations (Britain, China, and Hong Kong). In short, with such a decision-making structure lying outside the domain of the civic groups in Hong Kong, there is no direct access at all through which the policy outcome could be even slightly modified. In stark contrast to the robustness of the anti-nuclear movements in Taiwan and South Korea, the anti-nuclear movement in the territory was doomed to be a futile exercise from its beginning.

Conclusion

Despite its short life-span and failure to stop the Daya Bay Project, proponents of the anti-nuclear campaign in Hong Kong claim four major achievements. First and foremost, by mobilizing the general public to protest the nuclear project, the movement drew their attention to issues of nuclear facility safety. Second, it pushed the Legislative Council to organize a fact-finding study on nuclear power safety and contributed to a division and polarization of opinion with the Council on the movement's initiatives (Legco 1986). Third, it successfully forced the colonial government to respond to the safety concerns about the power station by adopting a contingency plan (Neal and Davies 1987; Guangdong DBNPS 1994). Lastly, the anti-nuclear movement strongly influenced the environmental agenda of the democracy movement in Hong Kong.

In South Korea, the ultimate target of the anti-nuclear movement was the closure of the nuclear power industry. But, given that the South Korean government thus far shows no sign of fundamental change in its nuclear policy and that the country's economy is structurally dependent upon nuclear power sources, this will likely remain a target. However, it has succeeded in cutting back—and bringing to a halt—plans for new nuclear power plants. The anti-nuclear activists' eyes remain set on the goal of eliminating nuclear power entirely. Toward this end they work to strengthen networks of local residents and concerned citizens living near nuclear plants, and actively explore legal and institutional actions to bring the nuclear program to an end.

For instance, at the center of South Korea's nuclear crisis is the monopoly of the production and distribution of electric power by the government-controlled Korea Electric Power Company (KEPCO). Anti-nuclear groups believe that a pluralistic market of power production and distribution will be conducive to the development of innovative ideas (e.g., non-nuclear forms of power generation). The government's continuing commitment to liberalize the state enterprises provides, therefore, a major avenue for the anti-nuclear groups to demand revision of existing energy-related laws and measures, and an end to KEPCO's monopoly.

In Taiwan, the battle over the nuclear issue since 1994 gradually shifted from civil society to party politics. From then, the anti-nuclear movement assumed parallel developments in both the civil and political spheres. However, with the legislators finally approving the construction of the fourth nuclear plant in late 1996 and even approving the yearly construction budget for 1997, anti-nuclear movement activists swung back to civil society in the form of violent street protests and riots on the construction site. Such a change of tactics can be interpreted as a distrust and disappointment on the part of the anti-nuclear movement activists toward the opposition parties and their politicians. Even with the semi-official policy announcement by the vice-premier in the National Energy Conference to re-evaluate the current energy development policy and to reduce Taiwan's reliance on nuclear power in the future, the local and national anti-nuclear movement forces are not convinced and certainly will not halt their protest in the future. Two possible options now exist in the minds of the anti-nuclear movement activists: one is to stage small and random protests during the long period of construction of the fourth plant as a means to continue their pressure against the state's nuclear agenda, and the other one is to rally further with opposition parties to force the state to change its energy policy completely so that there will be no further nuclear power plant projects on the island.

Indeed, although the construction of the fourth nuclear power plant has been approved, many immediate problems lie ahead during the ten-year construction period. For instance, residents of the proposed site have sworn to protect their homeland with their own lives if necessary and are determined to halt construction. Moreover, opposition legislators have threatened to veto the subsequent annual budgets for the project. In the long run, even if the construction of the new power plant is completed and it starts operating, the increasing amount of nuclear waste that needs to be disposed of will present a big headache for the government. The aborigines living next to the existing nuclear waste dumping site have already refused to take in any more waste and are demanding that the government remove the stored waste. The government's effort to find a new domestic dumping site has not been successful. After the news that several heads of poor villages and towns have secretly offered their land as dumping sites in exchange for a sizable amount of compensation was exposed in the media, all of these village heads withdrew their offers under immense local opposition.

In order to avoid being accused of instituting and perpetuating environmental racism against the aborigines, Taiwan's government decided to "export" the nuclear waste to other countries. In the past few years, Taiwan aggressively negotiated agreements with the People's Republic of China, North Korea, Russia, and some other countries to help dispose of its nuclear waste materials. The current dispute between Taiwan and South Korea over the former's shipment of nuclear waste to North Korea is putting Taiwan under immense international pressure. Taiwan's "export" of nuclear waste to North Korea is being criticized as a form of "environmental classism" at the international level, where a developed country deposits domestically undesirable products in a poorer country. The homeland of minority and socially disadvantaged groups in a poor country may be forced to suffer from the side-effects of unsafe nuclear waste disposal practices.

In the end, the export of nuclear waste from its country of origin to other destinations is only one dispute among many embedded in the intricacies of global nuclear politics. The proliferation of nuclear power technology, designed for either military or civilian purposes, has never been a purely national issue. It is inevitably an international one, because many countries that opt for the nuclear choice are plagued by problems caused by the incompleteness of their domestic nuclear chains, either in their effort to identify an acceptable site for the power plant or in their search for a socially acceptable method to properly dispose of nuclear waste. Given that the links in the nuclear chains in both South Korea and Taiwan will very likely remain incomplete or weak in the foreseeable future, and that these countries have to seek solutions outside their territorial boundaries, the anti-nuclear movements will continue to gain momentum and possibly develop into a regionwide project.

References

Association for the Referendum on the Fourth Nuclear Power Plant. 1995. *March for the Referendum on the Fourth Nuclear Power Plant.* (In Chinese.) Taipei: Jade Mountain Publishing.

Bello, Walden, and Stephanie Rosenfeld. 1990. *Dragons in Distress: Asia's Miracle Economies in Crisis.* San Francisco: Food First.

Burstein, Paul, Rachel L. Einwohner, and Jocelyn A. Hollander. 1995. "The Success of Political Movements: A Bargaining Perspective." In *The Politics of Social Protest,* edited by J. Craig Jenkins and Bert Klandermans, pp. 275–295. Minneapolis: University of Minnesota Press.

Chi, Chun-Chieh, H.H. Michael Hsiao, and Juju Chin-Shou Wang. 1996. "Evolution and Conflict of Environmental Discourse in Taiwan." Paper presented at the Association for Asian Studies Annual Meeting, Honolulu, Hawaii.

Chinese World Almanac. 1995. The Central News Agency.

Cho, Hong-Sup. 1990. "A Debate on Nuclear Energy: Technological Orientation or Ecological Orientation?" (In Korean.) *Society and Thoughts.* Special issue.

Cotton, James, editor. 1993. *Korea Under Roh Tae-Woo.* Canberra: Allen and Unwin.

Gamson, William, and Andre Modiglianai. 1989. "Media Discourse and Public Opinion on Nuclear Power." *American Journal of Sociology* 95: 1–37.

Guangdong Daya Bay Nuclear Power Station (Guangdong DBNPS). 1994. *Contingency Plan.* Hong Kong: Government Printer.

Guangdong Nuclear Power Joint Venture Co. Ltd. (Guangdong NPJV). 1988. *Guangdong Nuclear Power Station Progress Report.* Shenzhen: Guangdong NPJV.

Hart-Landsberg, Martin. 1988. "South Korea: The 'Miracle' Rejected." *Critical Sociology* 15(3).

Hsiao, Hsin-Huang Michael, Lester Milbrath, and Robert Weller. 1995. "Antecedents of An Environmental Movement in Taiwan." *Capitalism, Nature, Socialism* 6(3): 91–104.

Hung, Wing-Tat. 1993. "The Politicization of the Environment." In *Limited Gains,* edited by Cecilia Chan and Peter Hills, pp. 41–50. Hong Kong: Center of Urban Planning and Environmental Management, University of Hong Kong.

Jasper, James M. 1990. *Nuclear Politics: Energy and the State in the United States, Sweden, and France.* Princeton: Princeton University Press.

Jenkins, J. Craig, and Bert Klandermans. 1995. "The Politics of Social Protest." In *The Politics of Social Protest,* edited by J. Craig Jenkins and Bert Klandermans, pp. 3–13. Minneapolis: University of Minnesota Press.

Lai, On-Kwok. Forthcoming. "Environmental Movements Under Colonialism?" In *Social Movements in Hong Kong,* edited by Stephen W.K. Chiu and Tai-Lok Lui. Hong Kong: Hong Kong University Press.

Lam, Pun-Lee. 1996. *The Scheme of Control on Electricity Companies.* Hong Kong: The Chinese University Press.

Lee, Su-Hoon. 1997. "The Rise of Environmentalism in South Korea." A Working Paper, Centre on Development and International Relations, Aalborg University, Denmark.

Legislative Council of Hong Kong (Legco). 1986. *Report of the Legco Fact Finding Delegations on Nuclear Power Generation.* Hong Kong: Legco.

Neal, A.P., and M.C. Davies. 1987. *Contingency Planning.* Consultancy on the Environmental Aspects of the Daya Bay Nuclear Power Station for the Government of Hong Kong. Hong Kong: Government Printer.

Paterson, Walter C. 1984. *Nuclear Power at Daya Bay? A Report for Hong Kong Friends of the Earth.* Hong Kong: Friends of the Earth.

Thomas, S.D. 1988. *The Realities of Nuclear Power: International Economic and Regulatory Experience.* Cambridge: Cambridge University Press.

Yee, Herbert S., and Yiu-Chung Wong. 1987. "Hong Kong: The Politics of the Daya Bay Nuclear Power Plant Debate." *International Affairs* 63(4): 617–630.

11

The Contradictions and Synergy of Environmental Movements and Business Interests

*On-Kwok Lai, Hsin-Huang Michael Hsiao,
Hwa-Jen Liu, Somrudee Nicro, and Yok-shiu F. Lee*

Acronyms

CFCs	Chlorofluorocarbons	NIMBY	Not-In-My-Backyard
EOI	Export-Oriented Industrialization	SMEs	Small and Medium Enterprises
EPA	Environmental Protection Agency	TBCSD	Thailand Business Council for Sustainable Development
FoE	Friends of the Earth	TEI	Thailand Environment Institute
NGOs	Non-Governmental Organizations	TNCs	Transnational Corporations

---

Introduction

This chapter discusses the initiatives and counter-movement strategies adopted by the corporate sector in response to the rise of environmental movements in Asia. Taking a comparative perspective, this chapter emphasizes that environmental movements emerge not in socioeconomic vacuums but are embedded within and responsive to the processes of economic development. Moreover, the differential trajectories of environmental movements are influenced by pro- or counter-movement strategies adopted by business corporations (ranging from large national or transnational corporations, TNCs, to small and medium enterprises, SMEs) and their collective representations such as the Chambers of Commerce and Federations of Industries.

Specifically, the corporate sector has not just passively responded to the challenge of environmental movements but actively exerts influence on movement agencies and their leadership by the provision of differential (dis)incentives. In other words, private enterprises, within the domains of both local and global environmentalism, have increasingly learned from confrontational encounters with environmental groups. After dealing with decades of environmental challenges, they have learned not to cope with such challenges passively. Instead, private corporations have become increasingly engaged in discourses and actions aimed at shaping environmentalism as well as absorbing environmental appeals for their own corporate interests. Furthermore, in the 1990s it appears that business interests and environmental mobilization can go hand in hand without any problem.

The relationships between the corporate sector and environmental movements fall into a range of possibilities marked by two polar categories: antagonism and consensus. A closer examination of these relationships, which change over time, will help to specify the major contributory factors and the role of the state in molding and regulating such linkages.

Antagonistic relationships are best illustrated by the classic cases of conflict between corporate interests and environmental movements, as exemplified by Not-In-My-Backyard (NIMBY) social mobilization or by victimization processes arising out of site-specific hazardous industrial installations in the course of economic development. In this antagonistic relationship, environmentalists as well as the victims invariably adopt a confrontational approach that challenges the interests of the corporate sector.

However, consensual relationships have recently become the dominant mode of interchange between environmental movements' agencies and the corporate sector in the region. Both global environmentalism and local environmental movements prompted many private corporations, especially TNCs and large enterprises, to adopt a new proactive mode of interaction in bringing forth their own environmental initiatives. This is even more so as echoed by various environmental initiatives mooted by supranational and international organizations like the World Bank and the United Nations. The motives behind such a move on the part of the business sector are varied. Many intend to contain, if not capture, the impact of conflicting environmental mobilizations. But increasingly, most enterprises want to promote their own public image (as a part of an overall public relations strategy) and, for some, to further develop their businesses in the emerging green economy. Thus, we have witnessed a recent proliferation of pro-environmental engagement, including a surge of green-labeled products and services as well as corporate sponsorships of select environmental activities.

In the following, analyses of Taiwan, Hong Kong, and Thailand illustrate the historical contexts behind the transformation of environmentalism in each nation/territory. In particular, the roles of the state and a globalizing market in shaping local environmentalism serve as a backdrop to discuss the following two interrelated issues: How have environmental agencies responded to corporate sector environmental initiatives, and what has been the overall impact of corporate environmental initiatives on environmental movements? We then conclude by examining the prospect of environmental movements in these three regions in light of changing corporate environmental strategies.

Taiwan

Since the early 1980s, hundreds of regional and national protests regarding environmental issues have challenged the myth of "Taiwan's miracle" by revealing significant social costs incurred in the unconstrained pursuit of economic prosperity (Wu 1990; Chi et al. 1996). A sizable number of citizens suffered greatly from industrial pollution and hazard waste, whereby their living environment and health were adversely affected. The natural landscape was also rapidly degraded or destroyed by highly polluting industries. Invariably, grievances and anger have been directed at the culprits responsible for recent environmental catastrophes—profit-seeking enterprises and corporations.

We will single out the industrial sector and investigate its antagonistic relationship with the environmental movement in the following discussion. Compared to the industrial sector, the service sector seldom becomes the target of attacks from Taiwan's environmental movement; it hardly produces noxious gas or disposes of toxic wastes. Rather, in recent years this sector has become the engine promoting "green consumerism" and has profited from it. For example, financial institutions publicize "the credit card of environmentalism"; environmentalist meals are listed on restaurant menus; the food industry sells popsicles and mineral water with the environmental label. However, green consumerism per se differs from what has been defined as environmentalism. The former is an advertising effort initiated by the service sector to approach customers through building a positive image of a single enterprise—without shaking the foundation of the process of production; the latter, endorsed by the environmental movement, demands that all modern industries, especially pollution-generating industries, fundamentally reorganize the technology of production, labor force, and product nature.

The industrial sector is the major, if not the only, source of environmental pollution in Taiwan and also has become the target of criticism and demands by environmental activists. Throughout the 1980s, 90 percent of pollution disputes arose around factories or establishments of the chemical, fertilizer, petrochemical, metal, cement, paper, textile, electricity, and rubber industries (Hsiao 1988: 21–25). Similar patterns took place in the 1990s as well (Hsiao 1997). Since identifiable pollution sources disproportionately come from the industrial sector, it seems clear that the improvement of Taiwan's environment rests upon how the industrial sector reacts to and negotiates with the demands of both environmental activists and state regulations.

Since the early 1980s, victims of pollution have organized, demanded compensation from both private and state-owned enterprises, and blocked factory entrances in protests. An increasing number of local residents and activist scholars have opposed the establishment of new petrochemical factories and the construction of new nuclear power plants. Moreover, politicians, non-governmental organizations (NGOs), opposition parties, labor unions, and professional groups have become involved in various pollution disputes to resolve conflicting interests and demands. In short, these locally based grassroots protests and blockades have formed a wave of what Szasz (1994: 77–83) calls radical environmental populism, which has increasingly become a big headache for many enterprises.

In what ways, then, have Taiwan's enterprises responded to and interacted with such direct action-oriented environmental populism? And what has been their main strategy in dealing with the state's increasingly stringent environmental regulations, which resulted from the pressure of countless hostile local protests and the globalization of environmentalism? There is, as a whole, no common response pattern among the highly heterogeneous private sector. The strategies that cor-porations may adopt vary greatly, depending upon each firm's size, market orientation (domestic or overseas), product nature (pollution-affiliated or not), and availability of resources.

Generally speaking, it is safe to say that few opt to become "green" industries. Though accepting the notion of "not to pollute the planet where we reside" in a very broad sense, most of Taiwan's entrepre-neurs still view the "greening strategy" as counter-productive, costly, and undesirable. Compliance with new environmental regulations and responding to the demands of the environmental movement increases production costs (e.g., upgrading obsolete technology, replacing worn-out equipment, and reorganizing out-dated production processes), and few enterprises are willing to go to this expense except under heavy external pressure.

The most striking feature among Taiwan's businesses is the adop-tion of an "opportunist strategy" to deal with challenges arising from environmental populism. This opportunist reaction has largely discred-ited Taiwan's business sector as a whole for its stand on environmental protection issues. However, such a stand varies with the nature of the enterprise and is also influenced by government policies. Specifically, the major coping strategies of Taiwan's pollution-prone businesses (including manufacturing, construction, mining, and the electricity sec-tors) include *exit, bargaining,* and *pressuring the state.*

Since the late 1980s, challenged by cheaper labor costs in Southeast Asia and mainland China and by general competition in the global manufacturing market, Taiwan's government began to implement its second export-oriented industrialization (EOI) policy to reorganize the domestic economy. Incentives were provided for conglomerates to ex-pand domestic investments, selected medium-sized enterprises given financial assistance to produce higher value-added products, and me-dium- and small-sized enterprises of "sunset" industries encouraged to move out of Taiwan. The purpose of the policy was to strengthen Taiwan's competitive capacity by producing "high value-added items that are skill-intensive and require a more fully developed local indus-trial base" (Gereffi 1990: 17).

The impact of such a policy on the relationship between enterprises, enterprise pollution, and the environmental movement has been tre-mendous. Medium- and small-sized enterprises without sufficient capi-tal to invest in pollution abatement equipment were motivated by the government to move overseas, and many actually did just that. As a result, these relocated enterprises effectively escaped from domestic environmental regulations and transferred the social costs of industrial pollution to less developed countries with lax regulations. This is the first type of opportunist strategy called exit, which is very similar to that of some transnational corporations in Taiwan prior to the 1980s.

On the other hand, many big conglomerates and some medium-sized enterprises able to afford pollution-preventing investment have been unwilling to do so, questioning government resolve on environmental protection. Faced with rising labor costs, increasing environmental awareness, and multiplying pressures of environmental regulations, many conglomerates have threatened to leave Taiwan, staging an "investment strike" in order to bargain for "a better investment environment." Such a strategy of *bargaining* has had some immediate impact, because the Taiwan government and its political elites believe in keeping big industries (i.e., petrochemical, nuclear power, and other highly polluting industries) as signs of national economic strength. Regardless of very strong opposition from local residents and environmentally minded academics and professionals, the government continues to provide cheap land and water supply as well as to simplify environmental impact assessment (EIA) procedures to accommodate business demands. For years, the government also took suppressive attitudes and actions in dealing with local protests to allow and facilitate the construction of naphtha crackers (a highly polluting industry that refines oil products into precursors of plastics), nuclear power plants, and industrial parks that might threaten and destroy wetlands and forests around the island (Hsiao 1997).

Taking advantage of the government's ambiguous stand in the contest between economic growth and environmental protection, Taiwan's big conglomerates and large enterprises have adopted the third type of opportunist strategy of *pressuring the state* to favor economic growth at the expense of the environment. Moreover, Taiwan's big businesses have taken a variety of less costly and short-term tactics to deal with environmental protests. Instead of paying serious attention to long-term environmental management, they have chosen to trade for "the right to pollute" with (1) immediate fines or compensation when their pollution impact was discovered and disclosed by victims or environmental agencies; or (2) promises of rewards or monetary contributions to local public facilities in order to gain public support for new industrial projects. In short, in their minds, money could buy them the right to pollute.

In addition, although the government formulated "stricter regulations" in an effort to prevent pollution, whether or not these regulations and discentives were sufficiently stringent was questionable. Scholars and activists have long challenged the adequacy of the enacted regulations, charging that some crucial pollutant control standards were set at much lower thresholds than those found in other developed countries (Chang 1994: 296–297). Moreover, the extent to which these regulations were fully implemented appears doubtful. For example, during the 1992–95 period, the number of petition cases against pollution nuisances increased from 77,547 to 117,788, but the total amount of fines actually collected from pollution-causing enterprises dropped by approximately 11 percent (*Yearbook of Environmental Statistics* 1996).

Taiwan's environmental groups are not so concerned about enterprises fleeing the island; these groups mainly question the industries, especially big conglomerates and state-owned enterprises, that have opted for the strategy of buying the right to pollute. Their major tactics of environmental protest include petitions, demonstrations, blockades, and occasionally referenda. As Hsiao (1994) points out, since the 1980s, one of the major trends of Taiwan's environmental movement has been the radicalization of the repertoire of collective action. Peaceful and legal means of action proved futile at the initial stages, as almost all enterprises involved refused to admit their misdeeds or give a clear promise to improve.

At the same time, the Environmental Protection Agency and local environmental agencies feared offending either the culprits or the victims. They tended not to take sides or make any concrete conclusions, only intervening in a limited and timid way. "As a result, [the EPA] has angered people on all sides, establishing a reputation as weak and ineffective among environmentalists, but as troublesome within the government [and among enterprises]" (Weller and Hsiao 1994: 13). Outraged victims and environmental activists were thus forced to take increasingly disruptive actions. And invariably it was only after the confrontations heated up that pollution-causing enterprises gave in and agreed to pay compensation. It is therefore not difficult to understand why grievances were so pervasive among pollution victims and why most environmental activists distrust enterprises.

The conflict between the business sector's interests and the environmental movement has not been confined to local-level pollution sites, but has been extended to the public policy domain in Taiwan. For instance, demonstrations and referenda against the fourth nuclear power plant and other large-scale petrochemical industrial parks, as well as numerous public petitions demanding the conservation of natural resources, were eventually defeated by the industrial sector's pressure on the government to uphold the prevalent "economic growth goes first" policy. Protected, and in fact nurtured, by such a policy, Taiwan's businesses were under no political pressure to respond seriously to the challenges of the environmental movement. They have not established any direct dialogues or relationships with environmental groups through either co-option or sponsorship. Although many conglomerates, in their attempts to improve their corporate image, have established themselves as philanthropists by setting up non-profit charity organizations or sponsoring cultural and charitable activities, there are hardly any big businesses that have taken a progressive attitude toward the environment.

Hong Kong

Business interests and the environmental movement are intertwined in Hong Kong within the network of the colonial state's consultative politics and corporate-led green entrepreneurship and sponsorship. In response to global environmentalism and the burgeoning green market, there are various business sector initiatives fostering a green life-style. For instance, the recent establishment of the Private Sector Committee on the Environment and the Centre for Environmental Technology (both under the auspices of large corporations in Hong Kong) aptly indicates the responsiveness of the private sector to opportunities emerging in the greening global economy (Howroyd and MacPherson 1997).

Strategically speaking, private sector environmental initiatives more often engage in some kind of counter-mobilization against eco-fundamentalism such as that promoted by Greenpeace. Proclaimed in the name of environmental management, private sector initiatives are usually in fact a strong lobbying force against radical and progressive environmental policy initiatives. For example, they have recently organized media campaigns against the introduction of the polluters-pay principle in sewage treatment.

As already alluded to in the case study on Hong Kong, the history of the territory's environmental movement reflects an active engagement of the private sector in counter-acting, influencing, and shaping the movement. This has particularly been the case since the early 1990s, when many environmental NGOs became involved in the promotion of green life-styles within the community and, in the process, were drawn into the sponsorship network of corporate sector interests (Hung 1993; Pang 1994). Large private enterprises, particularly those in the service sector, are very concerned about their corporate image as well as overall costs of their operations. Environmental groups have been called in by some of these businesses to help provide expertise to improve the corporate public image through various in-house green initiatives like recycling programs. Alternatively, corporations have provided financial sponsorship to environmental groups to help promote environmental education activities.

Hong Kong's industrial relocation and upgrading have laid the foundation for a cordial relationship between the business sector and the environmental NGOs. On the one hand, massive relocation of manufacturing and other pollution industries across the border in mainland China has cut down the grievances of the NGOs against the business sector. On the other, industrial upgrading to high value-added, service, and tourist industries requires that business corporations possess an environmentally friendly image that appeals to "green consumers." Thus, Hong Kong's big corporations seek advice on the greening of the aviation business from some green groups. For instance, Cathay Pacific (a Hong Kong–based airline) has spent millions of dollars to promote a green corporate image and institute in-house green management. Recycling of in-flight wastes and the scheduling of no-smoking flights have been introduced to cater to the concerns of international customers over eco-friendliness. Obviously, market conditions, such as the extent of internationalization of a business's potential customers, do carry some weight in influencing corporate decisions on whether to engage in the promotion of in-house green entrepreneurship and the sponsorship of environmental group activities.

In addition to external factors such as the influence of global environmentalism on Hong Kong, the trend of increasing corporate interests working with environmental groups can be traced to some internal factors as well. Fundamentally, there has been a gradual change in the way corporations and the government perceive environmental NGOs in the territory. The latter are no longer considered as hostile pressure groups but as possible partners, leading to a rising level of cooperation among the three parties. Accordingly, almost all leading environmental NGOs have been granted green funds to help promote environmental education programs. Indeed, green funds from both the public and private sectors have become a major force in shaping Hong Kong's environmental movements. During the 1993–94 fiscal year, the colonial government established an Environmental Education Committee as well as an Environment and Conservation Fund amounting to HK$50 million (US$6.4 million). At about the same time, there was a burgeoning of another pocket of green funds made available by such major corporations as Caltex, Cathay Pacific, Shell, Esso, China Light & Power, Overseas Trust Bank, and the Provisional Airport Authority.

Perhaps because of the availability of green sponsorship, environmental NGOs adopted a softer approach to environmentalism in order to capture new opportunities. Similarly, other smaller environmental groups followed this same approach toward emphasizing environmental education under the new sponsorship regime. Indeed, the raising of environmental consciousness has been, and still is, the primary focus of almost all of the environmental NGOs. This is recently reinforced by the full-fledged recognition of environmental education programs as a part of extra-curricular activities in schooling. Environmental education has also been incorporated into the civic education program in the community and has become a fashionable theme in television and radio programs. Thus, through various sponsorship arrangements, environmental NGOs have been active in promoting environmental education activities in various social settings.

The main providers of sponsored environmental education programs include the established environmental NGOs (e.g., the Conservancy Association and the Friends of the Earth), smaller environmental groups (e.g., the Green Lantau Association and the Lamma Island Conservation Society), green groups in universities (e.g., Green Union of Students) and in secondary schools (e.g., Joint School Environmental Protection Association), as well as those in social service centers (e.g., the Caritas Social Service). With total membership of all of these environmental groups at around 10,000, the influence of environmental education programs should not be underestimated (HKCSS 1991; Lai 1993; Ng 1997).

There are four major benefits for an NGO to accept corporate sponsorship. First, financial sponsorship means more revenues for organizational operations. Financial consideration is important for the survival of most environmental NGOs, because membership subscriptions are rarely able to support them. Second, corporate sponsorship provides credibility and media exposure for the environmental NGOs' experimental projects (e.g., Green Power's projects of Green University, Green Primary School, and eco-tours). Third, the enhancement of the NGOs' public image in the mass media, in turn, helps their membership recruitment drives. This has been witnessed by the exponential growth of NGOs membership gained through sponsored educational programs. Finally, the sponsored activities can also indirectly help improve the visibility of the environmental leaders, raising their own profiles in the mass media.

On the other hand, corporate sponsorship can also be a source of conflict and tension for environmental NGOs. For instance, the Friends of the Earth (FoE) in Hong Kong lost its affiliation status from the worldwide FoE movement because it decided to accept sponsorship from environmental polluters. In addition, the marriage of corporate sponsorship and environmental groups has been controversial among environmentalists. In most cases, environmental NGOs have had to realign their mode of operation in accordance with the wishes of corporate sponsors. Eco-fundamentalists have questioned the extent of environmental NGOs' independence and pointed out the perils of the trivialization of environmentalism.

Thailand

In the past, due to negative impressions of each other, Thailand's public sector, private business sector, and NGO sector had no links with each other. The business sector, however, with its financial and managerial resources, has become an influential actor shaping the environmental movement.

In recent years, elements within the private sector have begun to show public concern for the environment and initiated environmental activities. For example, Khunying Chodchoy Sophonpanich, a member of the family that controls one of the leading banks in Thailand, formed the Thai Environmental and Community Development Association in 1984, which named its first environmental activity—the cleaning-up of Thailand's environment—the "Magic Eyes" program. The most prominent activity undertaken by this Association was the filing of a lawsuit against the Bangkok Metropolitan Authority and a private engineering firm, which were jointly responsible for the construction of the Bangkok Transit System, to demand that the latter make project information, including the Environmental Impact Assessment report, accessible to the public.

While the Thai Creation Association pioneered business involvement in environmental activities, it was not until 1990–91 that the private sector as a group showed increasing interest in environmental issues. This was the period when the Thai economy was rapidly expanding, and signs of natural resource degradation and environmental deterioration were becoming highly visible. Numerous environmental programs were introduced around that time, including a campaign to replace leaded gasoline with unleaded, the garbage elimination program, and the reforestation campaign. This period was also marked by the suicide of a conservationist, Sueb Nakasatien, a senior official of the Royal Forestry Department. This incident, widely recognized as a turning point in Thailand's environmental history, greatly enhanced environmental awareness among the general public; since then, environmentalism has had a growing impact on every part of Thai society, including the private business sector.

It should also be noted that in 1992, an important political event—the May bloodshed—took place in Thailand and led to major changes in many aspects of Thai society, including the environmental arena. Mr. Anand Panyarachun, a major Thai businessman, became prime minister after the incident. Under his tenure, some important environmental laws like the National Environmental Promotion and Conservation Act were revised. Together with Dr. Paichit Aurthaveekul (then the Minister of Science, Technology and Environment), Mr. Anand also formed the Thailand Environment Institute (TEI), where he serves as the president of the TEI Council.

Created to bypass the bureaucratic processes and other constraints under governmental regulations, TEI is a new form of NGO; its mission is to serve as a catalyst for initiating changes in the environmental field. Its board is comprised of important leaders from governmental agencies, the business sector, and environmental NGOs. One of TEI's major roles is to coordinate environmental initiatives and activities originating from these three sectors. For instance, the Institute has helped convince many business leaders to become members of the Thailand Business Council for Sustainable Development (TBCSD), established in 1993 with Mr. Anand as one of its founders. Among the many roles of the TBCSD is the promotion of ISO 14000 certification and the introduction of the idea of a Green Label in Thailand.

The private sector's decision to actively respond to rising environmentalism in their operations can be traced to several factors. First, corporations responded to changing preferences of consumers who were becoming environmentally concerned. Second, business operators were compelled to follow specific environmental rules and regulations. Third, for export-oriented businesses, international trade and international organizations such as the World Trade Organization and the European Union have served as major factors in shaping their corporate behavior vis-à-vis environmental standards and practices. Lastly, multinational corporations in Thailand were setting an example in the private sector by following environmentally friendly policies and practices initiated by their headquarters' offices.

In terms of specific environmental activities organized and/or supported by the private sector, several major categories can be identified. First, the most common form of activity is sponsorship of environmental awareness campaigns. Second, some large corporations participate in and support environmental projects designed by environmental NGOs. For example, the Bangchak Petroleum Co., Ltd. (a public corporation), and Plan Co., Ltd. co-organized the Annual Environmental Seminar in 1995 and 1996. Third, corporations responded actively to the rise of green consumerism. The TBCSD introduced the Green Label Project in 1993, encouraging its members to produce environmentally friendly products. Green businesses, such as shops selling natural products, as well as businesses managing recycled materials and providing waste management consultancy, increased in number. Finally, some corporations introduced environmental awareness programs among their staffs. For instance, the Thai Commercial Bank introduced some internal environmental measures, including the installation of a deep shaft waste water treatment system (*Prachachart Business Newspaper,* January 28, 1996, p. 3). Likewise, the Hotel Association of Thailand encouraged hotel operators nationwide to become members of the "Green Hotel" project, where they can be involved in the Green Building Project sponsored by the Electricity Generating Authority of Thailand and enjoy a 10 percent discount on their electric bills (*Manager Newspaper,* January 13–14, 1996, p. 7).

Among the major corporations in Thailand that have taken advantage of the rise of environmentalism, one company—Bangchak Petroleum Public Co., Ltd.—is recognized as the most prominent in terms of influencing environmental policy changes. Under the leadership of Mr. Sophon Suphapong, its president, this company has assumed an important role in coordinating the public sector, academics, NGOs, and local residents in efforts to address important environmental issues. Given its significant impact on the relationship between the private sector and the environmental movement in Thailand, the environmental concepts and strategies of Bangchak Petroleum and its president, Mr. Sophon, are highlighted below.

Bangchak's concept of the environment is quite different from that of other private companies. While other companies consider the environment as a marketing strategy, Mr. Sophon claimed that "[e]conomic development is just only a part of our life, not the whole." Moreover, his own field trips and exposure to people at the grassroots level for years have led him to the understanding that environmental problems stem from the problems of urban poverty. He thus further declared that "[e]nvironmental issues are a matter of morality," a belief shared by many grassroots NGOs; this formed the basis for his decision to establish a network with various NGOs throughout the country. Moreover, as a part of its overall environmental campaign strategy, Bangchak helped establish local cooperatives in the countryside to enable villagers to increase their incomes through participation in community-based businesses. A Lemon Green Shop was set up for the villagers to help them market insecticide-free vegetables as well as naturally made products.

Bangchak has also assumed an increasingly prominent role in organizing the Annual Environmental Seminar since 1995. First formalized in 1992, the Annual Environmental Seminar was born out of an informal annual gathering of environmental NGOs to discuss grassroots-level environmental concerns throughout Thailand. While at first it was organized by and for NGOs only, governmental agencies were gradually invited as participants. In 1994, the Department of Environmental Quality Promotion was the first governmental organization to take an important role in helping to organize the meeting, which was well attended by 147 organizations. In 1995, then, Bangchak became the main organizer of the annual event, marking the first time that the business sector was responsible for organizing the environmental meeting instead of the NGOs. The main objective of the annual meeting, however, has changed and now mainly concerns reporting on the activities undertaken by various environmental organizations and disseminating information on rural poverty to the general public, particularly the middle class.

Conclusion

The governments in all three cases discussed above are committed to rapid economic growth as an overall societal goal, to be achieved at all costs—including, if necessary, degradation of the environment. To varying degrees, the corporate sector in all three places is protected, and in fact nurtured, by the state's preference for economic expansion over environmental protection. In a way, the business sector in all three localities is not under any great political pressure to respond to the challenges of environmental movements. Yet only Taiwan stands out as an odd place in which the corporate sector has actually not bothered to respond to increasing environmental concerns over business operations. In contrast, the private and public corporations in Thailand have shown the greatest enthusiasm in responding to rising environmental concerns in their business strategies, so much so that some are now seen as dominating that country's environmental agenda. In Hong Kong, the private sector likewise has been actively responding to mounting environmentalism by counter-acting and influencing the environmental movement, albeit not to the same extent as that observed in Thailand.

In Thailand and Hong Kong, similar internal and external considerations affected the corporate sector's decision to take advantage of the rising tide of environmentalism in the 1980s. There is no doubt that many businesses incorporated the environmental factor in their operations as a result of increasingly stringent environmental rules and regulations promulgated in both societies. The most powerful influence on these firms' environmental disposition, however, comes from emerging domestic and international market opportunities to cater to the consumers' penchant for green products and services. The business sectors in both Thailand and Hong Kong are simply exploiting green consumerism by providing an increasing array of green or eco-labeled products. Beginning in the early 1990s, for instance, Hong Kong caught up with the latest fad of ecologically sound consumption appeals in the marketing and retailing of goods and services, such as the Body Shop movement (Bourdieu 1984). At about the same time, private corporations in Thailand started taking up the pursuit of ISO 14000 certification and Green Labels in their manufacturing processes and marketing strategies.

In both Thailand and Hong Kong, it can thus be argued that, under the shadow of a global greening of the market which is partly influenced by a green entrepreneurial strategy, the private sector strives for a green life-style approach to environmental issues that is structurally embedded in and enabled by the development of a green economy. This life-style approach (Chau 1991), however, has helped minimize a confrontational posture and reinforce a cooperative relationship between the business sector and environmental groups, as is evident in both societies.

Unlike Thailand and Hong Kong, however, Taiwan's unique political situation sheltered its private and public enterprises from the effects of global environmentalism. Since Taiwan is not a signatory of various international environmental agreements, the consensuses reached in these agreements have not applied to Taiwan's industries. The most salient example was that in 1990, when Taiwan's government was still granting permission for the production of chlorofluorocarbons (CFCs), already listed as a soon-to-be-banned material in the Montreal Protocol (Chang 1994: 289–95). However, even if Taiwan's business sector is not under any political pressure to form a liaison with the environmental groups to address the latter's concerns, what have prevented Taiwanese businesses from following in the footsteps of their counterparts in Thailand and Hong Kong in pursuing the expanding green consumer market? This has remained an unanswered question.

In conclusion, an increasing amount of corporate sponsorship of environmental initiatives and activities has exerted a strong influence on environmental movements in both Thailand and Hong Kong. There appears to be a high degree of mutual dependency between the environmental NGOs and their corporate sponsors. This dependency is mutually reinforced by budgetary considerations of the usually poorly funded NGOs and by the considerable attention given to public image on the part of the resourceful corporate sector. On the one hand, corporate sponsorship of non-confrontational environmental programs is now commonly used by the private sector as a PR strategy to enhance their corporate image. On the other hand, newly formed environmental NGOs, as well as those with strong environmental education profiles, are highly receptive to and influenced by corporate sponsorship.

Such a dependency relationship is most apparent in Thailand, where the Annual Environmental Seminar, originally initiated and organized by the NGOs, has been recently taken over by powerful players in the corporate sector. In Hong Kong, major corporations have focused their support for primarily environmental education campaign activities, which have led to the trivialization of environmentalism and a questioning of the NGOs' own independence. Indeed, the term "environmental" has been used as a magic catchword for most educational and entertainment programs in the cultural and media industries, as well as in many corporations' advertising and marketing campaigns. Since many of these campaigns are conducted through the mass media, these programs have gained public attention among a large audience. However, most participants are transient, passive onlookers, and the campaigns have not been able to generate large-scale, committed, sustained public participation in the environmental movement in the territory.

The above account strongly suggests that the course of environmental movements in Thailand and Hong Kong, but not (yet) in Taiwan, has already been heavily influenced by corporate strategies of appropriating the social space for environmental discourse through sponsorship of environmental education activities. The experience of Taiwan's environmental movement seems to suggest that the environmental NGOs in Thailand and Hong Kong, in order to strengthen their own identities, secure their own independence, and resist the counter-movement tactics of the business sector, would need to form liaisons and organize with grassroots-level social groups to bring forth a coherent agenda toward sustainable development.

References

Bourdieu, P. 1984. *Distinction*. Oxford: Blackwell.

Chang, Chin-Shi. 1994. "Greenhouse Effects, Ozone Layer, and Taiwan's Petrochemical Industries." (In Chinese.) In *Environmental Protection and Industrial Policies,* edited by Taiwan Research Fund, pp. 277–308. Taipei: Vanguard Publication Co.

Chau, Simon S-C. 1991. "The Environment." In *The Other Hong Kong Report— 1990,* edited by Richard Y.C. Wong and Joseph Y.S. Cheng. Hong Kong: The Chinese University Press.

Chi, Chun-Chieh, H.H. Michael Hsiao, and Juju Chin-Shou Wang. 1996. "Evolution and Conflict of Environmental Discourse in Taiwan." Paper presented at the Association for Asian Studies Annual Meeting, Honolulu, Hawaii.

Gereffi, Gary. 1990. "Paths of Industrialization: An Overview." In *Manufacturing Miracles,* edited by Gary Gereffi and Donald L. Wyman, pp. 3–31. Princeton: Princeton University Press.

Hong Kong Council of Social Service (HKCSS). 1991. "A Situation Report on Voluntary Agencies' Environmental Educational Protection Activities." *HKCSS Social Service Quarterly* 18 (Winter): 11–18.

Howroyd, S., and S. MacPherson. 1997. "Business, Environment and the Community." In *Community Mobilization and the Environment in Hong Kong,* edited by Peter Hill and Cecilia Chan. Hong Kong: CUPEM, University of Hong Kong.

Hsiao, Hsin-Huang Michael. 1988. *Anti-Pollution Protest Movement in Taiwan in the 1980s: A Structural Analysis.* (In Chinese.) Taipei: Environmental Protection Administration.

———. 1994. "The Character and Changes of Taiwan's Local Environmental Protest Movement: 1980–1991." (In Chinese.) In *Environmental Protection and Industrial Policies,* edited by Taiwan Research Fund, pp. 550–573. Taipei: Vanguard Publication Co.

———. 1997. *Taiwan's Local Environmental Protest Movement: 1992–1996.* (In Chinese.) Taipei: Environmental Protection Administration.

Hung, Wing-Tat. 1993. "The Politicization of Environment." In *Limited Gains,* edited by Peter Hill and Cecilia Chan, pp. 41–51. Hong Kong: CUPEM, University of Hong Kong.

Lai, Wing-Hoi. 1993. "Environmental Education in Social Welfare Agency." Unpublished master's thesis. Department of Social Work and Social Administration, University of Hong Kong.

Manager Newspaper. 1996. January 13–14, p. 7.

Ng, Mei. 1997. "Environmental Education." In *Community Mobilization and the Environment in Hong Kong,* edited by Peter Hill and Cecilia Chan. Hong Kong: CUPEM, University of Hong Kong.

Pang, S.F. 1994. *Influence of Environmentalism on Consumer Behavior.* Unpublished project report submitted to Dr. On-Kwok Lai.

Prachachart Business Newspaper. 1996. November 21, p. 19, and January 28, p. 3.

Szasz, Andrew. 1994. *EcoPopulism: Toxic Waste and the Movement for Environmental Justice.* Minneapolis: University of Minnesota Press.

Weller, Robert P., and Hsin-Huang Michael Hsiao. 1994. "Culture, Gender and Community in Taiwan's Environmental Movement." Paper for the Workshop on Environmental Movements in Asia, International Institute for Asian Studies (Leiden), and Nordic Institute of Asian Studies (Copenhagen).

Wu, Je-Ming. 1990. "Social Protests During the Period of Transformation of Taiwan's Political Regime." (In Chinese.) Unpublished master's thesis. Graduate Institute of Political Science, National Taiwan University.

Yearbook of Environmental Statistics, Taiwan Area, The Republic of China. (In Chinese.) 1996. Taipei: The Statistics Office of Environmental Protection Administration Press.

12

Conclusion

Yok-shiu F. Lee and Alvin Y. So

Acronyms

APEC	Asia-Pacific Economic Co-operation	NIMBY	Not-In-My-Backyard
		POs	People's Organizations
EPA	Environmental Protection Agency	TEI	Thai Environment Institute
GROs	Grassroots Organizations	WAND	Women's Action Network for Development
NEB	National Environmental Board		
NGOs	Non-Governmental Organizations	WTO	World Trade Organization

---

The differences and similarities among environmental movements in East Asia and Southeast Asia are heightened by comparative analysis. Three general characteristics are shared by Asia's environmental movements: they encompass a diversity of ideas and approaches; they are socially constructed by different political and community groups to serve their own interests; and they illustrate processes of cultural indigenization. At the same time, however, environmental movements in each society maintain a distinct identity that is easily distinguished by the dominant thrust of their major proponents. Thus, three major paths of environmental movements can be identified—namely, the populist path in Taiwan, South Korea, and the Philippines; the corporatist route in Thailand; and the postmaterialist mode in Hong Kong. Before identifying and examining the major factors that explain the divergent paths of Asia's environmentalism, let us first discuss the broad common characteristics shared by environmental movements in Asia.

General Characteristics

Asia's Environmental Movements Are Diverse

When we talk about environmental movements, we tend to think of a single movement in an Asian country. Many people refer to "the" environmental movement, as if it embraces an abstract, monolithic personality. In reality, our studies show that Asia's environmental movements are complicated phenomena. Environmental movements in Asia, as elsewhere, are made up of several different strands of environmental activities, including diverse social groups engaging in a variety of political actions. While these social groups may share some outlooks, in the course of generating and participating in a so-called "Asian environmental movement," their interests, motivations, and activities may not converge.

For instance, Hsin-Huang Michael Hsiao shows that there are three main streams of environmental movements in Taiwan: anti-pollution protests, which started as localized pollution victim protests organized solely by residents within the communities; the nature conservation movement—composed mainly of new middle-class members—engaged in rescuing endangered migratory birds, mangroves, rivers, forests, and coastal wetlands; and the anti-nuclear campaign, which aims at preventing the construction of additional nuclear plants in Taiwan. On the other hand, Stephen Wing-Kai Chiu et al. dichotomize Hong Kong's environmental movement into a community-based approach vis-à-vis a territorywide strand, because this distinction highlights the two most salient types of mobilizing strategies and orientations to environmental issues in Hong Kong. Whereas most local confrontational actions reveal a Not-In-My-Backyard (NIMBY) mode, which reflects primarily community groups' self-interest or concerns, most territorywide actions are driven by environmental pressure groups, which, despite their small-sized professional and elite-based memberships, proclaim to represent and defend the public's interests in the policy arena.

In Thailand, Alvin So and Yok-shiu Lee reveal a high degree of diversity of environmentalism in terms of the types of environmental initiatives put forth by social and community groups as well as a number of public and private agencies. A rough categorization of such environmental groups and agencies includes: grassroots organizations (GROs), civic groups, environmentally related development NGOs, environment-oriented NGOs, business-initiated environmental NGOs, and environmentally related NGOs. From a casual reading of their labels, this array of groups and organizations may be duplicating each other's activities. While it is likely that some of their functions overlap, they are nevertheless distinct categories as far as their organizational goals are concerned.

Given the wide variety of social groups and organizations encompassed by Asia's environmental movements, it is not surprising that these movements represent a loose network of diverse interest groups whose goals occasionally coincide, complement, and compete with each other. The diverse nature of environmental movements has two implications. First, the diversity of interests and resultant instability of multigroup alliances within most environmental movements make them somewhat less cohesive. Second, the diversity of interests leads to a "contingent politics of alliance." In Asia, some significant environmental conflicts involved a range of actors on various levels, whose interests coincide in a temporary, issue-specific manner rather than a long-term, structural manner. For instance, during the height of the Anti–Daya Bay Nuclear Plant Campaign in Hong Kong, a total of 107 local pressure and community groups converged to form the Joint Conference for Shelving the Daya Bay Nuclear Plant. The Joint Conference was itself an unprecedented coalition in terms of the sizeable number and diverse backgrounds of its constituents in the territory's environmental activism history. An excellent example of the notion of "contingent politics of alliance," the Joint Conference disbanded as quickly as it was formed when the campaign receded under a strong counter-attack by the plant's proponents.

Asia's Environmental Movements Are Socially Constructed

Similar to America's environmental movement, Asia's environmental movements are inherently political—fundamentally concerned with the allocation of resources in society. The political nature of environmental concerns is manifested in the unequal distribution of the costs and benefits of development. While such benefits may be measured financially, many costs are hidden and unequivocally environmental in nature, or are at least expressed politically as environmental.

Since the stakes are high, the state, local bureaucrats, middle-class environmental activists, local community residents, and business organizations tried their best to influence the contours and contents of the social discourses of environmental movements to promote their own interests and ideologies. Subsequently, when deemed useful by and beneficial to these groups and organizations, certain cultural and religious symbols are appropriated and invoked by (anti)movement activists to mobilize political and social support to achieve their goals.

Thus, Asia's environmental accounts are never simply about the environment per se. Environmental perspectives and related arguments are always motivated by particular interests, which may not be based on genuine concerns for environmental and ecological integrity. In other words, environmental movements are prone to be "used" according to the interests of movement interpreters.

Since state and business organizations strongly influence the mass media in many Asian countries, they generally have an upper hand in constructing an environmental movement to serve their own purposes. For example, Cathay Pacific spent millions of dollars to promote a green corporate image and foster green management. The recycling of in-flight waste and scheduling of no-smoking flights were introduced to appeal to the preferences of international airline customers for eco-friendly practices in the corporate sector.

In Asian countries where authoritarianism was dominant up to the late 1980s, many political activists turned to the environmental movements as a cover to promote the cause of democratization. For instance, opposition to the construction of the Chico River Dam in the Philippines was framed by proponents in a way not only to prevent ecological degradation but also to discredit the Marcos regime's economic agenda overtly favoring the interests of its big business allies. Nested in the strategic context of democratic struggles, it then became a standard procedure for Filipino activists to voice environmental demands together with their democratic call to remove the Marcos regime from power.

Asia's Environmental Movements Are Culturally Indigenized

In many Asian countries, the environmental movements can be, to varying degrees, traced to Western roots. Many proponents of environmental movements in Asia were educated in the West and/or strongly influenced by the social discourse on the environment found there.

Nevertheless, in the course of mobilizing community residents to protest, local activists have engaged in a process of indigenization through which Asian religions, cultural values, and rituals are incorporated into environmental movements.

When many Asian states were under authoritarian rule in the 1980s, local activists invoked religious sanctions to legitimize protest activities, to help unite community residents, and to consolidate their support against political repression and violence. In Taiwan, for example, local temples served as important sites of environmental protest. Local deities, religious parades, and the ghost festivals are key components of environmental protests against polluting companies. Besides religion, dominant Confucian values were also re-interpreted for environmental purposes: Chinese filial beliefs were invoked to condemn environmental culprits who were accused of threatening the local people's *zisun* (descendants); funerals were used to mourn the "deceased" environment; and the idea of "motherhood" was invoked to enlist the support of women to protect the wounded earth. Furthermore, local folk traditions were frequently invoked to protect indigenous communities' resources and life-styles. In the Philippines, the spirits of ancestors believed to reside in the mountains, trees, and lakes are used as claims by indigenous communities to thwart outside developers' attempts to poach from their natural environment.

It is this indigenization of Western environmentalism—attained through the incorporation of traditional Asian religious symbols, cultural symbols, values, and rituals—that empowered local environmental activists and enabled them to challenge the dominant authoritarian states in the 1980s. The fusion of local religious and native cultural values with contemporary environmental concerns thus created, in contrast to its Western counterparts, distinctive styles of Asian environmentalism.

In sum, Asia's environmental movements displayed several common characteristics; they are highly diverse, socially constructed, and culturally indigenized. Despite these similarities, however, it is important to acknowledge that significant variations remain with regard to the scope and contents of environmentalism among Asian societies. Moreover, although one can identify multiple streams in environmental movements in all Asian countries, in each country, a particular strand tends to assume a dominant position over the other streams and exercises strong influence over the movement's overall course of development. To facilitate a systematic comparative discussion, yet at the risk of oversimplification, it may be instructive to label a society's environmental movements by the dominant thrust of their major proponents. In what follows, we have identified three different paths of environmental movements in the Asian societies covered in this volume; namely, the populist movements in Taiwan, South Korea, and the Philippines; the corporatist path in Thailand; and the postmaterialist mode in Hong Kong.

Three Paths: Populist, Corporatist, and Postmaterialist

The Populist Path

In Chapter 7, Andrew Szasz characterizes the American toxics movement as "ecopopulism" because it is people-oriented, driven by "victim" consciousness, and fueled by grassroots mobilization. Unlike earlier phases of environmentalism strongly identified with nature preservation, establishment of national parks shielded from development, and protection of endangered species, the focal issues of ecopopulism are almost never simply about nature per se but always concerned with the question of how the transformation of nature threatens human interests, be they material (health, means of subsistence, traditional livelihoods) or moral (sense of unfairness, sense of being victimized by the powerful).

Similar to their U.S. counterparts, key environmental movements in Taiwan, South Korea, and the Philippines are moving toward the path of "ecopopulism." In the Philippines, for example, the Green Forum sought to promote: (1) the values of social equity and justice in the custodianship of natural resources; (2) ecologically sound economic activities whose primary beneficiaries are poor families and communities; and (3) authentic participation in governance and social transformation through popular empowerment. The key concepts expounded by the Philippines' populist environmental movement thus include "People's Participation," "Community Empowerment," "Environmental Justice," and "Sustainable Development."

Populist environmentalism in the Philippines, Taiwan, and South Korea is such a strong social force that it greatly influenced the orientation of other environmental campaigns in these countries. For example, in the Philippines, natural conservation issues are conceived as livelihood concerns, and the goal of nature conservation is pursued in conjunction with demands for equity, livelihood, and community resource rights. Even a previously apolitical environmental NGO, the Haribon Foundation for the Conservation of Natural Resources, declared in 1984 that "poverty and the distorted distributional effects of the political economy have grave ecological consequences." In Taiwan, a former conservation organization—the Bird Society—was drawn into political activism because of increased destruction of Taiwan's natural environment by the government's development-oriented projects.

The main actors of populist environmental movements in Taiwan, South Korea, and the Philippines include the following groups: local residents who are victims of environmental degradation; people's organizations (POs), whose leadership comes mostly from local communities; and non-governmental organizations (NGOs), whose leaders and members are supplied primarily by the new middle class. Whereas local residents and POs provide the grievances and energy for protests, NGOs provide needed organizational skills, mass media exposure, and overall strategy for the movements. It is the marriage of grassroots enthusiasm with middle-class organizational and leadership resources that explains the transformative power of Asian populist environmental movements.

Confrontational tactics were a major tool of protest adopted by populist environmental movements in Asia. Under authoritarian rule, such tactics are very often the only means available to local residents to challenge the state's decision to build a new power plant or protest the business sector's decision to build a paper mill in their community. Even after their countries went through intense social and political struggles to become democratic states, many environmental activists still embrace the militant approach, organizing grassroots-level mass protests, disrupting official meetings, or even throwing themselves in front of bulldozers and dumptrucks to express grievances and attain goals.

By steering their activities clearly onto the path of "ecopopulism," participants in environmental movements in the Philippines, South Korea, and Taiwan articulated a whole new discourse to present their claims. In addition to placing a substantial emphasis on social equity concerns in the allocation of natural resource benefits, Asia's populist environmental movements also advocated a community-based approach to sustainable development. The Green Forum in the Philippines, for instance, promoted a community-based model that attempts to incorporate ecological principles into economics and to integrate nature with society. They also argue that the twin objectives of environmental protection and social equity—two principal factors in sustaining a community—would be greatly facilitated through relinquishing power from the state to grassroots communities, and through a shift in the base of authority from political ideology to ecology.

In sum, the populist track charted by environmental movements in Taiwan, South Korea, and the Philippines is distinguished by its promoting grassroots activism, community empowerment, livelihood concerns, confrontational tactics, and social discourses on sustainability. In stark contrast, the environmental movement in Thailand took a totally opposite path—that of corporatist environmentalism—which is, in almost all of these aspects, the antithesis of "ecopopulism."

The Corporatist Path

While anti-nuclear crusades and other victim-based protests epitomize the populist environmental movements in Taiwan, South Korea, and the Philippines, the promotion of green labels, the campaign to use unleaded gasoline, and the sponsorship of the Annual Environmental Conference by the Bangchak Petroleum Co. Ltd. epitomize the corporatist environmental movement in Thailand.

The goals of corporate environmentalism in Thailand are to contain radical environmental protests, promote a socially responsible corporate image, and take advantage of business opportunities in the emerging green economy. First, since most NGOs in Thailand held negative perceptions of the private sector, corporate environmentalism developed as a means through which the latter could take movement initiatives away from the former. In the early 1990s, Anand Panyarachun, a prominent business figure turned prime minister, set up an Environmental Fund accused of favoring private businesses at the expense of NGOs; he organized a Business Council for Sustainable Development to oversee and influence environmental policy issues, and helped found the Thailand Environment Institute (TEI), located inside Bangchak Petroleum Co. Ltd.

Second, corporate environmentalism promotes a corporate image that is environmentally friendly and socially responsible. For instance, Bangchak Petroleum Co. has sponsored and organized the Annual Environmental Seminar since 1995, and the Thai Commercial Bank introduced several internal environmental measures, which include the installation of a deep shaft waste treatment system. Third, driven by

purely profit-seeking motives, corporate environmentalism helps pro-
pel, and benefits from, the growing fad of green consumerism. Thus,
the Thailand Business Council for Sustainable Development introduced the Green Label Project in 1993, and green businesses—such as
shops selling natural products, as well as businesses managing recycled materials and providing waste management consultancy—have
prospered in recent years.

In this respect, the main actors of the corporatist environmental
movement in Thailand are the business sector and the government. The
close connection between the two, aptly exemplified by the composition of the National Environment Board (NEB), is decisive in shaping
Thailand's environmental policies. In general, grassroots NGOs and
people's organizations are considered marginal groups and excluded
from crucial environmental decision-making processes. Since the establishment of the Environment Fund, for instance, only sixteen NGOs
have received some sort of funding support.

Corporate environmentalism strives to promote cooperation, as opposed to confrontation, between major stakeholders in the environmental arena. By cultivating a new social discourse on *benja phaki* (five
alliances)—which means cooperation among the five major social
groups of government, academics, NGOs, business, and the community—it attempts to claim that, despite their different perspectives and
priorities, each major actor can adopt a complementary role in serving
the larger common goal of environmental protection in the country.
This brand of corporate environmentalism even redefines "civil society" in a conservative way: the boundary of civil society is greatly
enlarged to include the state, the private sector, and the general public.
Key elements of this refined "civil society" form a partnership to work
together toward the same goal of environmental protection under a
civil network. The Thailand Environment Institute, for instance, can be
seen as serving an important bridging function in bringing together
such key components—business interests, the state, and the NGO sector—to work for the integrity of the Thai environment.

In short, corporate environmentalism in Thailand can be seen as an
environmentalism from above, in contrast to the populist environmental movements from below found in Taiwan, South Korea, and the
Philippines. Corporate environmentalism is initiated and dominated by
the business sector to serve its own interests. It also advocates a cooperative mode of operation and promotes a harmonious civil society

discourse. In this respect, it bears some similarities to the postmaterialist environmental movement in Hong Kong.

The Postmaterialist Path

Hong Kong's environmental movement also receives strong support from the business sector and endorsement from the colonial government. In terms of tactics, Hong Kong's leading environmental activists also advocate a non-confrontational, consensus-building approach. However, Hong Kong's environmental movement can be distinguished from its Thai counterpart by several peculiar characteristics.

Whereas Bangchak Petroleum's sponsorship and organization of the Annual Environmental Conference epitomizes corporate environmentalism in Thailand, environmental educational programs—such as organic farming, green carnivals, and green summer camps—epitomize the "postmaterialist" environmental movement in Hong Kong. Such a postmaterialist strand of environmentalism is dominated by the theme of creating and adopting a "green life-style." In order to protect the environment, prominent green groups in Hong Kong argue that it is necessary to promote a green consumption pattern, a green consciousness, and a green life-style through campaigns that discourage the use of plastic shopping bags and encourage waste paper recycling, eco-tours to tropical rain forests, and vegetarianism. The movement's tactic of raising public environmental awareness, using formal and informal environmental education programs as its principal tool of social mobilization, is aptly embodied in the slogans "Environmental Conservation Is Part of Your Life" and "Environmental Protection Starts with Me."

Although Hong Kong experienced a robust populist phase of environmentalism in the Anti–Daya Bay Nuclear Plant movement of the late 1980s, this populist sentiment was short-lived and largely evaporated by the early 1990s. On the one hand, political activists' energy was absorbed in the struggle for democracy in the remaining years of the colonial government, and their attention diverted to other social and political issues deemed more urgent than protecting the environment. On the other hand, leading environment groups have refrained from participating in the fight for democracy. Instead, they devoted much of their resources to drawing the mass media's attention to green life-style issues.

The main actors shaping the postmaterialist environmental agenda in Hong Kong are mostly young, new middle-class professionals such as scientists, academics, artists, clergymen, doctors, executives, journalists, and ex-radicals from the 1960s. Many received their higher education in the West and were strongly influenced by postmaterialist values prevalent in Western environmental movements. These young professionals developed good working relations with the business sector from which they obtained green funds to finance environmental education programs. Some also were accused of being co-opted into serving in the Hong Kong government's policy advisory structure. Despite such cozy relationships with both the private sector and the government, all environmental groups steadfastly declare that they maintain their autonomy in setting their own agendas. Most of these groups, however, do not initiate and/or maintain any sustained linkage to the grassroots communities or any populist organizations.

The postmaterialist environmental movement endorses a consensual approach to working with the business sector and the state rather than engaging in confrontations with the dominant power structure. According to Simon Chau, a charismatic leader of Hong Kong's postmaterialist environmental movement, raising green consciousness is a more important task than engaging in confrontation. Chau contends that the adoption of a green consciousness and the transformation of life-styles will produce the following results: (1) the number of supporters for the "green" movement will rapidly increase, and (2) serious societal problems such as those associated with the 1997 transition, and personal psychological pressures associated with making a living, falling ill, and searching for the meaning of existence will be satisfactorily resolved. As such, the ecological crisis will be averted accordingly.

With regard to the form and content of the discourse of postmaterialist environmentalism, leading Hong Kong environmental activists frequently appropriate traditional Chinese religious beliefs to justify and buttress their claims. For instance, Buddhism is said to attach great importance to the conservation and protection of the environment. Simon Chau cites a story saying Buddhist monks are forbidden to cut down trees: once, when a monk cut down a tree branch, the tree's spirit lodged a complaint with the Buddha, claiming that the monk had, in effect, cut off his child's arm. The moral of the story was that humans should respect and refrain from damaging all living things found in nature. Thus, the promotion of a Buddhist life-style on the part of some leading green groups has been an integral part of the environmental movement in Hong Kong. The most salient aspect of such a Buddhist life-style has been the rising popularity of a vegetarian diet, particularly among younger generations.

In a nutshell, the postmaterialist environmental movement in Hong Kong is distinguished by its proponents' emphasis on adopting a green life-style, a strong inclination to rely primarily on educational campaigns to raise green consciousness, a disinterest in grassroots mobilization, and a selective appropriation of traditional Chinese religious and cultural beliefs to justify and reinforce its assertions.

To reiterate, three major paths of environmentalism—populist, corporatist, and postmaterialist—can be identified with the various environmental movements in the five Asian societies that we discussed above. These environmental movements aspire to different goals (environmental justice versus a good business image versus a green life-style), consist of different stakeholders (grassroots groups versus business versus new middle class), adopt different tactics (confrontational versus co-optation versus consensual), and articulate different elements in their discourses (sustainable development versus civil society versus traditional Chinese religion).

What, then, explains these divergent paths of environmental activism in Asia? As the following discussion shows, anti-nuclear protests, democratization processes, and the business sector's reactions were all important factors, singularly and interactively, in shaping the contours of these different types of environmental movements in Asia.

Anti-Nuclear Campaigns, Democratization, and the Business Sector's Reactions

Anti-Nuclear Movements

Anti-nuclear movements emerged at almost the same time in Taiwan, South Korea, and Hong Kong in the second half of the 1980s. In these societies, the decision to set up nuclear power plants in the 1970s and the mid-1980s was made under highly centralized or authoritarian regimes by a small circle of bureaucrats and corporate managers. By the late 1980s, however, the political opportunity structure in these territories changed due to the advent of democratization and the retreat of authoritarianism. Subsequently, anti-nuclear voices from community residents and middle-class professionals rose; they were beginning to complain about the potentially harmful effects of nuclear waste disposal, nuclear plant accidents, and the undemocratic nature of nuclear energy decision-making processes. In Taiwan, the anti-nuclear campaign's alliance with political opposition parties provided the major impetus toward delaying and scaling down the Taiwan government's nuclear program. In South Korea, where no sharp cleavages can be detected among the political elite, it was the combined effects of grassroots mobilization and street protests that helped present a formidable challenge to the Korean government's nuclear decisions. However, in Hong Kong, despite an almost unprecedented success in forging a strong, territorywide coalition among numerous community and interest groups in the anti-nuclear movement, the activists were unable to shelve the construction of the Daya Bay Nuclear Power Plant, because it was built beyond the Hong Kong border with China.

In many Asian countries, popular resistance against nuclear power programs is an important, high-profile facet of local environmental protests. Fear of radioactive fallout, coupled with concerns over nuclear power plant safety and the problem of storing and disposing of nuclear waste materials, provide a powerful drawing card that brings diverse groups of people into the anti-nuclear campaign. As such, the campaign was conferred a special place in the origin of populist environmental movements in Asia. The reason is very simple: nuclear power is perceived by many as an extraordinary threat to the general public; it inspires so much dread and anxiety among local communities that it undermines whatever enthusiasm people may feel toward advanced modern technology. Subsequently, the success of anti-nuclear campaigns in South Korea and Taiwan boosted the environmental movements in these two countries onto the populist path, whereas the failure of anti-nuclear protests in Hong Kong and the absence of anti-nuclear struggles in Thailand help explain why environmental movements in these other two societies shied away from grassroots mobilization.

Democratization

Again, there is an interesting coincidence in timing with the onset of democratic transition and the advent of environmental movements in South Korea, Taiwan, the Philippines, and Hong Kong. In the comparative chapter on democracy, we examined the ways in which democratic transition and democratic consolidation shaped the contours of the environmental movements in these four Asian countries.

We find that during the critical transition from liberalization to democratic breakthrough, populist environmental movements and democracy movements are generally partners, cross-fertilizing and empowering each other. As two strong social forces, democracy and environmental movements shared the larger societal goals of mobilizing the grassroots communities: to resist and oppose authoritarian regimes, on the one hand, and to create a better living environment for local communities, on the other.

However, different relationship patterns occurred between the democracy movements and environmental movements when the democratic transition period shifted into the next phase of democratic consolidation. In societies where a fuller extent of democratization existed, as in the cases of Taiwan, South Korea, and the Philippines, the populist environmental movement acted either as a partner or as a guardian to the democratic forces, pushing the government toward adopting increasingly stringent and effective environmental protection measures. In the case of Hong Kong, however, where there were major difficulties in attaining democratic consolidation, the environmental movement was sidelined as a bystander in the continuing struggle for democracy. In Thailand, a country that has yet to embark on major steps beyond an initial democratic opening, the environmental movement went onto the corporatist path—the opposite of populist environmental movements found in the democratizing states of Taiwan, South Korea, and the Philippines.

Business Sector's Reactions

In the comparative chapter on the role of the business sector, we examined the various means by which it tried to exert influence on Asia's environmental movements. In Taiwan, populist environmentalism forced the private sector to adopt an exit option to relocate polluting industries overseas, to make concessions in negotiations with the government, or to trade "rights to pollute" with fines or compensations when polluting impacts are discovered.

In Hong Kong, due to the predominant service sector and booming economy, most businesses are not under intense pressure to clean up their acts. Instead, major firms have taken on the role of green sponsors to project a socially responsible and environmentally friendly corporate image, while others have developed new products and services to respond to an emerging tide of green consumerism. Green funding and sponsorship from Hong Kong's large corporations not only maintain a highly cooperative relationship between the private sector and leading environmental groups, but also direct the territory's environmental movement onto a postmaterialist path that emphasizes educational campaigns, green consciousness, and green life-styles.

In Thailand, taking advantage of the NGO sector's meager resources and capitalizing on this sector's close connection with the state, Thai businesses were particularly effective in initiating and advancing their own corporatist version of environmentalism to shape the agenda of the country's environmental movement. Thus, since 1995, Thailand's Annual Environmental Seminar has beem organized not by the NGOs, but hosted and sponsored primarily by the powerful Bangchak Petroleum Company.

Policy Implications

Universalizing an Environmental Discourse

By the late 1990s, Asia's environmental movements—irrespective of whether they were populist, corporatist, or postmaterialist—helped impose an environmental discourse in society as well as onto the state. In Asia, generally speaking, the public is increasingly receptive to and supportive of the agenda and acclamations of leading environmental groups. Asia's environmental movements are credited with the success of raising social awareness of the high costs of environmental degradation associated with high-speed, profit-oriented developmental policies. Environmental organizations are booming across Asia, not only in the urban centers but in rural communities as well. Ranks of environmental activists come not only from Western-educated, middle-class, professional ranks, but increasingly from grassroots communities and local people's organizations.

Robust environmental movements forced states and elites in Asia to adopt a pro-environmental discourse. For instance, President Ramos announced at the 1996 Asia-Pacific Economic Co-operation (APEC) summit meeting in Manila that he would position the Philippines as a "green tiger" in the twentieth-first century. In South Korea, every politician invariably presents himself/herself as a pro-environment candidate during election time, for in order to win, Korea's political contestants must address environmental issues in their platforms. In Taiwan, the opposition parties consistently maintain an anti-nuclear stand in their political platforms.

Beyond rhetoric, Asia's environmental movements are credited with some actual policy impacts. In Taiwan, widespread anti-pollution protests forced the government to adopt tougher measures on pollution controls. A specific Pollution Dispute Resolution Law was passed, the Environmental Impacts Assessment Act enacted, and the Environmental Protection Basic Law is now reviewed in the Legislative Yuan. In the Philippines, environmental activists have been recruited by the government to promote a participatory mode of local governance with regard to environmental issues.

Continuing Environmental Degradation

In spite of an increasingly cogent program of environmental activities and rising popularity of environmental discourses, Asia's environment shows no notable signs of improvement. In South Korea, Su-Hoon Lee remarks that the quality of water and air in the cities has not improved; the destruction of nature as a result of for-profit developmental projects (e.g., golf course construction) continues; and the country's pro-nuclear policy has, in essence, remained intact. In Taiwan, as Hsin-Huang Michael Hsiao notes, although local governments are now more responsive to environmental problems than in the past, the pro-growth ideology of the central government has hardly been challenged. The Environmental Protection Agency (EPA) and local environmental agencies in Taiwan still intervene in environmental disputes in a highly circumscribed manner. They fear offending either the polluters or the victims, so they usually refrain from taking sides or making concrete decisions. As a result, Taiwan's EPA upsets people on all sides, establishing a reputation as a weak, ineffective body among environmentalists, and as a troublesome unit among the government and private corporations.

How can we explain the paradox of rising popularity of environmental discourses, on the one hand, and continuing, if not worsening, environmental decline, on the other? As Su-Hoon Lee suggests, heightened environmental consciousness stems from the fact that environmental issues that received little attention in the past are now prominent in the mass media. At the same time, however, the state and the private sector succeed in containing the scope of environmental activism and diffusing potentially disruptive environmental disputes. They do this partly by proclaiming that they share the environmentalists' concerns, and partly by co-opting environmental activists into adopting a consensual, non-confrontational approach.

What, then, is the future prospect for Asia's environmental movements? Since the populist environmental movements in Asia show no sign of retreat, and since the corporatist and postmaterialist movements may shift toward the populist path if democratization consolidates in the countries concerned, there are reasons for optimism concerning Asia's environmental movements. However, to achieve the larger societal objectives of environmental justice and sustainable development, Asia's environmental activists must combine street protests with struggles in the legislative and bureaucratic arenas, grassroots mobilization with electoral mobilization, environmental critiques with critiques of society, politics, and culture. Only through a broadening of objectives and strategies can Asia's environmental movements move closer to achieving larger societal goals.

In particular, movement activists have to articulate an effective and thorough critique of rampant developmentalism that has been subscribed to indiscriminately by both the elite and the general population in the region. This is, admittedly, an uphill battle because there are only a few signs of a coherent green critique of industrial development being formulated in the region. The first aspect of such a critique relates to the unmasking of the concept of "progress" that lies at the heart of the ideology of industrial society. A look at the current social and environmental crises in the region aptly shows that "the belief in the progress is a cruel myth" (International Society for Ecology and Culture 1992: 13). After four decades of development, large majorities of people in the developing countries of Southeast Asia are still living in hardship and misery (Sachs 1993). The premise of superiority of the industrial development model has been fully shattered by a multitude of environmental accidents and disasters plaguing the newly industrialized economies of East Asia as well as the global ecological predicament (Finger 1994; Chatterjee and Finger 1994). It is imperative that movement activists in the region begin to formulate a coherent strategy, one that is informed by the new approach of global ecology, to question the very essence of industrial development and to challenge "the philosophical, moral, and religious underpinnings of modern society" (Taylor 1995: 5).

The second aspect of a full and thorough critique of developmentalism in the region has to be focused on Japan's experience, which is widely perceived by the peoples and governments in Asia as constituting a successful development model to be emulated. As succinctly pointed out by McCormack (1996: 290), an acute observer of Japan's postwar development history:

> The goal of attaining something like Japanese consumption levels has driven growth in much of Asia since at least the Vietnam War, and has come to define the kind of future to which people aspire. Japan is thought to have found, deciphered, and put into practice an alchemical formula for growth and prosperity. It constitutes both model and magnet, pulling upon the entire Asian region. Yet it is not possible to replicate the profligacy of raw materials and the carelessness of environmental impact practiced by Japan and the other advanced industrial countries. Japan therefore does not constitute a model, and it should be obvious that neither is there a model to be found in North America or Western Europe. Not only is Japan's affluence deeply problematic, but it pulls the region around it toward social and ecological disaster.

Articulating an effective critique of developmentalism in a region where most of the elites and general population alike have largely remained uncritical of the "industrial development model" as exemplified by Japan's postwar industrialization strategy undoubtedly presents a formidable challenge to the movements' activists. However, the fact that affluence has brought little sense of fulfillment to the Japanese people, who are supposed to be the richest in Asia but whose lives are actually "profoundly empty and alienated" would need to be exposed, emphasized, and brought to the attention of the rest of Asia (McCormack 1996: 18).

Future Research Agenda

This volume is a first effort to conduct a comparative analysis of the origins, transformation, and impacts of environmental movements in East Asia and Southeast Asia. It has particularly highlighted the crucial roles of anti-nuclear campaigns, democratization, private sector initiatives, and culture in shaping the contours of Asia's environmental movements. Many other issues of theoretical and practical concerns, however, have yet to be addressed and some of these are discussed below.

More Case Studies

This volume focused on only five cases: Taiwan, South Korea, Hong Kong, the Philippines, and Thailand. While these case studies provide important insights on Asia's environmental movements, this volume has not exhausted the divergent paths of environmental movements in Asia. Hence, additional case studies must be included in future research agendas on environmentalism in Asia.

For example, China's development experience provides fertile ground for further study. China now experiences rapid industrialization and rapid environmental degradation. Given the enormous population, China's environmental problems have serious implications not only for the Asian region but for the world as a whole (Smil 1993). The following questions could be asked: In what form will China's environmentalism take shape, and will this environmental movement pursue the populist or corporatist path? How will the Chinese state, which still claims to be socialist, respond to increasingly severe environmental problems and rising environmental activism?

Japan's development record offers intriguing materials for yet another case study of Asia's environmental movements. While economic powerhouse Japan appears to have maintained a better record of dealing with domestic environmental concerns than the U.S., her people have suffered greatly from various forms of industrial pollution (Ui 1992). Moreover, Japan has also been rightfully accused of exporting her pollution-prone industries to Southeast Asian countries, and of indirectly contributing to environmental degradation in these countries through her voracious demand for timber. Although Japan's environmental movement started much earlier than the ones examined in this volume, some analysts claim it to be a relatively ineffectual social force (Hoffman 1996). In view of the crucial role played by Japan in the regional political economy of the East and Southeast Asian regions, an in-depth study of Japan's environmental movement may help shed new light on the avenues available to, and constraints limiting, environmental activists both inside and outside of Japan in their efforts to thwart and reverse environmental decline in the region.

Gender

Another area of future research concerns the role of women in environmental movements. This volume has already touched upon the contributions made by women in Asia's environmental movements. For example, in Taiwan, the Homemakers' Union and Foundation is a very active group in dealing with environmental issues. For Taiwan's women, environmental protection and nature conservation are deemed important for protecting not just their own, but also their children's, health and future. In the Philippines, the symbol of *inang kalikasan* (mother earth), a prominent code in the Philippine culture, was adopted by the environmental movement. This symbol signifies women's nurturing, caring, and non-domineering attitude, which aptly and precisely informs the public how nature should be treated. In living up to and capitalizing on this ecological symbol, women's organizations became active constituents in the Philippine environmental movement. For instance, the Women's Action Network for Development (WAND), an alliance of more than 120 women's NGOs and POs, occupies one of the NGO seats in the Philippine Council for Sustainable Development.

Based upon the above observations, it is instructive to raise the following questions: In what ways have women played a role in Asia's environmental movements? To what extent have women assumed leadership positions of environmental organizations? What are the implications of gender becoming a symbol (e.g., mother earth) for Asia's environmental movements? To what extent, and how, have gender issues been incorporated into environmental discourse which, in turn, draws women into the ranks of environmental activists?

Global Linkages

Asia's environmental movements are not simply local or national issues, but are strongly influenced by global forces. Taylor (1995: 347) claims that the future of such local movements "will depend at least in part on how successful people's alliances will be in gathering resources from international sectors and making visible their local struggles for self-determination, local land control, and sustainable lifeways." However, it is not totally clear to what extent, and exactly how, global forces have brought forth positive or negative impacts on Asia's environment and on the region's environmental movements. On the one hand, global forces have played a positive role in advocating environmentalism in Asia. One notable example is the 1992 United Nations Conference on Environment and Development, popularly known as the "Earth Summit," which imposed an environmental discourse in Asia, forcing President Kim in South Korea and President Ramos in the Philippines to declare themselves "environmental presidents" of their respective countries.

On the other hand, in our studies of anti-nuclear campaigns, we find that the U.S. nuclear industry played an important role in promoting nuclear energy in South Korea and Taiwan. In Taiwan, all six nuclear reactors were imports manufactured by U.S. vendors such as General Electric and Westinghouse. Moreover, the World Bank was the main funding source of such controversial projects as the Chico Dam in the Philippines and the Pak Mool Dam project in Thailand. Furthermore, pro–free trade provisions recently agreed to by the developing countries with the World Trade Organization (WTO), as argued by many environmental activists, "will not only worsen the real economic and social well-being of their peoples, but will also massively and positively pollute and degrade their environment" (Ezenkele 1998: 3). They have therefore asserted that the WTO will be "the ground upon which a long series of key social-ecological battles will be fought" (Athanasiou 1996: 47).

Given the complexities of the interplay between global forces and local processes, we need to identify and examine the precise linkages between international factors and national/local environmental movements in Asia. Important research questions include: under what conditions will global forces contribute toward the advent and strengthening of Asia's environmental movements? And under what conditions will global forces turn into regressive factors limiting Asia's environmental activism? What is the best strategy for Asia's environmental activists to adopt to develop global linkages and advance their domestic agendas? We hope that the findings in this volume will stimulate researchers to conduct more studies, singularly and comparatively, on Asia's environmental activism.

References

Athanasiou, Tom. 1996. *Divided Planet: The Ecology of Rich and Poor*. Boston: Little, Brown.

Chatterjee, Pratap, and Matthias Finger. 1994. *The Earth Brokers: Power, Politics, and World Development*. London: Routledge.

Ezenkele, Agochukwu. 1998. Earth Times News Service, May 23.

Finger, Matthias. 1994. "NGOs and Transformation: Beyond Social Movement Theory." In *Environmental NGOs in World Politics: Linking the Local and the Global,* edited by Thomas Princen and Matthias Finger, pp. 48–66. London: Routledge.

Hoffman, Steven M. 1996. "The Influence of Citizen/Environmental Groups Upon Local Environmental Policy Process in Japan." Unpublished Ph.D. dissertation in Land Resources, University of Wisconsin-Madison.

International Society for Ecology and Culture. 1992. "The Future of Progress." In *The Future of Progress: Reflections on Environment and Development,* edited by Edward Goldsmith, Martin Khor, Helena Norberg-Hodge, and Vandana Shiva. Bristol: International Society for Ecology and Culture (no page numbers printed in publication).

McCormack, Gavan. 1996. *The Emptiness of Japanese Affluence.* Armonk: M.E. Sharpe.

Sachs, Wolfgang. 1993. "Global Ecology and the Shadow of 'Development.' " In *Global Ecology: A New Arena of Political Conflict,* edited by Wolfgang Sachs, pp. 3–21. London: Zed Books.

Smil, Vaclav. 1993. *China's Environmental Crisis: An Inquiry into the Limits of National Development.* Armonk: M.E. Sharpe.

Taylor, Bron. 1995. "Introduction: The Global Emergence of Popular Ecological Resistance." In *Ecological Resistance Movements: The Global Emergence of Radical and Popular Environmentalism,* edited by Bron Taylor, pp. 1–10. Albany: State University of New York Press.

Ui, Jun, ed. 1992. *Industrial Pollution in Japan.* Tokyo: United Nations University Press.

Contributors

Stephen Wing-Kai Chiu is associate professor in the Department of Sociology at the Chinese University of Hong Kong.

Laura Edles is assistant professor in the Department of Sociology at the University of Hawaii.

Hsin-Huang Michael Hsiao is research fellow of the Institute of Sociology and director of the Program for Southeast Asian Area Studies of the Academia Sinica, and professor of sociology at the National Taiwan University.

Ho-Fung Hung is a graduate student in the Department of Sociology at the Johns Hopkins University.

On-Kwok Lai is associate professor in the School of Policy Studies at Kwansei Gakuin University, Japan.

Su-Hoon Lee is professor in the Department of Sociology and director of the Institute for Far Eastern Studies at Kyungnam University, Seoul.

Yok-shiu F. Lee is associate professor in the Department of Geography and Geology at the University of Hong Kong and fellow (on leave) in the Program on Environment at the East-West Center, Honolulu.

Hwa-Jen Liu received her M.A. in sociology from the University of Minnesota and is now working at the Institute of Sociology, Academia Sinica, Taiwan.

Francisco A. Magno is associate professor and chair of the Political Science Department at De La Salle University, Manila.

Somrudee Nicro is director of the Urbanization and Environment Program at the Thailand Environment Institute, Bangkok.

Alvin Y. So is professor in the Division of Social Sciences at the Hong Kong University of Science and Technology.

Andrew Szasz is associate professor of sociology and provost of College Eight at the University of California, Santa Cruz.

Index